Building Database
Clouds in Oracle 12c

Building Database Clouds in Oracle 12c

Tariq Farooq
Sridhar Avantsa
Pete Sharman

♠♠Addison-Wesley

Boston • Columbus • Indianapolis • New York • San Francisco • Amsterdam • Cape Town
Dubai • London • Madrid • Milan • Munich • Paris • Montreal • Toronto • Delhi • Mexico City
São Paulo • Sydney • Hong Kong • Seoul • Singapore • Taipei • Tokyo

For information about buying this title in bulk quantities, or for special sales opportunities (which may include electronic versions; custom cover designs; and content particular to your business, training goals, marketing focus, or branding interests), please contact our corporate sales department at corpsales@pearsoned.com or (800) 382-3419.

For government sales inquiries, please contact governmentsales@pearsoned.com.

For questions about sales outside the U.S., please contact intlcs@pearson.com.

Visit us on the Web: informit.com/aw

Library of Congress Control Number: 2016936586

ISBN-13: 978-0-13-431086-2
ISBN-10: 0-13-431086-1
Text printed in the United States on recycled paper at RR Donnelley in Crawfordsville, Indiana.
1   16

Contents

Preface

Cloud Computing is all the rage these days. This book focuses on DBaaS (database-as-a-service) and Real Application Clusters (RAC), one of Oracle's newest cutting-edge technologies within the Cloud Computing world.

Authored by a world-renowned, veteran author team of Oracle ACEs/ACE directors with a proven track record of multiple best-selling books and an active presence in the Oracle speaking circuit, this book is intended to be a blend of real-world, hands-on operations guide and expert handbook for Oracle 12*c* DBaaS within Oracle 12*c* Enterprise Manager (OEM 12*c*) as well as provide a segue into Oracle 12*c* RAC.

Targeted for Oracle DBAs and DMAs, this expert's handbook is intended to serve as a practical, technical, go-to reference for performing administration operations and tasks for building out, managing, monitoring, and administering DB Clouds with the following objectives:

- Practical, technical guide for building Oracle Database Clouds in 12*c*
- Expert, pro-level DBaaS handbook
- Real-world DBaaS hands-on operations guide
- Expert deployment, management, administration, support, and monitoring guide for Oracle DBaaS
- Practical best-practices advice from real-life DBaaS architects/administrators
- Guide to setting up virtualized DB Clouds based on Oracle RAC clusters

In this technical, everyday, hands-on, step-by-step book, the authors aim for an audience of intermediate-level, power, and expert users of Oracle 12*c* DBaaS and RAC. This book covers the 12*c* version of the Oracle DB software.

Register your copy of *Building Database Clouds in Oracle 12*c for convenient access to downloads, updates, and corrections as they become available. To start the registration process, go to informit.com/register and log in or create an account. Enter the product ISBN (9780134310862) and click Submit. Once the process is complete, you will find any available bonus content under "Registered Products."

Acknowledgments

Tariq Farooq

I would like to express boundless thanks for all good things in my life to the Almighty ALLAH, the lord of the worlds, the most gracious, the most merciful.

I dedicate this book to my parents, Mr. and Mrs. Abdullah Farooq; my awesome wife, Ambreen; my wonderful kids, Sumaiya, Hafsa, Fatima, and Muhammad-Talha; and my nephews, Muhammad-Hamza, Muhammad-Saad, Muhammed-Muaz, Abdul-Karim, and Ibrahim, without whose perpetual support, this book would not have come to fruition. My endless gratitude to them as I dedicated more than two years of my spare time to this book, most of which was on airplanes and in late nights and weekends at home.

My heartfelt gratitude to my friends at the Oracle Technology Network (OTN), my colleagues in the Oracle ACE fellowship, my coworkers, and everyone else within the Oracle community and my workplace for standing behind me in my quest to bring this project to completion, particularly Dave Vitalo.

I had been contemplating authoring a book within the Oracle Cloud domain for a few years—the project finally started in 2013. I am very proud of my coauthors' industry credentials and the depth of experience that they brought to this endeavor.

From inception to writing to technical review to production, authoring a book is a lengthy labor of love and at times a painful process; this book would not have been possible without the endless support of the awesome Addison-Wesley team. A very special tip-of-the-hat goes to Greg Doench, the executive editor, and all the other folks at Addison-Wesley. Kudos to the technical reviewers, book reviewers, and editorial teams at Addison-Wesley for an amazing job on this book.

Many appreciative thanks to my buddies, coauthors, and technical reviewers, Pete Sharman, Sridhar Avantsa, Sandesh Rao, and Dr. Bert Scalzo

Finally, I express my gratitude to you, my dear reader, for hopping on this knowledge-laden journey. My sincerest hope is that you will learn from this book and that you will enjoy reading it as much as we did researching and authoring it.

Sridhar Avantsa

This, my second book, is specifically dedicated to my family. They make everything worth it at the end of the day. They encouraged me to take on a second book, in spite of knowing that this would disrupt family time.

To my wife, Gita Avantsa, you are the best thing that has happened to me. You are the pillar of our family and an absolutely amazing mother to our children. Twenty years of marriage and companionship have just flown by.

To my elder son, soon to be 10, Nikhil Avantsa, your physical and mental endurance at such a young age, the ability to see a silver lining in any dark cloud, and the protective shield you place on your younger brother are awe-inspiring. Tarun is indeed lucky to have you as his elder brother.

To my younger son, soon to be 9, Tarun Avantsa, you are the most mature, loving, and caring elementary-school-going child I have ever known and will ever know. Your willingness to sacrifice anything for Nikhil makes you the absolute best younger brother one could ask for.

To my parents, Krishna and Manga Avantsa, your love, sacrifices, and support are the foundations upon which my success is built. To my elder brother, Srinivas Avantsa, you were there to guide me at a most critical and crucial juncture of my life.

I want to thank my coauthors, Pete and Tariq, and the technical reviewers, Bert and Sandesh, for giving me the privilege and opportunity to work alongside some of the finest Oracle technologists to be found. To the amazing supporting team Addison-Wesley, I thank you for countless hours you have invested in the book.

Pete Sharman

Authoring or coauthoring a book is not for the faint-hearted; it's an incredibly intense labor that sometimes makes you wonder why the heck you even volunteered to do it in the first place! So my thanks to the wonderful team at Addison-Wesley, to Sridhar Avantsa, and especially to Tariq Farooq for keeping me on track.

As always, I dedicate this book to my lovely wife, Ann, and my wonderful (now adult) kids, Emma, Kit, and Sandi. Love you all to the moon and back!

About the Authors

 **Tariq Farooq** is an Oracle technologist, architect, and problem-solver and has been working with various Oracle Technologies for more than 24 years in very complex environments at some of the world's largest organizations. Having presented at almost every major Oracle conference and event all over the world, Tariq is an award-winning speaker, community leader/organizer, author, forum contributor, and tech blogger. He is the founding president of the IOUG Virtualization & Cloud Computing Special Interest Group and the Brain-Surface social network for the various Oracle Communities. Tariq founded, organized, and chaired various Oracle conferences, including, among others, the OTN Middle East and North Africa (MENA) Tour, VirtaThon (the largest online-only conference for the various Oracle domains), the CloudaThon & RACaThon series of conferences, and the first ever Oracle-centric conference at the Massachusetts Institute of Technology in 2011. He was the founder and anchor/show-host of the *VirtaThon Internet Radio* series program. Tariq is an Oracle RAC Certified Expert and holds a total of 14 professional Oracle Certifications. Having authored more than one hundred articles, whitepapers, and other publications, Tariq is the coauthor of *Expert Oracle RAC 12c* (Apress, 2013), *Oracle Exadata Expert's Handbook* (Addison-Wesley, 2015), and *Oracle Database Problem Solving and Troubleshooting Handbook* (Addison-Wesley, 2016). Tariq has been awarded the Oracle ACE and ACE Director awards.

 **Sridhar Avantsa** started his career with Oracle in 1991 as a developer. Over the years he progressed to become a DBA and an architect. Currently he runs the National Oracle Database Infrastructure Consulting Practice for Rolta AdvizeX (formerly known as TUSC). Sridhar's work as a technologist has been recognized by Oracle with partner awards on multiple occasions. His specific areas of interest and expertise include infrastructure architecture, database performance tuning, high availability/disaster recovery and business continuity planning, Oracle RAC and Clustering, and the Oracle engineering systems. Sridhar has been an active member of the Oracle community as a presenter and as a member of Oracle expert panels at conferences. Sridhar is the coauthor of *Oracle Exadata Expert's Handbook* (Addison-Wesley, 2015). Sridhar lives in Chicago with his wife and two sons.

 **Pete Sharman** is a database architect with the DBaaS team in the Enterprise Manager product suite group at Oracle Corporation. He has worked with Oracle for the past 20 years in a variety of roles from education to consulting to development, and has used Enterprise Manager since its 0.76 beta release. Pete is a member of the Oak Table Network, and has presented at conferences around the world from Oracle Open World (both in Australia and the US), RMOUG Training Days, the Hotsos Conference, Miracle Open World, and AUSOUG and NZOUG conferences. He has coauthored two books, *Expert Enterprise Manager 12c* (Apress, 2013) and *Practical Oracle Database Appliance* (Apress, 2014), and also previously authored a book on how to pass the Oracle8i Database administration exam for the Oracle Certified Professional program. He lives in Canberra, Australia, with his wife and three children.

About the Technical Reviewers and Contributors

Dr. Bert Scalzo is a world-renowned database expert, Oracle ACE, author, chief architect at HGST, and formerly a member of Dell Software's TOAD dev team. With three decades of Oracle database experience to draw on, Bert's webcasts garner high attendance and participation rates. His work history includes time at both Oracle Education and Oracle Consulting. Bert holds several Oracle Masters Certifications and has an extensive academic background that includes a B.S., an M.S., and a Ph.D. in computer science, as well as an M.B.A. and insurance industry designations.

Sandesh Rao is a senior director running the RAC Assurance Team within RAC Development at Oracle Corporation. He specializes in performance tuning, high availability (HA), disaster recovery, and architecting cloud-based solutions using the Oracle Stack. With more than 17 years of experience working in the HA space and having worked on several versions of Oracle with different application stacks, he is a recognized expert in RAC, database internals, and solving Big Data–related problems. Most of his work involves working with customers in the implementation of projects in the financial, retail, scientific, insurance, biotech, and tech spaces. His current position involves running a team that develops best practices for the Oracle Grid Infrastructure 12*c*, including products like RAC (Real

Application Clusters) and Storage (ASM, ACFS), which includes tools like Exachk, OraChk, and the Trace File analyzer framework for Diagnostic collections. Sandesh is involved with several projects for developing, deploying, and orchestrating components in the Oracle Cloud.

Database as a Service Concepts—360 Degrees

To understand the basic principles and concepts of database as a service (DBaaS), we must understand the meanings of both *database* and *service* and how the two interact. We also must understand the relationship between cloud computing and DBaaS. Cloud computing encompasses the IT infrastructure resources, which include networks, storage, servers, applications, and services. DBaaS is a subset of the overall cloud concept, specifically focused on the last two resources, applications and services.

The goal of this chapter is to explain the cloud computing implementation as it relates to DBaaS. Although the concept of DBaaS is generic, this book focuses on using Oracle technologies to implement DBaaS.

Cloud Computing: Definition and Classical View

The National Institute of Standards and Terminology (NIST) defines *cloud computing*[1] as follows:

> Cloud computing is a model for enabling *ubiquitous, convenient, on-demand* network access to a *shared pool* of configurable computing resources (e.g., networks, servers, storage, applications, and services) that can be *rapidly* provisioned and released with minimal management effort or service provider interaction. [emphasis added]

---

1. http://nvlpubs.nist.gov/nistpubs/Legacy/SP/nistspecialpublication800-145.pdf, p. 2.

This definition articulates the service goals that a cloud computing environment is expected to deliver:

- **Ubiquitous**: The resources are available and ready for consumption.
- **Convenient**: The consumer has easy access to the resources.
- **On demand**: Resource requests need not involve resource approval and acquisition tasks.
- **Shared pool**: The resources are shared, not dedicated, which provides mobility and flexibility in terms of assigning resources.
- **Rapid**: The time window between a resource request and its fulfillment is shortened or eliminated.

These service goals drive the physical implementation of any cloud computing model. Specifically, they provide the basis for the following core aspects of any cloud computing model, which are also interdependent on each other:

- **Roles** applicable within cloud computing—Who is sharing the resource pool?
- **Cloud type** from an infrastructure persepctive—What is the shared resource pool, and how is it deployed?
- The **security** framework within a cloud computing model—What are the basic rules that govern how the resource pool is shared?

Let us first look at roles within a cloud computing model. There are primarily two roles: end user and provider. The *end user* is the entity that uses the hardware resources and associated services that exist in a cloud environment. The *provider* is the entity that owns the physical hardware and infrastructure resources and is responsible for the services associated with delivering these resources to the end user.

Next, we look at the three types of cloud computing models prevalent: private, public, and hybrid.

- **Private cloud**: A cloud infrastructure provisioned for exclusive use by a single organization or entity, maintained by the entity and within the entity's network. The roles of provider and end user are represented by different groups within the entity.
- **Public cloud**: A cloud infrastructure provisioned in the public space such that multiple entities can use the infrastructure simultaneously. The provider is a third-party service provider that supports multiple clients or entities in the end user role.
- **Hybrid cloud**: A combination of the private and public cloud models.

The security model in a cloud environment must include the capability to define roles, responsibilities, and separation of duties for both the provider and end users. As a part of the overall cloud deployment model, the provider must develop, implement, and support a security system with proper access and privileges grants and administration in place.

The security requirements on all cloud environments follow the same basic model, with the difference that in a public cloud, the security controls have to be much wider and more stringent than in a private cloud. The security framework in both the public and private cloud models must also address data security and privacy protection between the provider and end users.

For public clouds, however, security usually requires a much stronger encryption algorithm than used in a private cloud as well as sufficient networking bandwidth to meet public needs. Furthermore, the administrator role at a provider is focused on managing the underpinning infrastructure of the private cloud itself.

To be able to define and create such a security framework, it is important to understand the roles associated with who is using the cloud. Once we understand who is using the cloud, we can translate that knowledge into requirements around access levels, roles, responsibilities, and separation of duties. Following are examples of these requirements:

- The role of a provider's cloud administrator is to manage the underpinning infrastructure of the cloud offering itself.
- The subscriber administrator role is filled individually by each subscriber entity on a cloud. The subscriber administrator manages resources and privileges for his or her own organization.
- The end user role applies to a specific user within a subscriber entity that requests and uses a subset of the resources.

Note

To the provider cloud administrator, the subscriber admnistrator role is the equivalent of an end user role with elevated privileges and rights.

To understand the impact and implementations of the security framework in a cloud environment, we also need to understand the models in which cloud services may be deployed. There are three main models:

- **Software as a service (SaaS)**: SaaS allows the consumer to use the provider's applications running on cloud infrastructure. The applications are accessible from various client devices through either a thin client interface, such as a web browser (e.g., web-based email), or a program interface. The consumer does not manage or control the underlying cloud infrastructure—not the network, servers, operating systems, storage, or even individual application capabilities—with the possible exception of limited user-specific application configuration settings.

- **Platform as a service (PaaS)**: PaaS allows the consumer to deploy any software or application onto servers deployed on cloud infrastructure. These applications may be consumer-created applications or consumer-acquired applications created using programming languages, libraries, services, and tools supported by the provider. The consumer does not manage or control the underlying cloud infrastructure but has control over the deployed applications and possibly configuration settings for the application-hosting environment.

- **Infrastructure as a service (IaaS)**: The capability provided to the consumer is to provision processing, storage, networks, and other fundamental computing resources where the consumer is able to deploy and run arbitrary software, which can include operating systems and applications. The consumer does not manage or control the underlying cloud infrastructure but has control over operating systems, storage, and deployed applications and possibly has limited control of select networking components (e.g., host firewalls).

DBaaS—A Special Case of Cloud Computing

DBaaS is a very specific implementation of cloud computing. Now that we have defined cloud computing at a generic high level, let's examine the characteristics that distinguish DBaaS.

To understand the principles of "database as a service," it's helpful to look at the terms *database* and *service* individually and then look at how they interact.

The Merriam-Webster online dictionary provides a definition of *database* that we are all familiar with: "a usually large collection of data organized especially for rapid search and retrieval (as by a computer)."

The term *service* is also one that we are familiar with. Merriam-Webster has quite a few definitions for this word, and following are some of the relevant ones that apply even in the specific case of DBaaS:

- "The occupation or function of serving"
- "The work performed by one that serves"
- "A facility supplying some public demand" such as "telephone service" or "bus service"

But these definitions are generic in nature and context. The core concepts of the definitions still apply in terms of an IT infrastructure as well—but with a few context-sensitive tweaks. In this section, we further explore the meanings and implications of *database* and *service*.

First, just to be clear, the concept we are discussing is not called "Oracle database as a service"—it is just "database as a service." Conceptually speaking, we can deploy DBaaS using Microsoft SQL Server, DB2, PostGres, MySQL, *or* Oracle. They are all software technologies that we can use to build and deploy DBaaS. The design and implementation of DBaaS includes choosing the underlying technologies that we use to implement the service. Oracle is a leader in database technology, and Oracle 12*c* focuses largely on feature sets, utilities, and functionality that enable cloud computing, making Oracle 12*c* a leading contender in terms of implementing DBaaS.

Now let us look at the service element of DBaaS. We must understand what services the end user expects and what components the provider must manage and maintain in order to deliver the expected services.

Let's start with the end users' expectations of DBaaS. Based on NIST's definition of cloud computing, we take the generic expectations implied by "services" and frame them around DBaaS-specific expectations.

Resource Utilization—Usage Instrumentation and Self-Service

One of the fundamental concepts of cloud computing is to provide end users of the cloud service the capability to monitor cloud resource usage and consumption. Therefore, a good cloud service should provide end users visibility into their resource usage, analytics, and chargeback.

With DBaaS specifically, the cloud service should provide the functionality or self-service capabilities to view resource usage and consumption as it applies to databases. The resources would include CPU consumption, storage consumptions, backup service consumption, and network bandwidth consumption.

Broad Network Access

By its definition, a core component of a cloud service is network access, or bandwidth. The cloud service network should be accessible over multiple devices and heterogenous platforms.

From a DBaaS perspective, the focus is on the protocols, quality, and efficiency of network access to the database. Network access concerns are applicable from an application standpoint as well as from an administration and management standpoint.

Resource Pooling

The reason a cloud service provides resource utilization statistics and analytics is to allow end users to tune consumption specifically to their needs. Remember, in a cloud, all the resources come out of a pool. End users should therefore be able to request additional resources when needed and reduce resource allocation and usage as needed. Remember, a cloud service must be able to optimize resources across the entire platform and at the same time maintain performance and availability according to service level agreements (SLAs) between the provider and end user.

Consequently, the service provider must enable end users to provision and decommission resources as needed without having to request resource increases or reductions through the provider. Based on resource usage statistics and business needs, end users should be able to manage and administer all resources, including CPU, network, storage, and backups.

Multitenancy is a key construct of the implementation of any cloud service. The service provider supports multiple clients within a cloud solution. The type of the cloud solution (private, public, or hybrid) determines who the allowed clients (end users) are.

In a DBaaS environment, multitenancy means that the cloud solution supports multiple databases across multiple clients, and each client has one or more databases.

From a DBaaS perspective, the end users, as consumers of services, do not manage the availability of resources or capacity-related issues. These concerns fall under the service provider's responsibility. The service provider must manage the resources at a holistic level across all the clients it supports.

However, there is a caveat here. The preceding statement is true as long as the end user requirements around security, privacy, and compliance are met. The provider has to ensure that the solution design meets the end user criteria.

Rapid Elasticity

Rapid elasticity is the logical next step and evolution of resource pooling. The cloud solution must be able to dynamically allocate or deallocate resources as requested by the end user. The service provided includes the ability to dynamically add or remove resources based on workload volume and nature. In other words, the solution needs to be adaptive and flexible to adjust resource requirements on the fly.

Measured Service

The culmination of all of the preceding concepts of resource usage intrumentation, pooling, and elasticity is the ability to measure resources across an entire service and at each individual cloud subscriber level. Therefore, resource usage should be monitored, controlled, and reported upon, providing transparency for both the provider and the consumers of the utilized service.

Another way to put this is that the cloud solution is based on multitenancy—multiple clients being supported from a single cloud solution, which leads to the question of who should be charged for resources. Obviously, the cost should be based on what resources are actually used. In other words, the cloud solution must be able to support *chargeback* capabilities. The chargeback can be based on what is provisioned or, more popularly, on what resources are actually used.

Services Applicable to DBaaS

We now have a solid foundational understanding of what cloud computing is and how it applies to DBaaS. In this section, we outline the specifics around services as they relate to DBaaS and what they mean to end users as well as to the provider in a cloud computing environment.

The services offered by the DBaaS provider to the end user fall into three main categories: provisioning, administrative, and reporting. Some of these services are optional, and others are mandatory.

Provisioning services provided to end users include some or all of the following:

- The ability to requisition new databases.
- The ability to choose database options as needed (partitioning, advanced security, Real Application Cluster, etc.).
- The ability to add resources (storage, CPU, network bandwidth, etc.) to existing databases. This includes the ability to scale up as well as to scale down.
- Database backup capability using provided backup resources.

Administrative services include some or all of the following:

- The ability to perform on-demand database restores and recoveries
- The ability to perform database clones using existing database backups
- Database monitoring capabilities, including basic 24/7 incident reporting management capabilities

Reporting services include some or all of the following:

- Performance management, which is the ability to look at a database from a performance and tuning standpoint, whether in the form of reporting or in the form of application and GUI database restore and recovery capability

- Resource consumption and usage reports, which let end users compare the resources provisioned and the actual usage so they can fine-tune resource needs to accommodate workload
- The ability to view resource chargeback based on resource allocation and consumption
- The ability to track provider compliance to the SLAs

The ability to track provider compliance to the SLAs is an especially critical point to understand. To ascertain whether or not the requested services are being provided at an appropriate level, end users must first define what "appropriate level" means. For each service, there may be more than one SLA. The higher the SLA, the more technology and resources are needed to satisfy the SLA. Pricing is also affected by the level of service detailed in the SLA.

For example, for I/O performance guarantees, the SLA would specify the input/output operations per second (IOPS) and megabytes per second (MBps) would specify I/O service times. Based on the SLA, the provider determines the actual storage layer provided to the end user. It is the provider's responsibility to ensure that the service delivered to the end user is within the accepted limits.

If we look at I/O performance as an example, the SLAs could be structured as follows:

- **Bronze standard**: Small block average I/O service times equal to or under 15 ms
- **Silver standard**: Small block average I/O service times equal to or under 10 ms
- **Gold standard**: Small block average I/O service times equal to or under 5 ms
- **Platinum standard**: Small block average I/O service times equal to or under 1 ms

Based on these SLAs, the provider may choose to

- Place bronze customers on low-end storage arrays using primarily serial advanced technology attachment (SATA) disks
- Place silver customers on high-performance storage arrays using serial-attached SCSI (SAS) drives
- Place gold customers on high-end storage arrays with a combination of SAS drives and solid-state drives (SSDs)

- Place platinum customers on high-end storage arrays based entirely on SSDs or flash memory

The key is that, once end users make their choice, the provider has to

- Define the exact key performance indicators (KPIs) required to meet the service level expectation
- Ensure that the KPIs required for the SLA are measured and monitored
- Plan for expansion to continue to be able to meet and provide the expected KPI metrics both now and in the long term
- Provide end users with reports that support or, if necessary, justify the provider's service performance capabilities

Architecture of an Oracle-Based DBaaS Implementation

DBaaS started primarily as a consolidation exercise for reducing capital expenditures (CAPEX), but as it evolved, organizations started looking into other key drivers, such as self-service, showback, and chargeback. Before we look at the details of how to implement DBaaS, we need to have some understanding of the underlying consolidation models and deployment issues that are common to all DBaaS flavors and some of the terminology that we use when defining DBaaS.

Consolidation Models

The various consolidation models that can be used to provide DBaaS are shown in Figure 1.1. The simplest and most prevalent form of consolidation exists around server virtualization. Server virtualization offers a simple way of running multiple operating system instances on the same hardware. A better model, platform consolidation, consolidates multiple databases on the same operating system, or a *cluster*. However, in both cases, database sprawl is still an issue that invariably leads to larger administrative overheads and compliance challenges. An even better consolidation model is the capability to host multiple schemas from different tenants within the same database, using Oracle Database 12*c*'s multitenant architecture.

Before we describe such methodologies, however, it is important to have a common understanding of the components that make up the underlying architecture.

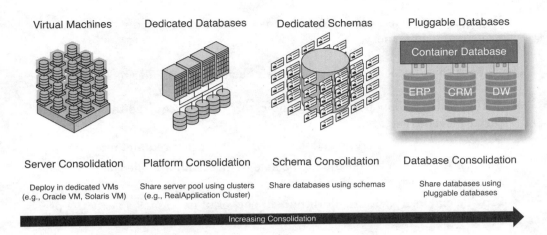

Figure 1.1   Consolidation models

Architecture and Components

In Oracle terminology, hosts containing monitored and managed targets are grouped into *logical pools*. These pools are collections of one or more Oracle database homes (used for database requests) or databases (used for schema requests). A pool contains database homes or databases of the same version and platform—for example, a pool may contain a group of Oracle Database 12.1.0.1 container databases on Linux x86_64.

Pools can in turn be grouped into *zones*. In the DBaaS world, a zone typically comprises a host, an operating system, and an Oracle database. In a similar vein, when defining middleware as a service (MWaaS) zones, a zone consists of a host, an operating system, and an Oracle WebLogic application server. Collectively, these MWaaS and DBaaS zones are called *platform as a service* (PaaS) zones. Users can perform a few administrative tasks at the zone level, including starting and stopping, backup and recovery, and running chargeback reports for the different components making up a PaaS zone.

In the DBaaS view of a PaaS zone, self-service users may request new databases, or else new schemas in an existing database can be created. The databases can be either single instance or a Real Application Cluster (RAC) environment, depending on the zones and service catalog templates that a user can access.

Diagrammatically, these components and their relationships are shown in Figure 1.2.

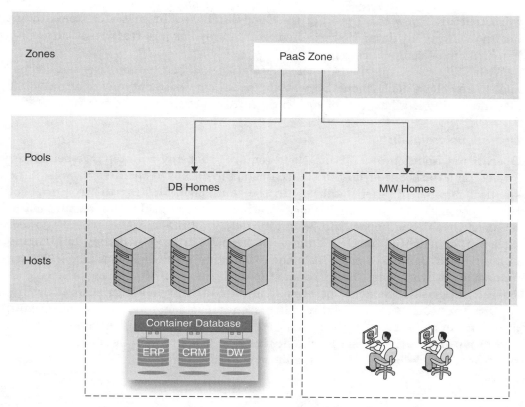

Figure 1.2 Components of a PaaS zone

Deployment Issues

Now that we understand the architecture and components that are used in the different consolidation models, let's examine some standard deployment issues that need to be addressed. These include security, operational, resource, and fault isolation issues, as well as scalability and high availability. It is very important to understand that delivery services and the SLAs around those services will drive the actual architecture, design, and implementation. Therefore, architecture, design, and implementation also play directly into the chargeback and metering aspect of the services.

Security Isolation

Security isolation is often the first point that management worries about in any cloud model. Is my data safe? What options do I have for securing my consolidated infrastructure? How can I prevent the cloud database administrator from accessing and viewing my data? How can I ensure that my network traffic is secure? Can I ensure I meet compliance regulations?

With all of these questions, security isolation has become an essential component of any cloud deployment. Security breaches can arise not only externally but also internally, so all aspects of your cloud infrastructure must be secure.

Operational Isolation

Operational isolation in a DBaaS cloud requires that any maintenance being performed on a database or on the environment the database operates in affects the smallest number of other databases in the same pool. Meeting this requirement clearly becomes more problematic for operating system or grid infrastructure maintenance, though the impact can be minimized by rolling upgrades where allowed. Isolation for patching an Oracle database kernel can be provided by minimizing the number of databases per Oracle home, but adding Oracle homes also increases management overheads. Database startup and shutdown would normally be considered database-dependent operations, but administrative errors such as setting the wrong ORACLE_SID can lead to unforeseen impacts on other databases. Again, isolation can be provided at the ORACLE_HOME level and by having different user IDs and group IDs at the kernel level, but this also leads to more management overhead, and, it must be said, more likelihood of human error.

Resource Isolation

In a DBaaS cloud, resource isolation deals with the allocation and segregation of resources such as CPU, memory, network (public and private), and storage (I/O per second and overall capacity). Management concerns include questions such as How does the CPU usage of my database affect other databases in the DBaaS cloud? How much memory should I allocate to a specific database? Can I restrict the network utilization, both at the public network and interconnect levels, to not impact other databases? Likewise, how can I guarantee storage capacity and IOPS for my databases?

Fault Isolation

Fault isolation in a DBaaS cloud is normally provided at the database level, since that is the unit of granularity in the multitenant architecture. Each database and its associated instance (or instances, in RAC environments) need to be isolated from other databases. Even when all databases are run from a single ORACLE_HOME, database faults are normally isolated to a failing instance, so fault isolation is maintained by fencing off the offending instance. However, other failures may require handling at different levels. For example, concerns include how to deal with a server, network, or storage failure. Such failures are normally handled by some form of redundancy such as multinode setups, active/passive switches, bonded networks, or redundant storage such as Automatic Storage Management (ASM) redundancy.

DBaaS Scalability

Scalability is a fundamental characteristic of DBaaS architectures by virtue of their support for self-service, elasticity, and multitenancy. Oracle's database technologies provide a number of ways to support scalability when delivering database services, including resource management and quality of service, addition of extra storage through functionality such as multiple Exadata Database Machine frames, horizontal scaling via RACs when service demands increase beyond the capabilities of a single machine, and scalable management resources where Oracle Enterprise Manager can add management nodes as the number of targets under management grows.

DBaaS High Availability

Not all consumers require the same level of availability in a cloud environment. Oracle's DBaaS self-service catalog allows the capability to include different levels of availability using a metals model, as shown in Table 1.1.

For example, the bronze standard provides a single-instance database service (possibly via RAC One Node), whereas the other extreme, platinum, would normally include a RAC database with multiple standbys. These standbys might include a near standby in the same data center as your RAC database and a far standby in a completely separate remote data center. These measures help to improve the high-availability and disaster recovery goals you have for that database. In Oracle Enterprise Manager 12.1.0.4, with the added support for Data Guard, you now have the ability with just a few clicks to provision the primary and multiple standbys across different data centers. The standbys can be either single instance or a RAC configuration.

Table 1.1   Availability Levels

Service Level	Description
Bronze standard	Single instance databases/RAC One Node databases
Silver standard	Single instance with standby
Gold standard (HA)	RAC databases
Platinum standard	RAC with standby

Business and Technology Benefits of Having DBaaS Enabled

DBaaS, or a database cloud, is becoming a very popular concept with organizations of all sizes across the spectrum of industry. Placing database infrastructure concerns with the DBaaS provider frees an organization's IT and technology departments to focus at an organizational level rather than at an application or department level. With the focus at an organizational level, the IT and technology teams are more closely aligned with the organizational and business needs. The fundamental requirements of an organization have never really changed—they have always aimed for lowered operational expenses (OPEX) and total cost of ownership (TCO). What has changed is the emergence of new platform architecture and software technologies that, working together, deliver on those needs. The opportunity to reduce OPEX and TCO is precisely what is driving the improved acceptance and adoption rate of DBaaS.

Let's look at some of the intrinsic benefits of deploying DBaaS, which include the basic benefits associated with any cloud solution:

- **Time-to-market**: The nimbleness with which a company reacts and adapts to changing market conditions, competition, and consumer needs and expectations is critical. A core component of any cloud solution is self-service and automation. With a well-planned cloud solution, there is no need to deploy hardware for new projects, and with self-service and automation, the business units become more self-reliant.

- **Scalability**: The combination of inherent concepts of elasticity, consolidation, and resource pooling at a wider organizational level drives scalability in a cloud computing environment. For custom built solutions, the value and benefit of this automatic scaling is even more potent and impressive.

- **Empowerment**: Cloud computing solutions typically have a web-based interface for users. They can be accessed by employees, customers, and partners no matter where they are. With a cloud database, everyone gets to work with the same set of information, and spreadsheet chaos is a thing of the past.

- **Availability**: Combining the benefits of standardization (hardware, software, procedural best practices) and empowerment (self-service, on demand scalability) automatically delivers improved availability.

Let's go a step further and look at why databases are worthy of their own class in the cloud solution world. We do not see phrases such as "application servers as a cloud" or "web servers as a service" or "exchange servers as a service." Logically and technically, these concepts can exist, but they do not. Why is that?

Databases are used to store data. As we are all aware, the amount of data being generated, used, and stored is growing exponentially. This ever-growing volume of data needs to mined and analyzed to generate intelligent, actionable information. Now, more than ever, data means everything—it drives financial, operational, and tactical decisions and strategies in every business. But along with all this data come the headaches of tasks such as managing performance, scaling capacity, and backup and recovery strategies.

Databases are often considered the single point of serialization of application processing and logic, usually because application design is not focused on how databases work or the best way to use them. What this means is that designing, managing, and performance tuning databases represents a unique set of skills and talents.

From a computing perspective, resource consumption characteristics and performance needs of a database are unique in nature. Databases, especially untuned databases, can be resource hogs when it comes to storage, CPU, and network resources.

Scaling of databases also presents unique challenges. Scaling can directly impact expenditure on multiple components of the platform and infrastructure, including on the storage subsystem (due to storage volume or performance) and on throughput (in IOPS or MBps).

Databases are a complex component of the application stack. Consequently, the underlying database technology can potentially have a severe impact, positive or negative, on the overall scalability, availability, business continuity, and performance aspects of any given application. When the applications in question are business critical and/or revenue generating, the potential for impact makes the databases a very visible, highly scrutinized component.

From an economics perspective, databases can prove to be one of the costliest, if not *the* costliest, component of any given application deployment. The database's application stack, for example, can drive the overall solution cost in the following ways:

- Database licensing costs and annual support costs.
- Database-specific infrastructure costs, especially those driven by performance initiatives, such as high-performance compute servers, high-performance storage, and in some cases even high-performance networking.
- Staffing and resourcing costs for maintaining the database (design, administration, performance tuning, etc.).
- Cost of high-performance backup management, storage systems, and infrastructure based on the uptime, recovery point objectives (RPOs), and RTO expectations. (In today's age of data explosion, databases tend be quite large, and database backup and recovery becomes key.)

Cloud computing, as a concept and a solution, is aimed at resolving these economic concerns. When you add the uniqueness of databases to the mix, you can see the value of deploying a database cloud, or in other words, deploying a DBaaS solution.

Great First Step for Transitioning into the Cloud

Moving an organization's IT infrastructure from the old server-based model to a cloud-based model can be a daunting task, regardless of whether the destination is a private cloud or a public cloud. Implementing a cloud solution on a very focused, self-contained technology stack, such as database technology, can be a very useful first step into cloud computing.

The toolkit available for database technologies is wide, extensive, mature, and multivendor. The same is true for the infrastructure components, such as the server, storage, and backup infrastructures. Dedicated, fully contained, engineered appliances have been a part of the database technology stack for a while now.

Another key aspect to consider is the significant amount of automation that exists in the database arena. This is primarily due to the unique and complex nature of databases plus the sizes of the databases that are common nowadays.

Security is an important aspect of any cloud solution and is yet another consideration that has long been a part of any overall database solution. Databases have their own dedicated security model that is mature and can fairly easily integrate into the larger organization model (single sign-on [SSO]- and Lightweight Directory Access Protocol [LDAP]-based authentication and integration, etc.). Database security models have matured to include data encryption for data backups, data at rest, as well as data in flight.

Finally, the amount of data existing within organizations is huge, and its rate of growth is exponential. Almost every application deployed will need a data repository or data store of some type. This growth in data must be supported by corresponding growth in infrastructure.

The combination of the mature toolkit, the engineering inherent to database solutions, the preexisting automation especially in the administration aspects of databases, and the existence of a mature security model provide a solid foundation upon which organizations can build and deploy their first cloud solution.

The existing domain knowledge and the highly experienced skill set available provide the technical basis for learning and fine tuning the various aspects of cloud computing.

According to some reports and surveys, database technology–related expenditure for midsize to large-size companies can be up to 40 percent or more of the annual IT budget. Having a defined organization-wide strategy for databases will help organizations manage the growth of data and at the same time keep database costs down. The fact that databases can drive up to 40 percent of the IT budget makes the database a very attractive focus area to use to kick off cloud computing as a long-term IT strategy.

Summary

Cloud computing is a generic architectural concept that encompasses the entire gamut of technology as it relates to infrastructure. Cloud computing is more than just another fancy term for "virtualization." All of the new "as a service" models are implementations of cloud computing. Infrastructure, platform, database, software, network, and storage as a service all are implementations focusing on specific concepts of the technology stack within infrastructure. These terms are sometimes used interchangeably, but in reality, cloud computing is a concept, whereas the as-a-service models are implementations.

The very definition of "cloud computing" has introduced a fundamental change in thinking when it comes to ownership, roles, responsibilities, and expectations. This is not to say that ownership, roles, responsibilities, and expectations were missing or lacking before the advent of cloud computing. They have always existed, but cloud computing has changed the lens through which they are seen.

Introducing the core concept of "service" into the overall architecture brings about these changes. We saw that in order to deliver a service that is meaningful, cloud computing had to introduce "elasticity, flexibility, and rapid and easy deployment" into its core concept and architecture.

DBaaS implementations are not much different from other cloud implementations. Database clouds have some unique challenges when it comes to cloud implementations, driven by their complex and temperamental nature. We need to understand these core concepts specifically as they apply to databases in order to deploy a successful and meaningful DBaaS.

This chapter is the beginning of understanding the cloud computing framework, specifically when it comes to database clouds or DBaaS.

2

The Database Cloud Administrator—Duties and Roles

In Chapter 1, "Database as a Service Concepts—360 Degrees," we introduced the core concepts that define and drive cloud computing in general. We went into some detail about how the concept of cloud computing applies to the database world, and we talked about the roles and interactions that exist in a cloud environment at a very high level.

In this chapter, we explore what it means to be an Oracle database administrator (DBA) in the cloud computing world. The basic role and functions of the DBA working in a cloud environment are not much different than in a traditional, on-premises environment. What does change with the cloud paradigm is the thought process and viewpoint.

DBA Responsibilities in a Traditional Environment

In the traditional database paradigm, the DBA role falls loosely into two categories: the application DBA and the operational DBA (see Figure 2.1). They work on the same database but look at it from two different perspectives. DBAs in both roles must understand the core concepts and internals of the database to perform their job. They also need to understand the various database features, how they work, and how to best use them.

Depending upon the role or interests, DBAs may gravitate to functionality at an object level (partitioning, indexing, compression, virtual columns), to functionality

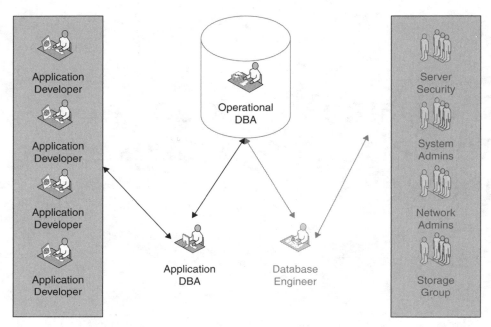

Figure 2.1   DBA responsibility in a traditional model

useful to programmers and database users (results caches, advanced queueing, or Java within the dataset, XML processing, etc.), or to functionality applicable at the database level and focused on infrastructure needs (Data Guard, Real Application Clusters [RAC], recovery management, encryption, etc.).

Application DBAs tend to work with databases from a *logical* implementation viewpoint. They look at the database from an application- and data-centric focus. They are more in tune with relational data models and star schema warehouse models, data relationships and usage, and database features directly consumable by the application team, such as partitioning, queueing, replication, Procedural Language/Structured Query Language (PL/SQL) features, and enhancements.

Operational DBAs, by contrast, tend to look at the database from a *physical* implementation perspective. They administer the physical aspects of the database, such as backups, database storage allocation and capacity, database server health, disaster recovery, and consolidation. Operational DBAs are focused on database features that are directly consumed by the infrastructure side of the equation. The benchmark of success is meeting key performance metrics around I/O and network latencies.

The roles of the application DBA and the operational DBA are equally important, and in many areas, they overlap. Both must understand the core concepts of the database and how it functions. Both are concerned with performance tuning, availability, and scalability.

Take performance tuning as an example. An application DBA tunes the database with the purpose of optimizing the application and its use of the database. An operational DBA tunes the database with the purpose of optimizing the physical infrastructure—reducing I/O latencies or pressure, relieving memory pressure, improving operating system performance, and fine-tuning the network.

More specifically, both DBAs tune SQL. The application DBA tunes SQL by understanding the application and how it uses the data and by working with the development team to optimize that process. The operational DBA tunes SQL by looking at Explain Plans, I/O characteristics, and latencies.

The most successful DBAs are those who can look at the same problem from both viewpoints. The best solution is the one that balances infrastructure and application concerns.

DBAs are often seen as the gatekeepers of the databases. They see the database as "their" property and themselves as the guardians of their database. Server administrators, storage administrators, backup administrators, and network administrators share this outlook as it applies to their areas. Consequently, IT infrastructure management is often seen as a collection of siloed groups, much like an island nation of small, individual islands.

In actuality, there is a smaller and relatively unknown group of DBAs that we call *database engineers*. This group of DBAs straddles the fence between the various groups responsible for the IT infrastructure, and their role is similar to that of application DBAs. Database engineers work closely with the infrastructure teams—with the storage team to build adequate storage, with the server team to choose servers and operating systems to best support database operations, and with the network teams to configure the networking, all to ensure that the database performance can be maximized and optimized.

What's Changed with DBaaS

With the evolution of cloud computing, the roles and viewpoints of the DBAs also have evolved. Cloud computing introduces a fundamental change in database ownership and responsibility. This change has a ripple effect felt throughout the entire workflow between applications and the database. As a result, each individual role is now distinct, visible, and critical in its own way.

As defined in Chapter 1, the database cloud, or database as a service (DBaaS), is all about providing a platform that frees the application development teams from having to worry about servers and hardware, allowing them to focus all of their attention on application ownership and development.

In other words, DBaaS splits the ownership and responsibility into two tracks, one at an infrastructure layer and the other at an application layer. DBaaS divides performance responsibilities by differentiating between application-owner performance and infrastructure-owner performance:

- Infrastructure teams own and are responsible for performance at a hardware and infrastructure layer.
- Application teams own performance responsibility from an application perspective, which includes how the application interacts with the database.

DBaaS divides scalability responsibilities, once again, by differentiating between application scalability and infrastructure scalability:

- Infrastructure teams own the responsibility of creating a platform that is elastic and scalable on demand. In other words, infrastructure teams own managing capacity in anticipation of growth.
- Application teams own the responsibility of creating an application that is scalable on demand and, more important, understanding and obtaining what the application needs for scaling.

Availability responsibilities also are divided by ownership. It is crucial to understand the distinction between performance and scalability, on the one hand, and availability, on the other. Performance and scalability have a direct impact on availability.

The database and infrastructure team is responsible for availability of the service itself, and the application team is responsible for availability at the application layer. This statement is broad and rather useless unless we better define and distinguish *service* availability and *application* availability.

To start with, let us agree that if the application is unresponsive to the end user, it can be considered as being unavailable. The real question is, *Why was the application unresponsive to the end user?* The difference between the availability of the DBaaS and the availability of the application is rooted in the problem that is making the application unavailable in the first place.

From the DBaaS team's perspective, if the database is up and running and is able to respond to a login request, it is considered as being available. But that seems too generic and simplistic; therefore, we add quality of service (QoS) and the corresponding service level agreements (SLAs) to this definition of availability. The SLA might state availability requirements in terms of I/O response time as compared to I/O throughput expectations, such as input/output operations per second (IOPS), megabytes per second (MBps), and CPU capacity. Therefore, from a DBaaS provider perspective, the database is considered as being available if it is up and running, accepting database login requests, and producing QoS metrics that show all SLAs are being met.

Some examples where the DBaaS provider will be responsible for the outage and for identifying and resolving the issues are as follows:

- The archive destination space was not managed properly and fills up as a result. The database is unavailable because the archiver has insufficient space to archive and release the online redo logs.
- There was an issue at the storage area network (SAN) layer, which caused the I/O performance to drop dramatically.
- A database backup job kicked off at the wrong time or has been running for too long and is impacting the data file I/O performance.
- The database or the server crashes or aborts due to either a hardware or a software bug.

The key point is that, from a business unit perspective, availability is based on the ability to perform the business function according to the SLA. In other words, this is the availability of the entire application the business uses to deliver the function. For an application to be available, therefore, the infrastructure must be available and the application must be able to use and capitalize on the infrastructure strength. Let us take a deeper look at availability from a database perspective.

Database availability is defined in terms of the database being open and able to accept connections and respond to a beacon set of requests within a defined response-time window. Events that would constitute the database itself being down include, but are not limited to, the following:

- The database is hung in an archiver stuck mode.
- The database is failing requests due to lack of space.
- The database is up and running, but the listener is down, and therefore the database is not available.

Once the database is deemed available, the application owners and developers are responsible for identifying and resolving the issue that is interfering with availability. The reason this rather hard line is drawn here is that the application development team has the ownership of and authority over the application design and architecture. In such cases, an availability hit is recorded against the application, and it is the application team's responsibility to identify and remediate the situation. Following are a few examples where availability is impacted by application design and architecture:

- Excessive row-level locking and blocking causes an unresponsive application.
- The application does not manage its connection pool properly and consequently exceeds the configured maximum number of connections. As a result, the application receives an error when establishing connections and is rendered unresponsive and unavailable.
- The database load and throughput exceed the volume specified by the SLA for the solution design.
- Availability requirements of the database have increased since the original solution design.

In terms of cloud service, these examples emphasize the need for proper and clear definition of what is called the *service catalog*. The service catalog describes all the responsibilities and expectations of the cloud provider as well as of the cloud subscriber. From an availability perspective, for example, the service catalog would describe

- The definition and expectations on overall SLAs related to the database infrastructure
- The QoS and beacons used to measure and report on SLAs
- The definition of planned outages versus unplanned outages and their durations

Note

Defining uptime SLAs is relatively easy, but defining and developing an overarching QoS is where the difficulties arise. The QoS must also take into account the infrastructure capabilities, such as automated relocation of resources.

This discussion leads directly to the topic of feature set and capabilities of a good DBaaS solution. Not only must the solution be proactive in terms of ability to handle pure infrastructure issues, it must also be able to assist application owners in identifying, addressing, and managing application availability. In other words, a good DBaaS solution is one that provides the features and toolkits that enable the consumer and provider to be proactive. For example, the solution should have in place

- A monitoring and alerting system that is comprehensive and customizable in terms of metrics monitored and who receives the notifications
- A dashboard system that clearly shows how the service is performing against the QoS goals and SLAs
- A system that allows the consumers of DBaaS to scale and grow on demand

What this really means is that DBaaS has changed the database paradigm by redefining and redrawing the lines of ownership and responsibility and, at the same time, combining the individual infrastructure fiefdoms into a single role, at least from the end user viewpoint. End users expect a service delivered at an agreed-upon quality level, with the toolkit and functionality that gives them visibility, control, and flexibility. The consumer is not—and does not want to be—aware of the mechanics of how that service is delivered.

The New Role of the Cloud DBA

In the earlier sections, we talked about application DBAs, operational DBAs, and database engineers. With the introduction of DBaaS, these roles are now spread out and sometimes even decentralized. What we mean is that some aspects of the DBA role must logically move under the umbrella of the application development teams, while others are centralized to a much greater extent:

- The application DBAs work with the application development team very closely. They are the point of integration between the developers and infrastructure team. In other words, they can speak the developers' language as well as the infrastructure team's language and bridge that gap.
- The operational DBAs are now part of the centralized group, taking care of the day-to-day care maintenance of the underlying infrastructure for the database.
- The database engineers are the integration point between the application and operational DBAs. They are the ones who work with the application DBAs to define the QoS metrics and SLAs.

In order to understand these roles and how they map into the overall DBaaS platform and concept, we need to define the roles and responsibilities in greater detail.

The Application DBA Role in DBaaS

As we said earlier, the application DBA is a part of the application development team working closely with the developers. To be able to influence the application design and architecture, the application DBA role is now decentralized and embedded within the application development team.

The application DBA's primary responsibility is to work with the application developers and architects early on and throughout the application development lifecycle to

- Ensure the application development team understands how databases work and uses them appropriately.

- Ensure the application development team understands how the database events can impact an application.

- Work with the application development team to understand how database events and outages are manifested to the application. This understanding enables the application development team to build in mechanisms to gracefully handle and manage these events.

- Work with the application development team to design and build the logical database using the appropriate features to maximize performance.

- Facilitate communications between the application development team and the core DBaaS teams.

- Translate the application development team's performance, availability, and infrastructure requirements into terms and metrics the DBaaS team can use to properly size, design, and deploy a solution.

- Translate the DBaaS team's assessments, statements, and findings such that the application development team can understand and use the information appropriately. This information includes projections for storage space, CPU requirements, I/O metrics, uptime, and availability.

In other words, application DBAs are key during the application design and development phase. Their role becomes one of ensuring that both the database and the application in terms of how it uses the database are architected and designed properly. The best way to achieve this goal is for the DBA to be embedded early on in the process and to work with the application teams proactively on potential issues. As a result, the application DBAs work closely with both the application teams and the database engineers on the DBaaS team.

The Operational DBA Role in DBaaS

The operational DBA role still remains pretty much intact and crucial in the new paradigm created by DBaaS. The operational DBA's primary responsibility in a DBaaS environment is still one of ensuring that the ancillary processes around managing the database are managed and controlled effectively. These responsibilities include things such as the following:

- As the first line of defense for a database, triage and handle database-related alerts.

- Work with the DBaaS team to ensure that the database is being managed to meet and exceed agreed-upon QoS and SLA requirements. For example:

  - Ensure database backups are being performed per the defined SLAs.

- ▪ Ensure I/O performance is compliant with the stated SLAs.
- ▪ Ensure patching and maintenance work is being performed in compliance with the end user availability SLA as well as being communicated to the end user teams.
- ▪ Ensure database performance issues occurring due to infrastructure problems are being identified and resolved as per the specified SLAs.
- Communicate with the application development team, especially the application DBA, on application-owned performance bottlenecks and issues. These issues could include, for example, excessive application-level row locking, excessive redo generation, or inefficient use of partitioning leading to query plans that perform an excessive amount of I/O.
- Communicate with the application development team when the database is coming close to utilizing all the assigned resources and needs more. Resource usage could be in terms of CPU utilization, I/O limits, and storage space.

In other words, operational DBAs perform key roles once application databases are promoted into production. They are the primary recipients of the monitoring system's alerts and thus work very closely with the application DBAs and database engineers to ensure a database is performing as expected or better than expected.

The Database Engineer Role in DBaaS

The database engineer role is not necessarily a new role in terms of function, but it is a new role in terms of its singular focus and attention. Database engineers focus on designing, building, and deploying the overall DBaaS. The primary responsibilities of the database engineer therefore include the following:

- Define, design, and build the DBaaS tiers based on QoS and SLA requirements.
- Define the solution architecture to deliver databases based on the defined metrics.
- Define and develop the operational tools and procedures required to support the ongoing database maintenance and management.
- Define and develop the tools and dashboards that enable the service consumer to measure and validate service delivery and to manage capacity needs on demand.
- Plan and manage capacity growth and demands at the DBaaS offering level rather than at a single database level. Capacity planning efforts account for storage volume, storage performance, and compute capacity, as well as network bandwidth and capacity.

Let us look at a few examples of these tasks, high availability being the first. There are many technologies and methods available to provide for database-level high availability. For example, the most often used technologies include Oracle RAC, Oracle Data Guard, Oracle Golden Gate Replication, storage replication, database sharing, virtualization techniques and features, and so on. One solution stack might be as follows:

- Use Oracle RAC along with Oracle Data Guard to deliver the highest level of availability.
- At the next level, deploy single-instance with Data Guard.
- At the third and lowest level, deploy single-instance databases with nightly backups.

From an I/O performance perspective, the DBaaS could provide tiered storage, starting with a low-end Internet small computer system interface (iSCSI) Network File System (NFS) storage going all the way up to high-end SAN using tiered storage and solid-state drives (SSDs) or flash memory drives.

For capacity and scaling, the solution could either be RAC, wherein compute capacity is added by growing the system horizontally, or it could be based on a virtualization tool, allowing for vertical scaling by adding virtual CPUs, and so on.

Another crucial aspect of the overall DBaaS is database backup. Once again, multiple options and technologies are available for performing database backups. The most common examples are Oracle Recovery Manager (RMAN)-based backups to either active or standby databases and RMAN in conjunction with storage technology such as snapshots and mirror splits. These backups can be written to different locations or devices to meet the backup speeds or RTO objectives. Options for database backup destinations include dedicated backup devices such as the Oracle Zero Data Loss appliance or the Data Domain appliance or cheaper SANs being managed as virtual tape libraries.

Preparing to Be a Cloud DBA

Depending on the organizational structure and whether it is a private cloud or a public cloud, the following roles can be fulfilled by DBAs in different parts of the organization:

- In the case of the public cloud database provider, the database engineer and operational DBA roles are with the cloud provider, but the application DBA is embedded into the application development team.

- In the case of large institutions building a private cloud database that is shared across the entire organization, the same structure is followed.

- In the case of private cloud, these roles may be combined under the same organizational entity as well.

It is important to understand that the DBA organizational structure may morph from one structure to another based on organizational needs and demands. Figure 2.2 represents the DBA roles that exist in the DBaaS-based solution. As stated earlier, the same roles existed before but are now much more visible and distinctly defined.

As a DBA working in the current traditional model who is preparing to move into the DBaaS model, the transition is not just about skill sets. You would obviously need to possess or acquire the specific skills needed to execute your responsibilities within the role. The transition is more about mindset. The transition into DBaaS or database clouds is also about *delivering a service and being accountable for it.*

The approach to DBaaS is more consultative and democratic than dictatorial in nature. To take it a step further, the very concept of DBaaS is based on free market and demand and supply. The DBaaS provider is providing a service. End users will consume the service if it meets their needs in terms of functionality, cost, ease of use, and more. On the flip side, the provider cannot accept any requests

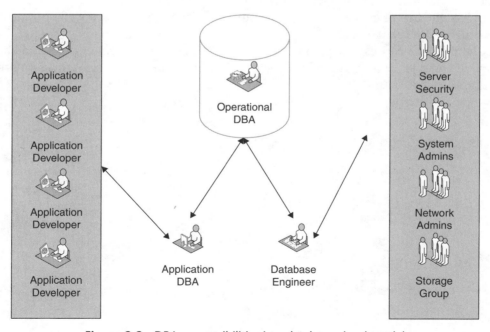

Figure 2.2 DBA responsibilities in a database cloud model

or conditions that it cannot deliver, which leads us to the second mindset change: adaptability and flexibility (within reason).

From a technical perspective, DBAs in the DBaaS paradigm, particularly operational DBAs, still need a lot of the same skills as those in a traditional database environment. Database engineers and application DBAs will need to pick up some ancillary supporting technologies.

Application DBAs are going to work with developers more closely, so they should learn and understand some of the new technologies in the application space, development languages (Java, Ruby, etc.), technologies supporting applications such as application servers, web servers, and even new concepts such as big data and NoSQL.

Database engineers and cloud architects also need to become familiar with technologies and concepts in the infrastructure space, including server, virtualization, storage, and networking technology improvements and changes. These technologies are the underpinning of DBaaS and therefore essential to a successful database cloud service.

Summary

The purpose of this chapter was to help database technologists understand the implications of database cloud services to their environments and jobs. DBaaS is an offshoot of infrastructure as a service and platform as a service, which are well-entrenched and successful technologies.

Cloud DBAs can expect to interact with a larger set of technologies than they have in the past and therefore will need to expand their existing database-related skills.

## 3

Cloud Computing with DBaaS—Benefits and Advantages over Traditional IT Computing

We have covered the basic ideology and concepts around cloud computing and understand that database as a service (DBaaS) is a special case of infrastructure as a service (IaaS) and platform as a service (PaaS). We know that with DBaaS, the roles and responsibilities of the DBAs need to be adjusted.

In this chapter, we look at the various technologies and options that Oracle has developed that make it possible to deliver DBaaS along with all of its demands and expectations. We will see how these technologies can benefit an organization, enabling it to manage infrastructure resources efficiently while at the same time delivering the expected performance with resource elasticity on demand.

DBaaS Evolution: Pre–Database Cloud Strategies

When it comes to managing databases and the infrastructure supporting them, the focus has been on database consolidation. One approach to database consolidation is to consolidate multiple databases into one physical database, which can be done in two ways:

- Convert independent databases into dedicated schemas within a single database.
- Use pluggable databases, a new feature of Oracle 12*c*, and combine multiple databases into a single, larger-container database.

A second approach is to consolidate multiple databases onto a single piece of hardware, which also can be done in two ways:

- Consolidate multiple databases, as is, on fewer, larger servers and hardware.
- Use virtualization technologies to convert physical servers to virtual servers sharing server resources via the hypervisor.

Consolidating databases as schemas has some obvious drawbacks and restrictions, because of which schema-level consolidation is not a scalable and manageable option. Schema-level consolidation assumes that

- The candidate databases do not have any object namespace collisions. We can avoid this if we qualify object names with the schema owner prefix, but that solution impacts the portability to a large extent.
- The candidate databases do not have object ownership or security privileges and permission-level collisions.
- All the candidate databases have the same performance, uptime, and availability requirements. Another key aspect to consider is the peak load times when consolidating databases. Multiple databases with the load peaking at the same time may present a capacity and scaling issue.

Object name, user, and security privilege collisions can either imply application-level modifications or expose security risks. We cannot combine a database that has an 8 a.m. to 5 p.m. uptime expectation with another that has a 24/7 uptime expectation without compromising on uptime.

An alternative approach is to consolidate multiple databases onto a physical server that is larger in terms of both memory and CPU power. Once again, we must consolidate databases that share the same uptime requirements or risk failing to meet the uptime or flexibility requirements database.

In either case, we still must handle the problem of resource allocation and management. In a combined database (multitenant) environment, it's possible that one of the databases issues a query or runs a process that can get out of control and consume more than its share of resources, negatively affecting the other tenant databases. Until now, the toolkit to measure, quantify, and throttle resource consumption across databases has had limited capabilities.

To overcome some of these challenges, a new alternative was developed: consolidating databases on a virtualized platform. Assuming a one-to-one correlation between database and the virtual server, virtualization allows us to allocate resources (CPU and memory) to a database by allocating the resources to the virtual servers they run on. However, there is one caveat to this approach: oversubscription of resources is a real possibility. Oversubscription of resources is the case where the sum of virtual resources allocated is larger than the sum of the physical resources available.

It is important to keep in mind that oversubscription almost always occurs. Not having oversubscription directly implies excess capacity not being used and thus being wasted. The key with a cloud deployment is how to combine workloads to share resources efficiently.

In other words, in a situation where the workload on the virtual servers is high across multiple virtual machines (VMs) simultaneously, resource starvation and contention occurs, which in turn can lead to performance and stability issues.

Comparatively speaking, it is relatively easy to manage memory by ensuring oversubscription does not occur, especially since the servers are capable of scaling to more than 1 TB in memory. CPU resource usage is directly related to processing workload. Processing workloads can vary by time of the day as well as by workload type. In other words, demands on and usage of CPU resources are not uniform but rather temporal and time sensitive in nature.

If we were able to add the capabilities of moving CPU resources around in a dynamic fashion, while at the same time guaranteeing performance, virtualization becomes an extremely viable alternative.

Delivering DBaaS with Oracle Technologies

Oracle has developed new or enhanced existing hardware technologies, database software options, and features as well as ancillary software options and features that are aimed specifically at delivering DBaaS. These technologies and enhancements are best used in conjunction with existing Oracle database features:

- Pluggable databases, new in Oracle 12c, to support multitenancy
- Oracle Flex Clusters and Flex Automatic Storage Management (ASM), new in Oracle 12c
- Oracle Enterprise Manager
- Oracle Engineered Systems
    - Oracle Exadata Database Machine and Oracle Database Appliance are specifically targeted for database implementations.
    - The Oracle Virtual Compute Appliance is a more generic, multipurpose converged appliance with virtualization technologies built in using Oracle Virtual Machine.

What Is Database Multitenancy?

Multitenancy is a generic term referring to the situation in which multiple individual entities reside in the same physical space and share the same resources. Schema-level consolidation, server consolidation, and server virtualization represent earlier methods and techniques used to achieve multitenancy.

With Oracle 12c, Oracle introduced a new approach, with the same goal of resource optimization. This approach is called *pluggable databases* and represents a hybrid approach between schema-based and server-level consolidation. Pluggable databases represents the single most important fundamental and conceptual change in Oracle's approach to database consolidation. *The shared resource unit is an Oracle database (container database), and tenants are fully self-contained databases (pluggable databases).*

The core concept of database-level multitenancy is not new; it has long been a part of the SQL Server and Sybase core architectures and structures. Pluggable databases represents an adaptation of the SQL Server and Sybase multitenancy model into the Oracle database architecture. The fundamental concepts that differentiate Oracle in the database space (V$ performance views and wait events model, read consistency model, row locking, and nonescalating locks) have not changed. In other words, the pluggable databases represent the best of both breeds (architectures).

Oracle's 12c multitenancy option addresses the issues and concerns that have proven to be challenges with the server consolidation approaches available to date. Pluggable databases have taken the benefits of the various options that have been used in the past and adapted them specifically to focus the implementation on Oracle databases and at the same time eliminate the challenges of the current approaches.

Pluggable Databases—Multitenancy in Oracle 12c

The Oracle 12c database multitenancy architecture requires that we add a few new terms to the Oracle lexicon:

- The *container database (CDB)* is the database that is capable of supporting multitenancy.
- The *noncontainer database (non-CDB)* is used to identify the databases as we know them from previous releases. These databases do not support the Oracle 12c multitenancy architecture.
- A CDB has a *root container* that is used to manage CDBs and to maintain system metadata and objects only. The root container is also referred to as CDB$ROOT.
- The application databases that contain user data and metadata are called *pluggable databases (PDBs)*.

The primary goal of using multitenancy is to address some very common but key customer challenges:

- Maximize consolidation density by using the shared resources more efficiently.
- Reduce operating expenses by simplifying administrative tasks. Administrative tasks that are normally performed and repeated at the non-CDB or PDB level are now performed at the CDB level. The gains are a result of consolidating and eliminating repeated tasks into a single task. Examples of tasks that can be simplified include backups, patches, and upgrades.
- Simplify database provisioning.
- Simplify capacity management.

The word *pluggable* is used to describe multitenancy in Oracle 12*c* for a very specific reason: a PDB can be unplugged from one CDB and plugged into a separate CDB with little effort and impact to the rest of the system (see Figure 3.1). A PDB is a complete database from a logical and application standpoint, whereas the root container's primary function is to store and manage the metadata needed for PDBs.

A single CDB can support up to 252 PDBs all connected to and managed by the root container. In order to achieve this mobility, CDBs have to be able to support the mobility of the metadata appropriately. At the same time, we also need to be able to support administering both the CDB as a whole and the individual PDBs.

Therefore, in the case of CDBs, some central structures, such as control files, online redo logs, undo tablespace, and system metadata (i.e., data dictionary), are

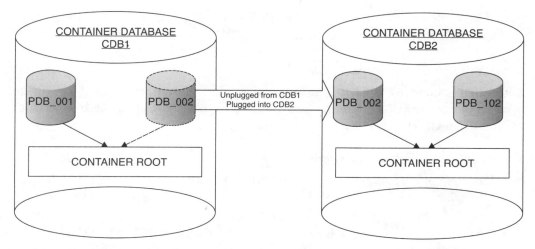

Figure 3.1   Oracle 12*c* multitenancy—unplug and plug in a pluggable database

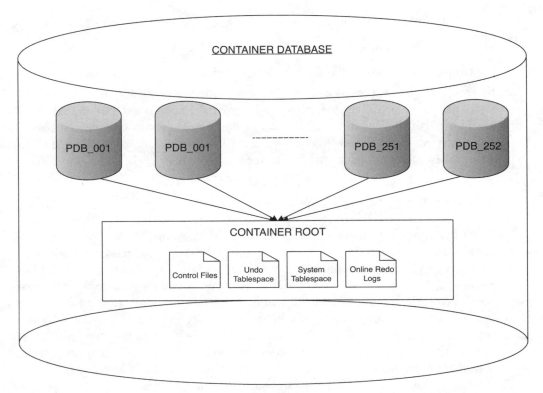

Figure 3.2   Oracle 12*c* multitenancy pluggable database model

owned by the root container. These are then either logically or physically virtual-ized by the CDB from the root container to the PDB (see Figure 3.2).

Basic Concepts of Pluggable Databases

The resources under the CDB that are common and shared across all the PDBs go beyond just physical CPU and memory. Following are some of the core functional aspects of an Oracle database:

- Most of the background processes are shared.
- The memory structures associated with the system global area (SGA) are shared by the PDBs. The SGA for each PDB is a logically virtualized view of the SGA managed by the CDB.
- The V$ or GV$ views are based primarily on the contents of the SGA and therefore now contain a CON_ID field, which identifies the database context for the information.

- The internal structures and objects that any database requires to function are managed and maintained at the CDB level. These include SPFILEs, control files, online redo logs, standby redo logs, and undo tablespace.

- Users and privileges can be maintained at the CDB layer or can flow down to an individual PDB from the CDB.

The chart in Figure 3.3 is taken from an Oracle white paper[1] and gives us an idea of the gains pluggable databases are capable of delivering from an overall capacity and performance standpoint.[2] The comparison is between consolidation of traditional standalone databases and consolidation using pluggable databases.

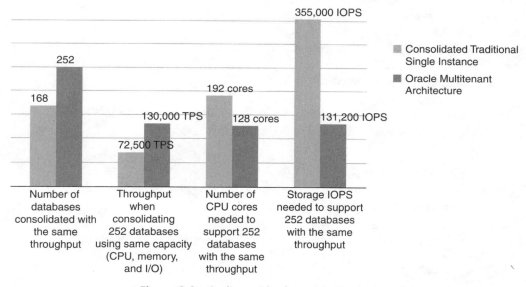

Figure 3.3   Scaling with pluggable databases

Following are the key points to take away from this example:

- Using pluggable databases, we can consolidate 50 percent more databases while maintaining the same throughput (168 versus 252).

- Comparing throughput when consolidating 252 databases in each method, pluggable databases delivered an 81 percent improvement in transactions per second (TPS).

1. "Oracle Multitenant on SuperCluster T5-8: Scalability Study," April 2014, www.oracle.com/technetwork/database/multitenant/learn-more/oraclemultitenantt5-8-final-2185108.pdf.

2. "Oracle Multitenant," June 2013, www.oracle.com/technetwork/database/multitenant-wp-12c-1949736.pdf.

- The improved throughout was delivered with a 33 percent reduction in CPU resources required (192 cores reduced to 128 cores).

- With pluggable databases, the same throughput was delivered and at the same time eliminated approximately 63 percent of the I/O (355,000 I/O operations per second [IOPS] reduced to 131,200 IOPS).

The data dictionary of an Oracle database contains metadata about both the Oracle system structures and the application (see Figure 3.4). In the case of a CDB, the data dictionary is physically partitioned between the PDB and the root. The root contains system metadata only, and the PDB contains application-specific metadata only.

A new CDB-specific set of data dictionary views have been added. For each DBA_* data dictionary view, there is now a CDB_* view. The CDB_* views contain information for all objects in the CDB across all the PDBs.

Oracle 12c pluggable databases are compatible with all other Oracle technologies, including Oracle Real Application Cluster (RAC), Data Guard, GoldenGate, and Data Pump. In other words,

- We can use pluggable databases with the CDB being Oracle RAC aware. The PDBs also automatically become Oracle RAC databases.

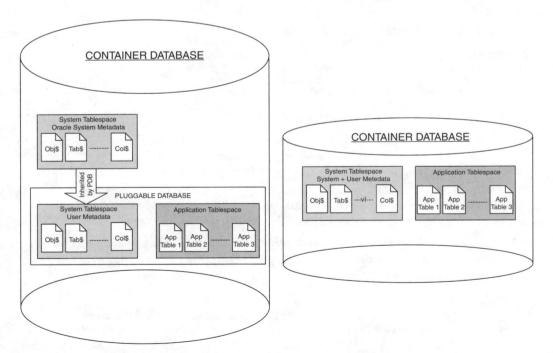

Figure 3.4 Data dictionary virtualization in a pluggable database/container database

- We can set up GoldenGate replication between PDBs or between a PDB and a non-CDB.

- Recovery Manager (RMAN) database backups are executed from the context of the CDB (not the PDB). However, RMAN allows us to perform a point-in-time recovery (PITR) restore of a PDB without impacting the availability of the other pluggable databases.

- Data Guard works exactly the same way but is configured and set up at the CDB level. What this means is that when we execute a switchover or failover operation, the entire CDB undergoes the role change.

The reason RMAN and Data Guard are configured and managed at a CDB level is that they are dependent on the online redo logs, which are defined and managed at the CDB level. *The online redo logs (as well as the undo) are logically virtualized*; that is, each redo log entry is annotated with the CON_ID of the CDB where the change occurred. The undo tablespace is also virtualized the same way as from a database recovery perspective; the undo and redo go hand in hand.

From an application perspective, there is no difference between a PDB and a regular database. The application will connect to the PDB directly over SQL Net in exactly the same as always. The use of pluggable databases does not place any requirement upon the application to be CDB, root container, or pluggable container aware.[3] The security model associated with PDBs is covered later.

With the base assumption that the application has been tested and validated against a non-CDB Oracle 12c database, Oracle guarantees that the application will see no change in behavior or response from a pluggable database versus a non-CDB database. In other words, any application SQL against its application-owned objects will execute and perform exactly the same way, PDB or not. This guarantee comes with a caveat and, in the opinion of the authors, a technically sound and valid one at that.

There is a very small, specific subset of SQL statements that are database-context aware and sensitive and that cannot be issued when connected to a PDB. These commands are almost entirely administrative in nature and will generate an ORA-65040 error code when issued against a PDB:

- Altering system commands modifying initialization parameters marked as non

- Creating a pluggable database when the user is not connected to the root container

- Attempting to close the SEED PDB

---

3. Certain limitations and requirements exist when creating CDB-level users. For example, the username for the common user must be prefixed with *C##* or *c##* and contain only ASCII or EBCDIC characters.

However, if the application code is designed and developed following industry-accepted best practices and standards, there is no reason it would need to execute such statements. The only exception to this statement would be if database administration tools and software, such as Enterprise Manager, should require such capabilities.

Reasons such as these are why we strongly recommend application-level regression testing prior to actually going live with PDBs.

Pluggable Database Features

The ability to unplug a database from a CDB and plug it into another CDB by itself is a huge game changer. The benefits derive from the flexibility and simplicity inherent in this ability. The reason patching exercises are simplified with this approach is that the PDB application metadata is separated from the CDB root container metadata. Remember, the PDB inherits the core Oracle system information from the root container.

With PDBs, patching and upgrades become a lot easier and incur a lot less downtime. To patch a database, you simply unplug the PDB from the lower-version CDB and plug it into higher-version CDB. This same unplug/plug functionality can also be used in the reverse to downgrade or back out a database patch. The existing rules for downgrades and backing with respect to the setting of the "compatible" parameter being at an equal or lower version than the target still apply. Effectively, the time and effort to create a new CDB at the higher patch level is a one-time effort and is amortized across the entire database upgraded using the CDB.

> **Note**
>
> In some instances, the upgrade/downgrade processing cannot be done implicitly. In such cases, the DBA is notified that a particular Oracle-provided script has to be run.

Another way to perform patching exercises is to patch a CDB that owns and manages multiple PDBs. With one patching exercise, all the PDBs within a single CDB are patched simultaneously. If a CDB contained 10 PDBs, it would take the same amount of time, effort, and outage windows to patch 10 PDBs as it would take to patch one non-CDB database. Effectively, we have saved the time, effort, and outage time of nine non-CDB patching exercises.

From an availability perspective, we can react quickly to situations such as server or CDB loss. With the simple task of unplugging and plugging, a PDB can be relocated to another server. This relocation exercise may be in response to a capacity planning decision or it may be due to server loss or the loss of a CDB.

Pluggable databases also simplify and speed up processes related to provisioning. Each CDB comes with a seed database, which is used to instantiate a new PDB within a CDB. All that needs to be provided in the "create pluggable database" command, apart from the name of the database, is a valid path prefix and creation of local administrative roles.

PDBs also come with many options and methods of cloning a PDB to create a replica. This ability is extremely useful when it comes to development and test database refreshes. The multitenant architecture allows for

- Cloning to be created within the same CDB
- Cloning across CDBs using Oracle SQL Net connectivity
- Cloning based on storage-level snapshot functionality if available

Another important point to note is that PDBs are fully compatible with and extend existing Oracle database functionality and features. As stated earlier, Oracle RMAN and Data Guard are supported and managed at the CDB itself. By managing database backups and Data Guard at a CDB level, the administrative overhead is significantly dropped. Once again, the operating cost of managing backups and DR for all PDBs is reduced to that of managing one non-CDB database. This cost of administering one non-CDB is amortized across all the PDBs—managing backups of one PDB or 10 PDBs is the same.

PDBs are fully RAC compliant and compatible. The difference is that the CDB in such a case is a RAC-enabled, RAC-aware CDB. The PDBs inherit the RAC functionality when plugged into a RAC CDB. The PDBs can be made available across all the nodes or across a subset of nodes. Access to the PDBs is managed exactly as it would be in single-instance configuration using Dynamic Database Services. Combining RAC with PDBs gives us local high availability, capacity management, and scalability from Oracle RAC and the flexibility and ease of administration of PDBs.

Database resource management has been enhanced now to be CDB/PDB aware. The ability to create a resource governance plan has been around for a while, since each PDB is a fully compliant database by itself. With Oracle 12c, under the multitenant architecture, we can now create resource governance plans at a CDB level. The CDB resource governance plan can be used to control the number of concurrent sessions, CPU usage, and parallel server process usage across PDBs. With Exadata, file I/O resources can also be controlled with CDB-level directives, as it is used with I/O Resource Manager (IORM).

The resource governance is based on the share and cap model. Resources are broken into shares, and each resource is given a set of resources to use but can also be capped on the high side of resource usage. For CDB-level plans, the resource shares and caps are assigned to the various PDBs by creating CDB plan directives.

Security under Multitenancy

A pluggable database maintains and extends the already existing strong database security model to include and support Oracle 12c multitenancy. As we can see in

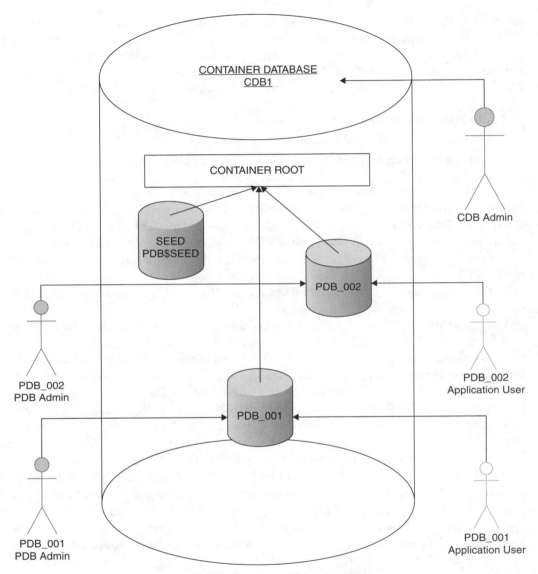

Figure 3.5 Security model under pluggable databases model

Figure 3.5, we can have users at different levels, with access and privileges at either a CDB level or at each individual PDB level. Similarly, application accounts can be created individually for each PDB.

A user ID (usually called a USERID) can be created at the CDB level. All user-defined common user IDs must be created with a prefix of *C*##. You can give the common user access to a specific subset of PDBs by granting the user the "create session" privilege. The privileges granted to the same common user can vary across each of the PDBs the user has access to. The common user's schema on each PDB he or she has access to is unique at a PDB level.

Local user accounts, by contrast, are created individually at the PDB level. The standard user naming convention applies to local user names. The same local user can exist on different PDBs, but these user IDs have no other commonality between them. Local users can access only the PDB in which they are created and have no access to any of the other PDBs or even to the CDB.

The same concept also applies to roles. A common role is a database role, defined and created in the root container. A common role can be assigned only to "common users," and all the privileges cascade down to the PDB level. A local role, on the other hand, is created at the individual PDB level and can only contain roles and privileges applicable to administering at the individual PDB.

The same concept is used to extend the standard database auditing features and functionality. A common audit configuration is created at the CDB level and visible to and enforced for each of the PDBs within the CDB. A local audit configuration is defined and created at the individual local PDB level and therefore applies only to the specific PDB it was created in.

Other Oracle Database Technologies and Features

Pluggable databases and multitenancy are key features of Oracle 12c, especially from a consolidation and database cloud perspective. Other features of Oracle 12c are useful and applicable specifically to database cloud implementations and initiatives.

Oracle RAC functionality is core to database cloud implementations for obvious reasons. First, Oracle RAC has a lot of potential for high availability because Oracle RAC, by definition, provides the ability to withstand and survive a cluster node loss or a database instance loss situation. The second reason is that Oracle RAC provides scalability and capacity planning. We can scale the environment out horizontally by adding servers to the RAC cluster.

Another important feature in the Oracle clustering space is Oracle Flex Clusters. Oracle Flex Clusters is an enhancement to the core Oracle Clusterware functionality available through the grid infrastructure. It is not an enhancement of Oracle RAC.

Oracle Flex Clusters basically contain two kinds of cluster nodes: hub and leaf nodes (see Figure 3.6). Regardless of the node type, each node belongs to the basic grid infrastructure cluster and uses the private interconnect for interprocess communication. The hub nodes are tightly coupled and have access to the shared storage as well. Leaf nodes are a part of the grid infrastructure cluster but do not have access to the shared storage. Each leaf node communicates with a dedicated hub

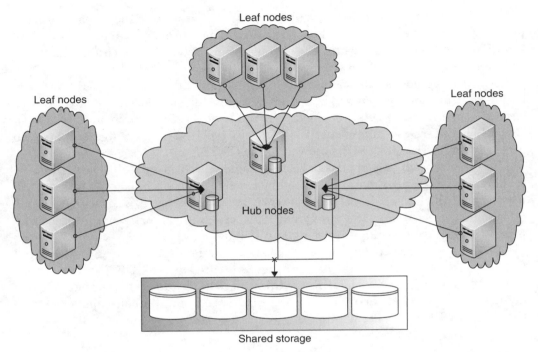

Figure 3.6 Oracle Flex Cluster

node that it connects to for data requests. In a Flex Cluster, we can have up to 64 hub nodes and a much higher number of leaf nodes.

What this means is that the hub nodes with access to the shared storage are where the databases are running. The leaf nodes are not part of the database cluster, since they do not have access to the shared storage. The leaf nodes are used to run application-level software that uses the core grid infrastructure functionality to provide fault tolerance for the application tier in much the same way as it does for the database tier.

In a Flex Cluster, the grid infrastructure provides additional functionality that allows us to change the role or mode of a node, going from a leaf node to a hub node, or vice versa. As a part of the role change, the grid infrastructure Clusterware will start and stop the services as needed.

In a more traditional RAC, all nodes in the database cluster will be running their own ASM instances. Therefore, the background processes on each database node in the cluster communicate with the local ASM instances to execute and implement the I/O requests at the storage level. In the event an ASM instance is lost, the database instances would also crash. More important, during patching updates, the ASM instance is also shut down, which results in service interruptions to the databases.

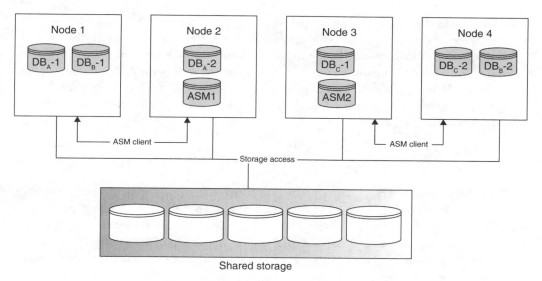

Figure 3.7   Oracle RAC with Flex ASM

Within Oracle clustering, there is another concept called Flex ASM (see Figure 3.7). Flex ASM is a solution to many of the availability-related issues discussed previously. In order to run Flex ASM, the cluster needs to be configured in Flex mode. In Flex ASM, the one-to-one relationship between ASM and database instances is decoupled. ASM is actually running on only a few of the hub nodes. The database instances are talking to the ASM instances remotely over a separate network called the *ASM network*. In the event an ASM instance is lost, all the database instances will be redirected to a surviving ASM instance and the loss will not cause an interruption of service.

Oracle Enterprise Manager Cloud Control 12*c* (EM12*c*) is another key component to deploying Oracle database in a DBaaS model. EM12*c* supports all the database functionality available and makes administration much easier. In addition, EM12*c* is focused on delivering an administration tool that is cloud aware and includes support for a lot of the cloud computing functionality. EM12*c* functionality and applicability to database clouds is covered extensively in later chapters, so we do not go into much detail here.

Following are some of the other features that can be used to great advantage when it comes to deploying Oracle 12*c*:

- Enhanced functionality for resource management and allocation using RMAN.

- Use of instance caging to limit CPU resource allocation at a database level. This helps ensure that no single database is causing a CPU bottleneck by consuming more than its fair share of resources.

- In Oracle RAC, there is a concept of admin-managed versus policy-managed clusters. Admin-managed configurations basically use the standard Oracle RAC administration and configuration functionality. Policy-managed configurations use the concept of server pools. A server pool is an arrangement of the Oracle RAC nodes into logical groups. Database instances are then mapped to the server pool. Based on load, new servers can be added to or removed from a server pool.

Oracle Engineered Systems

Apart from the software stack, Oracle also has a complete array of hardware that is database aware, tuned specifically from the point of view running an Oracle database. These systems are able to provide some extreme-level performance and have a significant amount of capacity as well as expansion capabilities. Depending on the requirements and expectations, one or more of these platforms may be applicable to a given scenario.

At the entry level, Oracle has the Oracle Database Appliance (ODA) X5-2. Each ODA consists of two compute nodes, and each node has two sockets of an 18-core Intel processor. Additionally, included with ODA is a storage shelf that can deliver up to 64 TB of raw space. An additional storage cabinet can be added to the configuration, which in effect doubles the raw storage capacity.

At the next level, Oracle has introduced the Virtual Compute Appliance (VCA). This is an engineered system with built-in Z File System (ZFS) storage, capable of supporting up to 25 compute nodes, and it uses Oracle Virtual Machine (OVM) as the virtualization platform. The VCA comes with an appliance manager that simplifies the administration, provisioning, and scaling of servers under the umbrella of OVM.

Last but not least, Oracle delivers the Exadata Database Machine, which is a highly specialized Oracle database–focused black-box appliance that includes storage, network, and compute capacity needed to run the solution. The Exadata provides a lot of database-aware features and tuning that help it deliver extreme performance. Even the storage in an Exadata is database and SQL aware, and consequently can thoroughly optimize the performance. Specific to database consolidation and database clouds, the Exadata also includes I/O resource manager (IORM). IORM allows the Exadata administrator to specify and control I/O prioritization at an inter-database level and not just an intra-database tier.

Another key point built into the Exadata model is its capacity scaling model. An organization can start with what is known as an *eighth rack* and scale up to a quarter rack, half rack, full rack, and across eight full racks. In terms of compute capacity, using the X5 model standards, that is equivalent to saying that we can start with two compute nodes with 18 cores each (eighth rack), expand to two compute nodes with 36 cores each (quarter rack), expand further to four compute nodes with 36 cores each (half rack), then to eight compute nodes with 36 cores each (full rack), and all the way up to 64 compute nodes, each with 36 cores (8 full racks daisy chained). With Exadata X5, Oracle enhanced the licensing model to be more flexible and based on capacity.

Cloud Computing with DBaaS

The hardware and software required to deliver robust, scalable, manageable DBaaS functionality using Oracle as the database platform exist. Any organization of any size can deploy a DBaaS service that will deliver on the following primary goals:

- **Agility**: Respond to requests and resource needs in a fast, real-time manner.
- **Availability**: Deliver a service that meets the defined goals of performance and availability.
- **Elasticity**: Provide the ability to shrink or expand resource footprints as needed to meet computing demands.
- **End user reporting and accounting**: Provide the ability to capture and present usage metrics, performance against key performance indicators, and so on.

Benefits and Advantages

The benefits to an organization that can successfully deploy a DBaaS solution can be measured in two ways: by operating costs and by customer satisfaction criteria. Operating costs can be lowered by

- Deploying a database architecture that can scale in the just-in-time (JIT) model. The organization saves on infrastructure and licensing costs by not having to acquire resources well in advance of their actual need. A combination of consolidation using engineered systems and deploying an Oracle 12*c* multitenant architecture, Flex Clusters, and RMAN models are key here.
- Deploying an architecture that is agile enough to relocate idling resources to the areas of demand. A combination of policy-managed clusters and Oracle 12*c* multitenant architectures will drive the reduction of costs from an agility perspective.
- Deploying a solution that is standardized and has the toolkit available to monitor, alert, and administer the environment efficiently. A combination of technologies such as Oracle RAC, Oracle 12*c* multitenant architectures, and EM12*c* can be used to drive this administrative aspect of cost reduction.

- Deploying a highly resilient, flexible architecture to drive down outage windows (both planned and unplanned) and thus drive down costs associated with outages. Oracle 12*c* features such as RAC, Flex ASM, and multitenancy are key to driving down outage costs.

- Deploying an Oracle database–aware consolidation strategy to streamline and thereby reduce the capital expenditure in infrastructure costs. Oracle RAC and the multitenant architecture will play an essential role here.

- Deploying a user-friendly, portable system that allows end users to review, report, and manage their resource allocation. Such a deployment will drive down resource costs by eliminating wait times and streamlining processes and procedures.

Customer satisfaction will be a direct outcome of being able to design and deploy a solution that

- Reduces downtime and outages
- Improves time to respond to user requests and questions
- Provides the end user with tools to achieve self-sufficiency and control

The same set of technologies that drive operating cost savings will go a long way to promoting customer satisfaction.

Challenges

The path to achieving the suggested goals and requirements requires careful upfront planning and design. As a part of the planning process, we recommend scheduling periodic checkpoints to validate that your organization is on track to achieve the target platform and environment.

Another aspect to consider during planning is the dedication of resources focused entirely on the design and build out of the new architecture. Without this focused effort, the probability for distraction is extremely high, and resources would be sucked right back into the day-to-day administrative tasks.

We also recommend that the organization plan for building and training the team in the new technologies being introduced. No matter how good the implementation, without a properly skilled staff to administer and deliver the service, the service is doomed to failure.

Standardized processes, procedures, and offerings contribute greatly to the success of DBaaS. These processes should be defined early and evangelized with the remainder of the organization from day one.

Summary

In this chapter, we looked at the various technology offerings available that can help an organization design, build, and deploy a robust DBaaS or database cloud solution. This chapter discussed several technologies that subsequent chapters will cover in more detail.

Oracle 12*c* has a host of new features that are perfectly suited for this purpose. The key new features included with Oracle 12*c* are

- Pluggable databases
- Resource management
- Oracle Flex Clusters
- Oracle Flex ASM

EM12*c* not only supports these new features, but its design and architecture are focused on supporting the core concepts associated with cloud solutions in general and database clouds in particular. The proper design and implementation of this combination is the key to a successful database cloud implementation.

At an infrastructure level, Oracle-engineered systems provide a platform that can be useful in deploying a database cloud service, but we do not imply that this is the only way to implement a database cloud. Virtualization technologies such as VMware also have functionality and tools that can be used to implement a database cloud solution. The new features in Oracle Database 12*c* and EM12*c* can also be used to complement and enhance these solutions.

Schema Consolidation in Enterprise Manager 12*c*

Schema as a service provides database consolidation by allowing administrators to host multiple application schemas within a single database. This offers the capability of database as a service (DBaaS) to possibly hundreds of application users without creating database sprawl. Users can perform day-to-day actions such as provisioning, monitoring, and backup all from a single self-service console. Schema as a service leverages database features such as Oracle Resource Manager and Oracle Database Vault to isolate users of the cloud. These features are complemented by metering and showback/chargeback capabilities, which provide visibility and transparency into resource consumption by each user.

However, schema as a service also has problems, the main one of which (covered in detail later in this chapter) is namespace collision. Having said that, until the introduction of Oracle Database 12c with the multitenant option, schema as a service was really the only viable way of consolidating multiple applications into a single database, and many Oracle customers used it successfully.

Before we look at the details of using schema as a service, there are two areas we need to cover:

- We need to have an understanding of the components that make up the underlying architecture. This is important for both schema consolidation (covered in this chapter) and database consolidation (covered in Chapter 5, "Database Consolidation in Enterprise Manager 12*c*").

- We also need to understand the deployment issues that have to be addressed when undertaking a consolidation exercise. Again, these are common to both schema and database consolidation, but the way we address those issues will vary between the different consolidation models. We'll come back to these deployment issues after we've discussed setting up and using schema as a service.

Let's start by looking at the architecture and components.

Architecture and Components

Oracle Enterprise Manager Cloud Control 12*c* delivers the complete spectrum of database consolidation, as depicted in Figure 4.1.

In Oracle terminology, hosts containing monitored and managed targets are grouped into logical pools. These pools are collections of one or more Oracle database homes (used for database requests) or databases (used for schema requests). A pool contains database homes or databases of the same version and platform—for example, a pool may contain a group of Oracle Database 12.1.0.1 container databases on Linux x86_64.

Pools can in turn be grouped into zones. In the DBaaS world, a zone is typically composed of a host, an operating system, and an Oracle database. In a similar vein, when defining middleware as a service (MWaaS) zones, a zone comprises a host, an operating system, and an Oracle WebLogic application server. Collectively, these MWaaS and DBaaS zones are called *platform as a service (PaaS) zones.* Users can

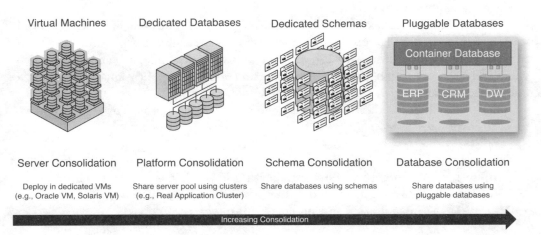

Figure 4.1   Consolidation models

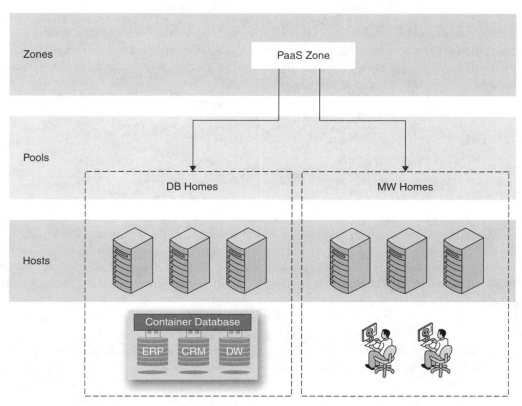

Figure 4.2 Components of a platform as a service zone

perform a few administrative tasks at the zone level, including starting and stopping, backup and recovery, and running chargeback reports for the different components making up a PaaS zone.

In the DBaaS view of a PaaS zone, self-service users may request new databases, or new schemas in an existing database can be created. The databases can be either single instance or a Real Application Clusters (RAC) environment, depending on the zones and service catalog templates that a user can access.

Diagrammatically, these components and their relationships are shown in Figure 4.2.

Schema as a Service Setup

Now that we've looked at the architectural components that make up a consolidation environment, let's look at the details of how it is set up.

Schema as a service can be used to provide profiles and service templates for both an empty schema service and a schema service with seed data. In each case, the cloud infrastructure setup is very similar to the pluggable database as a service (PDBaaS) model, which we discuss in the next chapter. Typically, these steps are done only once and consist of the following:

- Configuring the software library
- Defining roles and assigning them to users
- Creating PaaS zones and pool
- Configuring request settings for the DBaaS cloud
- Configuring quotas for the self-service roles

The only difference with schema as a service from the setup perspective is how the pool is defined. For schema as a service, you must define a different pool, which will contain a pool of databases to which the schemas are deployed.

Before we drill into the details, let's talk about the environment we'll be using to set this up. It's a fairly simple environment consisting of two hosts, host1 and host2. host1 contains the production (prod) database, which is our reference or master database containing the HR schema, which is the schema we will be replicating with schema as a service. host2 contains the test database. The databases need to exist before we set up schema as a service. Diagrammatically, it looks like what is shown in Figure 4.3.

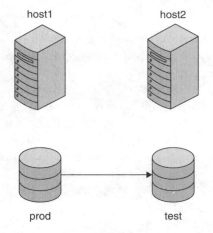

Figure 4.3   Schema as a service environment

Creating a Directory Object

Schema as a service uses a directory object to export the data from the reference database—in our case, the HR schema in the prod database—so we need to create a directory object and grant HR read/write access to it. Obviously, you can do that through SQL*Plus, but I'll be honest—I can never remember the syntax, so it's quicker for me to do it through Enterprise Manager than to look up the syntax in the documentation.

1. This step is done from the prod database home page by following the path Schema → Database Objects → Directory Objects. After logging in, you see the screen, shown in Figure 4.4, where you can click the Create button.

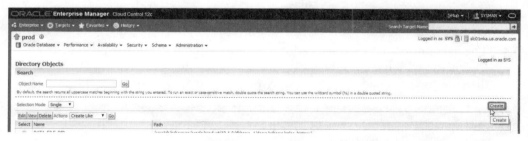

Figure 4.4 Creating a directory object, step 1

2. On the Create Directory Object page, you need to provide a name for the directory object (in this case, I'm using DBaaS_Schema_Export) and an operating system path to the directory you will be using (e.g., /u01/oracle/ schema_export). You can click the Test File System button to validate the path is correct (see Figure 4.5).

Figure 4.5 Creating a directory object, step 2

3. On the next screen, you are shown the host name and Oracle Home location, and you can enter credentials to validate the path. In this case, you already have a named credential, so you select that and click Login (see Figure 4.6).

Figure 4.6   Creating a directory object, step 3

4. The system will now log in as that user and validate that the path exists. Provided you have not made any typos, you should see a message that the directory exists, and you can simply click Return (see Figure 4.7).

Figure 4.7   Creating a directory object, step 4

5. You need to assign the correct privileges on the directory object to the HR user. To do that, you click the Privileges tab (see Figure 4.8).

Figure 4.8   Creating a directory object, step 5

6. A list of users defined in the prod database appears. You can scroll through that list until you find the HR user, then select it and click OK (see Figure 4.9).

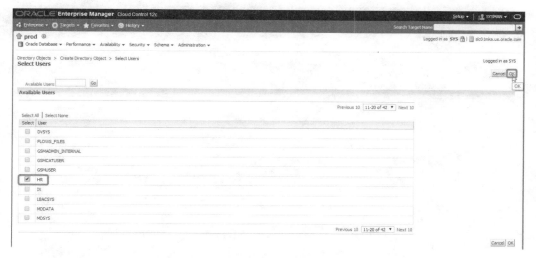

Figure 4.9   Creating a directory object, step 6

7. Select both Read Access and Write Access, and click OK (see Figure 4.10).

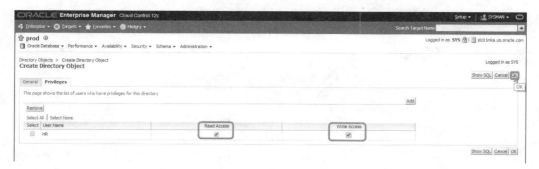

Figure 4.10   Creating a directory object, step 7

8. You should now see a message that the directory has been created successfully, and the directory should be listed in the directory objects list as well (see Figure 4.11).

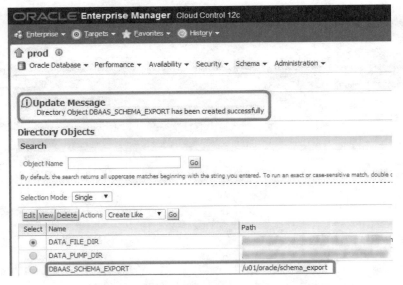

Figure 4.11 Creating a directory object, step 8

Creating a Database Pool

Now that we've created the directory object, we can go through the rest of the process of setting up schema as a service.

1. Start by following the path Setup → Cloud → Database (see Figure 4.12).

Figure 4.12 Creating a database pool, step 1

2. As mentioned earlier, we need a database pool that has been created specifically for Schema as a Service. For this task, you select For Schema from the Create dropdown list (see Figure 4.13).

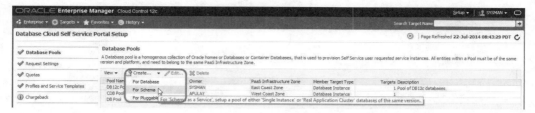

Figure 4.13   Creating a database pool, step 2

3. We need to provide the pool details, credentials, and PaaS infrastructure zone details, then click Add to select databases for the pool (see Figure 4.14).

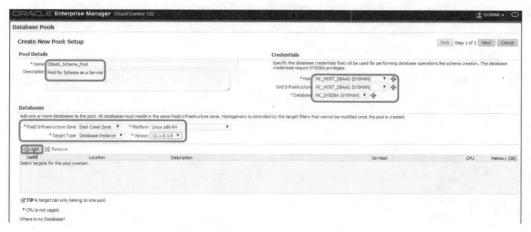

Figure 4.14   Creating a database pool, step 3

4. On the Select and Add Targets pop-up, you can select multiple databases to add to the pool, and in a real cloud environment, you normally would do exactly that. In the small-scale lab that I'm using, I simply select the TEST database row and click Select (see Figure 4.15).

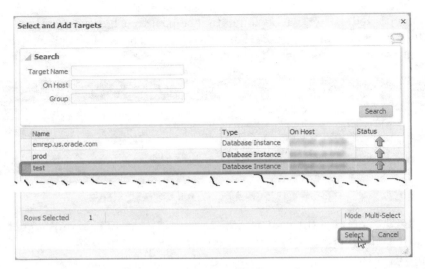

Figure 4.15   Creating a database pool, step 4

5. Back on the Setup page, you have now entered all the values you need, so you just click Next (see Figure 4.16).

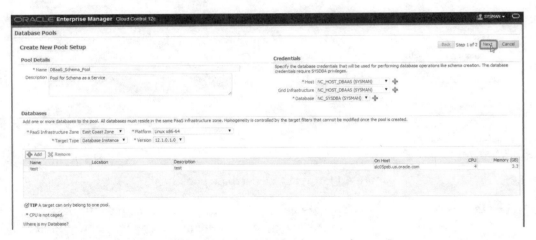

Figure 4.16   Creating a database pool, step 5

6. The Policies page is where you set up the placement policies for the resources in the pool. You can place constraints on the maximum number of schemas that can be created on a database in the pool (via the maximum number of database services), as well as set up the maximum workload parameters for

each service. The placement algorithm uses these parameters to determine
in which database the schema is placed (when there is more than one
database in the pool, obviously). In the example shown in Figure 4.17, you
have set the maximum number of database services to 15 and enabled the
workload limitations and Resource Manager. All that remains to do is click
Submit.

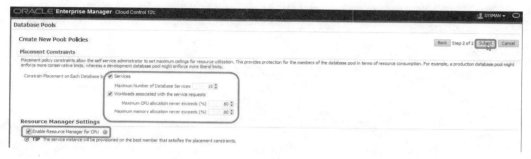

Figure 4.17   Creating a database pool, step 6

7. You will then see a message that the Database Pool has been created successfully (see Figure 4.18).

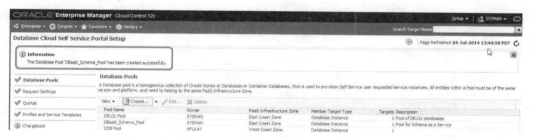

Figure 4.18   Creating a database pool, step 7

Creating a Profile and Service Template

Now that we've created the pool, the next step is to create a Profile and a Service
Template for schema as a service.

1. To start this process, click Profiles and Service Templates (see Figure 4.19).

Figure 4.19 Creating a profile, step 1

2. First, create a profile by clicking Create in the Profiles region (see Figure 4.20).

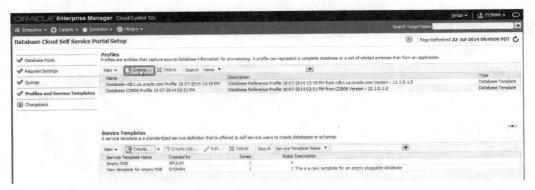

Figure 4.20 Creating a profile, step 2

3. The first screen of the wizard requires you to select the magnifying glass to search for a reference target (see Figure 4.21).

Figure 4.21 Creating a profile, step 3

4. In a small environment, you can already see the prod database listed, but you could search for it if there were lots of targets. Once that row is chosen, you click Select (see Figure 4.22).

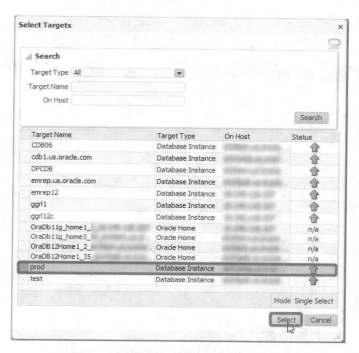

Figure 4.22   Creating a profile, step 4

5. On the Create Database Provisioning Profile: Reference Target page (see Figure 4.23), two regions need attention. First, for the Reference Target region, uncheck the Database Oracle Home checkbox, click the Structure and Data radio button, and select the Export Schema Objects radio button. Second, in the Credentials region, provide the relevant named credentials for the host and the database. Then click Next.

Figure 4.23   Creating a profile, step 5

6. On the Content Options wizard step, choose the HR schema from the Available Schemas list and move it to the Selected Schemas list (see Figure 4.24).

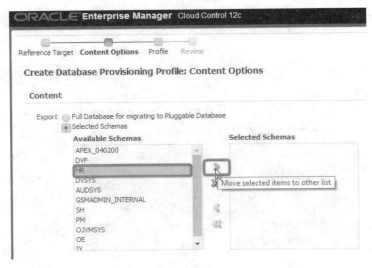

Figure 4.24   Creating a profile, step 6

7. The Dump region tells you where the export files for the schema being exported will be placed. In my environment, this directory is an NFS mount point I used when I created the directory object earlier. Click Add to specify the dump directory (see Figure 4.25).

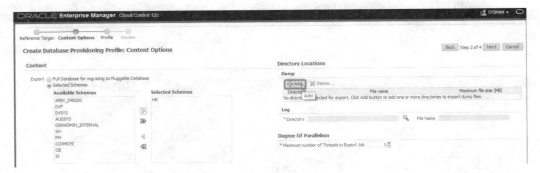

Figure 4.25   Creating a profile, step 7

8. Next, choose the row containing the directory object you created earlier, and click Select (see Figure 4.26).

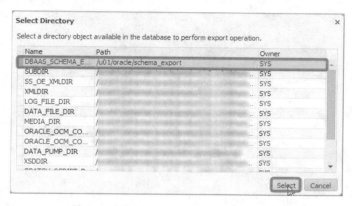

Figure 4.26 Creating a profile, step 8

9. Back on the Directory Locations region, you need to specify the log directory. Personally, I would prefer that this default to the same directory added for the dump file—maybe I should add that as an enhancement request! You can click on the magnifying glass to do this step (see Figure 4.27).

Figure 4.27 Creating a profile step, 9

10. As you haven't created a separate directory object for the logs to go to, you simply select the same directory object again and click Select (see Figure 4.28).

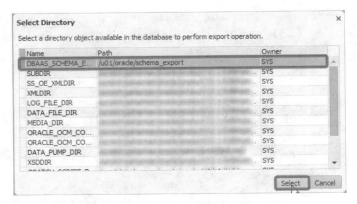

Figure 4.28   Creating a profile, step 10

11. If you are exporting a decent sized data set, you can also specify the degree of parallelism for the export job. However, the HR schema isn't particularly large, so we leave the degree of parallelism at the default of 1 and click Next (see Figure 4.29).

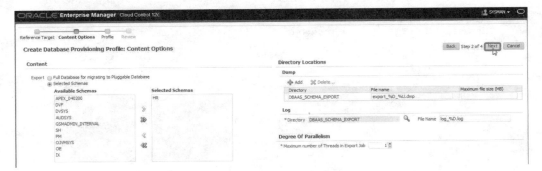

Figure 4.29   Creating a profile, step 11

12. On the next screen, give the profile a meaningful name and click Next (see Figure 4.30).

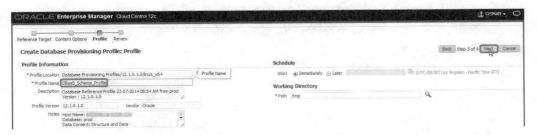

Figure 4.30   Creating a profile, step 12

13. On the Review step, you can double check that everything is as expected, and then click Submit (see Figure 4.31).

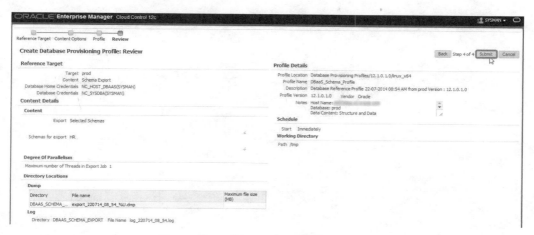

Figure 4.31   Creating a profile, step 13

14. At this stage, a procedure is created and executed, and you are redirected to the Procedure Activity screen. You can click View → Expand All to see all the steps that will be executed in the procedure. You can also change the View Data refresh rate in the top right corner so you can see the procedure activity status refreshing until it is complete. Once the procedure completes successfully, you'll see a screen like the one shown in Figure 4.32.

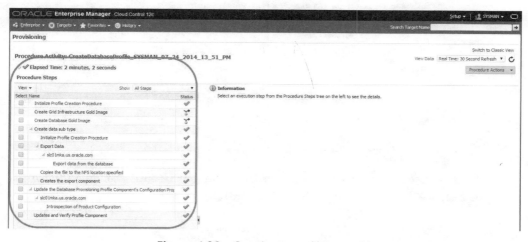

Figure 4.32   Creating a profile, step 14

Now the profile you're going to use is created. Next, you need to create a service template using the following steps:

1. Go back to the Database Cloud Self Service Portal Setup page by following the path Setup → Cloud → Database (see Figure 4.33).

Figure 4.33   Creating a service template, step 1

2. Again, you click Profiles and Service Templates (see Figure 4.34).

Figure 4.34   Creating a service template, step 2

3. This time, you want to select For Schema from the Create dropdown list in the Service Templates region (see Figure 4.35).

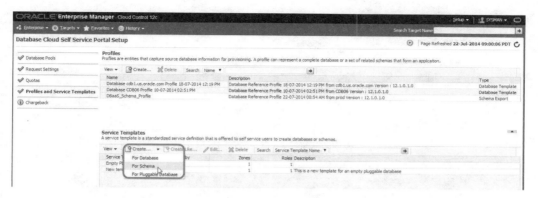

Figure 4.35 Creating a service template, step 3

4. Provide a meaningful name and description for the service template, then click the magnifying glass to select a profile to import the schema from (see Figure 4.36).

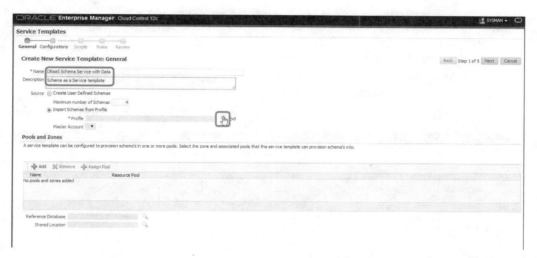

Figure 4.36 Creating a service template, step 4

5. Select the DBaaS_Schema_Profile profile you created in the previous section and click Select (see Figure 4.37).

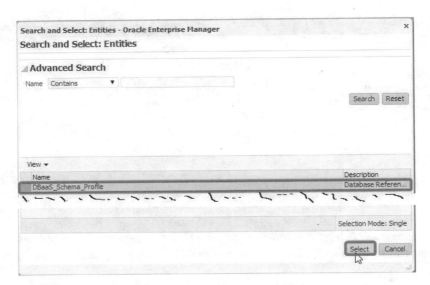

Figure 4.37   Creating a service template, step 5

6. Back on the General step of the wizard, you would normally select a "master account" that will have the necessary privileges to manage objects owned by other schemas in the export. In this case, of course, the profile has only one schema in the export, so the master account should be automatically set to HR. Make sure that HR has been selected, and click Add in the Zones region (see Figure 4.38).

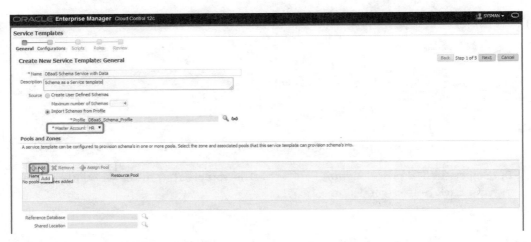

Figure 4.38   Creating a service template, step 6

7. In my example, I'm using the East Coast Zone, so I select that row and click Select (see Figure 4.39).

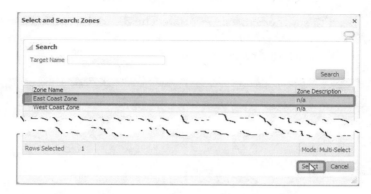

Figure 4.39 Creating a service template, step 7

8. Select the East Coast Zone again, and this time click the Assign Pool button to assign a pool to the zone (see Figure 4.40).

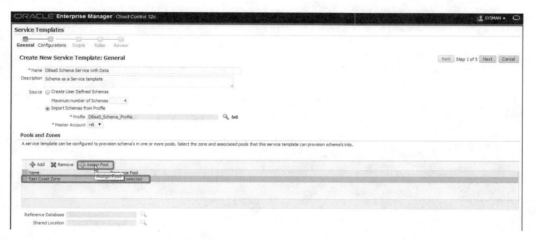

Figure 4.40 Creating a service template, step 8

9. This time, you select the DBaaS_Schema_Pool pool, and click Select (see Figure 4.41).

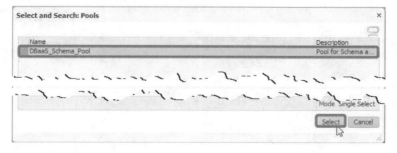

Figure 4.41 Creating a service template, step 9

10. Now you need to set the Shared Location. The Shared Location is a filesystem where the export files are located, so click the magnifying glass next to the Shared Location field (see Figure 4.42).

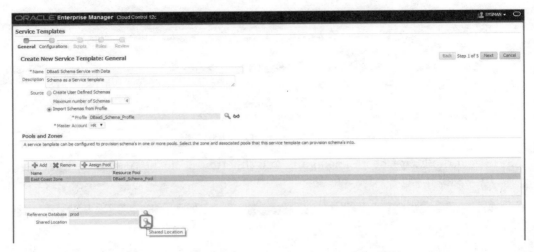

Figure 4.42   Creating a service template, step 10

11. Locate the OS directory you used for the directory object created earlier, then click OK (see Figure 4.43).

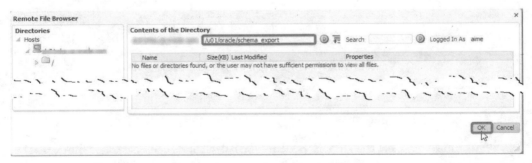

Figure 4.43   Creating a service template, step 11

12. That's all you need to provide on the General wizard step, so you can click Next (see Figure 4.44).

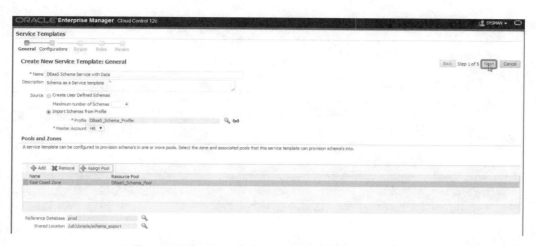

Figure 4.44 Creating a service template, step 12

13. On the Configurations step, you want to set up different workload sizes that can be chosen by the self-service user at runtime, based on the CPU, memory, and storage requirements of a particular service. To do this, you click Create (see Figure 4.45).

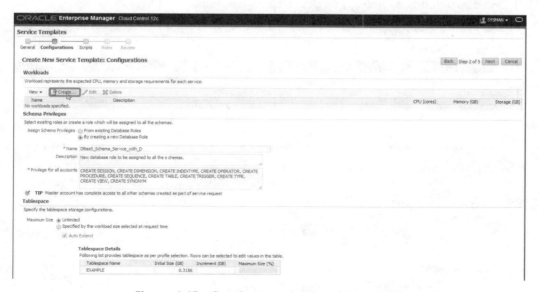

Figure 4.45 Creating a service template, step 13

14. In this case, the workloads are likely to be fairly small, so allocate 0.03 cores, 0.03 GB of memory, and 1 GB of storage at the low end, and click Create (see Figure 4.46).

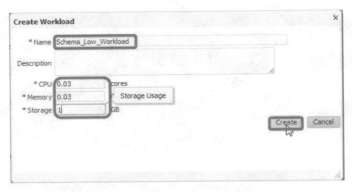

Figure 4.46   Creating a service template, step 14

15. Likewise, you can create a couple of other workloads by repeating the same steps. In the Schema Privileges region, you can provide a name for the database role that will be associated with the master account for the service, and you can define a tablespace that will be created for the service as well. In my example, I've left the default role name and set the tablespace to be specified by the workload size selected at request time. Then click Next (see Figure 4.47).

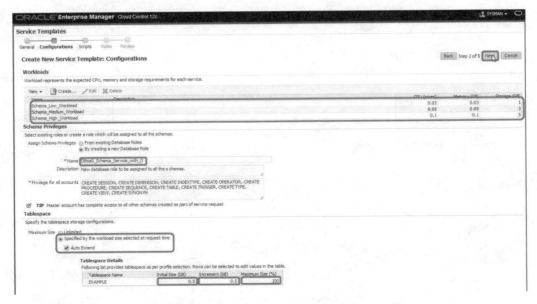

Figure 4.47   Creating a service template, step 15

16. On the next step of the wizard, you can set scripts to be run before and after creation and/or deletion of the service instance. We are not going to do that, so just click Next (see Figure 4.48).

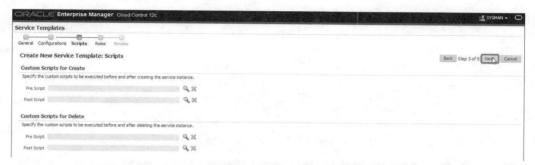

Figure 4.48   Creating a service template, step 16

17. A service template can be configured with one or more roles, so click Add to add the DBAAS_CLOUD_USERS role created earlier (see Figure 4.49).

Figure 4.49   Creating a service template, step 17

18. Select the row for that role, and click Select (see Figure 4.50).

Figure 4.50   Creating a service template, step 18

19. That's all you need to do on the Roles step, so just click Next (see Figure 4.51).

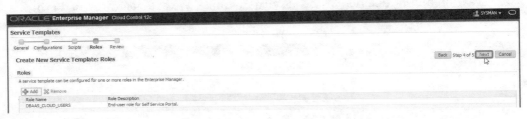

Figure 4.51   Creating a service template, step 19

20. Finally, you can review all the settings for the Service Template, and click Create to create the new service template (see Figure 4.52).

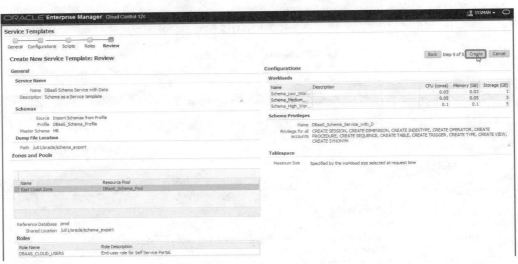

Figure 4.52   Creating a service template, step 20

21. You should now see a message that the service template has been created successfully, and see the template listed in the Service Templates region (see Figure 4.53).

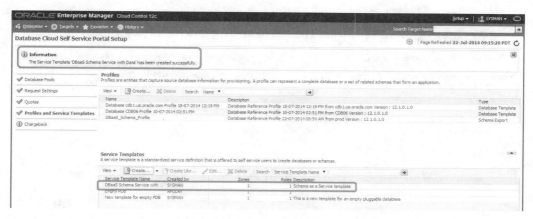

Figure 4.53 Creating a service template, step 21

Now we are done. The next step is to start using schema as a service.

Using Schema as a Service

The first step when using use the Database Cloud Self Service Portal with schema as a service in Enterprise Manager 12.1.0.4 is to log in as the self-service user (not the self-service administrator [SSA]).

1. Provide the right username and password, and click Login (see Figure 4.54).

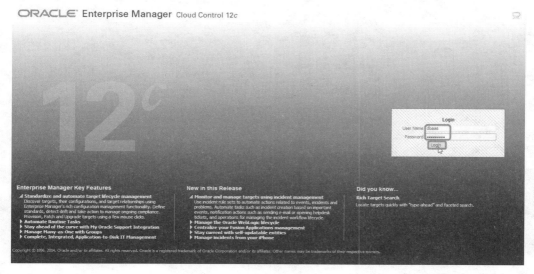

Figure 4.54 Using schema as a service, step 1

2. By default, you are taken to the Infrastructure Cloud Self Service Portal page. Select Databases from the Manage dropdown list (see Figure 4.55).

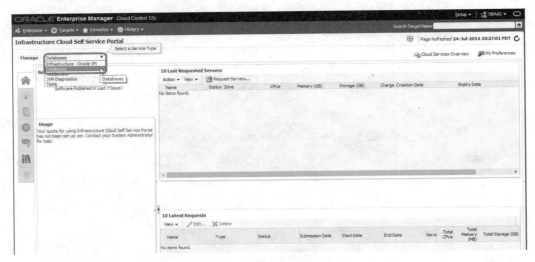

Figure 4.55   Using schema as a service, step 2

3. Next, request a schema from the Database Service Instances region (see Figure 4.56).

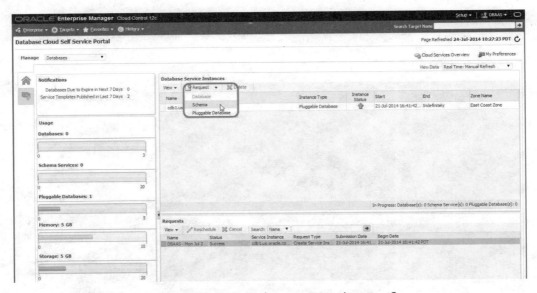

Figure 4.56   Using schema as a service, step 3

4. On the Select Service Template pop-up, select the DBaaS Schema Service with Data template you created earlier, and click Select (see Figure 4.57).

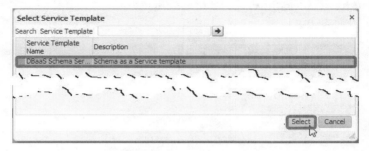

Figure 4.57   Using Schema as a Service, step 4

5. On the Create Schema page, you need to provide information for three regions:

- **General**: In this region, you provide a request name, select the zone the schema will be created in, provide a database service name, and choose a workload size from the workloads we created earlier.

- **Schedule Request**: This is where you define when the request will start and an end date after which the service instance will be removed. You also have the option to keep the service instance indefinitely.

- **Schema Details**: Here you define schema details, the master account, and the tablespace that will be defined as part of the service instance. While most of the other information you provide is self-explanatory, some of this region may be a bit unclear, so let's look at these fields in more detail:

  - **Schema Details**: The schemas that will be created as part of this self-service request, which is dependent on the service template chosen. You can choose to create multiple schemas at once if your template was based on that, but in this example, I only selected the HR schema. Each schema will be remapped to another name, based on the provided prefix, so in this example, you will end up with a new schema called DBAAS_HR. Note also that you can choose to have different passwords for each schema if your request has multiple schemas, or alternatively, if you're lazy like me, you could keep the same password for each schema. Obviously, it's better from a security perspective to not be lazy.

  - **Master account**: The master account is the account that has privileges over all the schemas created as part of this service request.

  - **Tablespace**: This is the name of a tablespace that will be created to contain the schema objects as part of the service request.

The fields on this page that are marked with an asterisk (*) are mandatory fields, so you need to make sure you provide values for those fields at least. Once you have filled those in, you just click Submit to start the service request processing (see Figure 4.58).

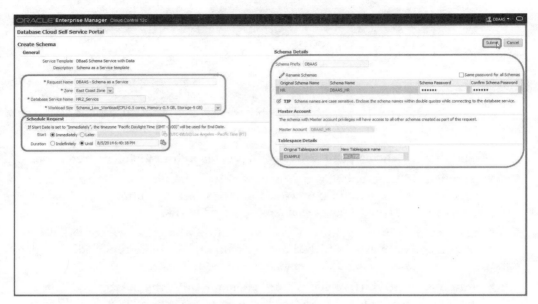

Figure 4.58   Using schema as a service, step 5

6. Back on the Database Cloud Self Service Portal page, you can swap the refresh rate from manual to every 30 seconds (see Figure 4.59).

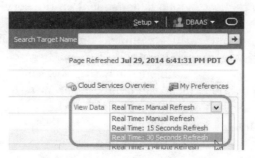

Figure 4.59   Using schema as a service, step 6

7. You should also notice the Usage region has been updated to reflect the newly submitted request (see Figure 4.60).

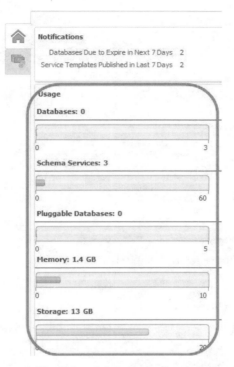

Figure 4.60   Using Schema as a Service, step 7

8. After a short period of time, you will notice the HR2_Service instance has now been added to the list of Database Service Instances. If you want to see more details, you can click on the link in the Status column for the Requests region. (Depending on the screen refresh timing, you will see either the word *Running* or the word *Success* there—the fact that you now have a new instance in the Database Service Instances list is your real indication that the service instance was created successfully.) You should also notice that we actually added *two* requests in this case—one is to create the service instance and the other is to remove it, as we had specified a duration of 7 days for the service instance lifetime (see Figure 4.61).

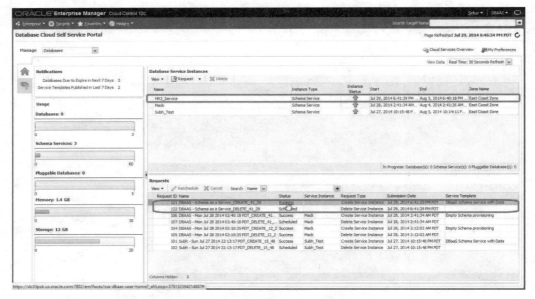

Figure 4.61   Using schema as a service, step 8

9. If you click on either Running or Success, you can see the Request Details pop-up (see Figure 4.62).

Figure 4.62   Using schema as a service, step 9

Selecting any of the execution steps will show more details in the Execution Details region for that particular step. You can also see that some steps weren't needed (like the custom scripts), so they will show a status of Skipped. You can click OK to close that window.

Deployment Issues

Now that we understand the architecture and components that are used in the different consolidation models and how schema as a service is both set up and used, we need to examine some standard deployment issues that must be addressed. These issues include security, operational, resource, and fault isolation, as well as scalability and high availability. See Chapter 1, "Database as a Service Concepts—360 Degrees," for definitions of these terms. Here we look at how each of these issues affects schema as a service.

Security Isolation when Using Schema as a Service

In the schema as a service environment, the effect of granting a privilege or role is contained to the schema where the grant was made, thus ensuring greater security. One of the main issues (if not the main issue) in a schema as a service environment is namespace collision. Namespace collision may be mistakenly resolved by creating public synonyms, which of course is not recommended from a security perspective. The result is that while, by itself, schema as a service does not lead to reduced security, the decisions of the administrator can end up meaning security is decreased when compared to PDBaaS.

For most configurations, Oracle's out-of-the-box database security profiles are sufficient to limit access to data in the schema as a service environment. However, it is also possible to provide deeper security using functionality such as encryption, Database Vault, and Audit Vault.

Operational Isolation when Using Schema as a Service

From a backup and recovery perspective, schema as a service tablespaces can be both backed up and recovered individually, even recovered to different points in time. This capability increases the operational isolation significantly.

As more schemas are consolidated into a single database, operations that affect an ORACLE_HOME will affect more schemas. However, this drawback is offset to a certain extent by the ease with which transportable tablespaces can be used to move the schemas to a different database. Having said that, moving a schema in this way is not quite as straightforward as moving a pluggable database, so schema as a service doesn't rank as highly as PDBaaS for that reason. In addition, schema-based consolidation lacks isolation from both the database lifecycle management and independence of patching and upgrades perspective.

However, the area that makes schema as a service much more difficult from an operational perspective is the issue of namespace collision. Namespace collision occurs because a single database cannot contain multiple copies of the same database object in a single schema. Namespace collision means there can only be one EMPLOYEES table owned by the HR user at any one point in time.

For schema as a service, this is not so much a concern at the database layer as it is at the application layer. The implementation of schema as a service in Enterprise Manager requires you to provide a schema prefix when you issue a Create Schema as a service instance request, and it creates the new schema with that prefix.

For example, if you were using the HR schema from the prod database to create a copy of the HR schema in the test database, and you provided the schema prefix MYHR, the test database would have a schema called MYHR_HR owning a copy of the prod HR database objects.

From the database perspective, then, we can indeed create multiple copies of a schema in a single database, and each schema will be named using the naming convention SCHEMA_PREFIX_ORIGINAL_SCHEMA_NAME, removing the issue of namespace collision.

However, from an application perspective, there is clearly still an issue, as any application based off the original HR schema will expect the objects to be owned by HR. There are at least three ways to address this issue:

- **Private synonyms**: For each user in the database who will be accessing the HR application, create a set of private synonyms for each object used in the HR application. This task would need to be performed for every object used in the HR application and for every user who would be accessing the application. Obviously, it can be done in a scripted manner but still involves manual intervention by the database administrator.

- **Public synonyms**: One way to address the need for creating private synonyms for every user, as just shown, is to use public synonyms instead. However, by their very nature, only one public synonym can be created for an object owned by a specific user, so this approach removes the ability to consolidate multiple schemas into a single database and therefore is not really a resolution we can use.

- **Logon trigger**: Create a logon trigger for each user who will use the application to include a statement of the form ALTER SESSION SET CURRENT_SCHEMA=MYHR_HR. Again, this would require manual intervention after the schema has been created.

Of course, we could also modify the application code to change every HR schema reference to MYHR_HR, but that is rarely something that is easily achieved. The end result of this approach is that, from an application layer, namespace collisions cause a lot of difficulty in the schema as a service paradigm.

However, prior to the advent of PDBaaS, schema as a service was the consolidation model that allowed greatest consolidation to occur, and a number of customers have successfully used one of the preceding namespace collision resolutions in production environments.

Resource Isolation when Using Schema as a Service

Schemas created by schema as a service are just the same as any other database schema. As a result, it is quite simple to use Oracle Resource Manager to create resource consumer groups, map sessions to those groups, and then assign resources to those groups based on resource plan directives.

However, because you do not know which database schemas will be created in when using schema as a service, these sorts of methods are all interventions by the DBA after the schema creation. Following are two methods that do not require this manual intervention after the service has been created:

1. Create and select workloads sensibly. If more than one workload is created, SSA users can specify the workload size that will best meet their requirements.

2. Properly define placement constraints at the database pool level. When a database pool is created, the self-service administrator can set maximum ceilings for resource utilization as placement constraints. These constraints can define

   a. The maximum number of database services for each database

   b. The maximum CPU allocation for the service request

   c. The maximum memory allocation for the service request

   The service instance will then be provisioned on the member that best satisfies these placement constraints.

Fault Isolation when Using Schema as a Service

Fault isolation in a schema as a service request is normally provided at the schema level, so application faults in one schema will not cause other applications to fail.

It is also possible that login storms or an improperly configured midtier will impact other applications.

In addition, the more schemas that are consolidated into a single database, the more impact a fault at the database level will have. Of course, there are some faults (such as dropping a table incorrectly) that can be resolved at the schema level, thus isolating the fault from other schemas in the same database.

Once a fault has been isolated and resolved, there are two parts of the database architecture that allow fast recoverability and thus smaller mean time to repair (MTTR) in any database, including one used with schema as a service.

1. Flashback functionality, including both Flashback Drop and Flashback Table:

   a. Flashback Drop allows you to reverse the effects of dropping a table, including any dependent objects such as triggers and indexes.

   b. Flashback Table allows you to undo the effects of accidentally removing (or indeed adding) some or all of the contents of a table, without affecting other database objects. This feature allows you to recover from logical data corruptions (such as adding or deleting rows from the table) much more quickly than you might otherwise.

2. Point-in-time recoverability can be performed at the individual tablespace level, so if you have multiple schemas affected by an issue, you can issue parallel point-in-time recovery commands to improve MTTR.

Scalability when Using Schema as a Service

Scalability is a fundamental characteristic of DBaaS architectures by virtue of their support for self-service, elasticity, and multitenancy. Oracle's database technologies provide a number of different ways to support scalability when delivering database services, all of which are applicable in schema as a service. These include

- Resource management/quality of service
- Addition of extra storage through such functionality as multiple Exadata Database Machine frames
- Horizontal scaling via RAC when service demands increase beyond the capabilities of a single machine
- Scalable management resources where Enterprise Manager can add management nodes as the number of targets under management grows

High Availability when Using Schema as a Service

As we discussed in Chapter 1, not all consumers require the same level of availability in a cloud environment. Oracle provides different levels of availability to accommodate the unique needs of consumers in the cloud environment. Table 4.1 (reproduced from Chapter 1 for convenience) shows the availability levels offered through Oracle's service plans.

Table 4.1 Availability Levels

Service Level	Description
Bronze standard	Single instance databases/RAC One Node databases
Silver standard	Single instance with standby
Gold standard (HA)	RAC databases
Platinum standard	RAC with standby

Summary

In this chapter, we looked at the architecture and components that make up a consolidated environment, as well as the deployment issues that need to be faced when undertaking a consolidation exercise. We also walked through the details of setting up and using schema as a service.

From the application layer, namespace collisions can cause substantial difficulty in the schema as a service paradigm. However, prior to the advent of PDBaaS, schema as a service was the consolidation model that allowed the greatest consolidation to occur, and a number of customers have successfully used one of the namespace collision resolutions outlined in this chapter in production environments. In the next chapter, we cover using PDBaaS, which addresses the namespace collision issue very successfully.

5

Database Consolidation in Enterprise Manager 12c

In Chapter 4, "Schema Consolidation in Enterprise Manager 12c," you learned how to set up and use schema as a service and were introduced to the issue of namespace collision. Let's move on now and look at an even better consolidation model that deals with the namespace collision issue using Oracle Database 12c's multitenant architecture—the capability to host multiple schemas from different tenants within the same database. From the cloud perspective, this model is known as pluggable database as a service (PDBaaS). PDBaaS enables the highest degree of consolidation. A pluggable database (PDB), which can be described as portable sets of schemas, schema objects, and related structures that appear logically to an application as a separate database, provides enhanced database consolidation. Users can perform day-to-day actions such as provisioning, monitoring, and backup all from a single self-service console. Metering and showback/chargeback capabilities that provide visibility and transparency into resource consumption by each user complement pluggable databases.

The steps to set up PDBaaS can be broadly outlined as follows:

1. Enable database as a service (DBaaS), including setting up the software library, privileges, and users.

2. Set up one or more platform as a service (PaaS) infrastructure zones.

3. Create a database pool for PDBaaS.

4. Configure request settings.

5. Define quotas for each self-service user.

6. Create a database provisioning profile. This step is optional and is unnecessary if you are creating an empty pluggable database.

7. Create a service template, either for an empty pluggable database (i.e., created with an empty schema) or for a pluggable database from a profile (where you can import schemas from a database provisioning profile, including applications with data such as eBusiness applications).

8. Configure chargeback.

9. While deploying a database, select the service template that you have created.

Let's look at the details.

PDBaaS Setup

Cloud administrators configure the PDBaaS cloud, define cloud governance with policies and quotas, expose it to certain users, and decide the total amount of resources each user can reserve before the self-service portal can be used.

The first step in the process requires the Oracle Software Library to be configured. The Software Library is a repository that stores software patches, virtual appliance images, reference gold images, application software, and their associated directive scripts. It allows different versions, maturity levels, and states of entities. The software entities can be automatically mass-deployed to provision software, software updates, and servers using Oracle Enterprise Manager Cloud Control 12*c* (EM12*c*) in a reliable and repeatable manner. These provisioning operations, which are unattended and can be scheduled, lead to substantial cost savings.

Besides acting as a repository for certified software entities, the Software Library is a logical interface between the deployment models and the automation framework required to perform a large number of patching and provisioning tasks. To configure the storage location for the Software Library, follow the path Setup → Provisioning and Patching → Software Library, and set a location for the Oracle Management Server (OMS) Shared File System, as shown in Figure 5.1.

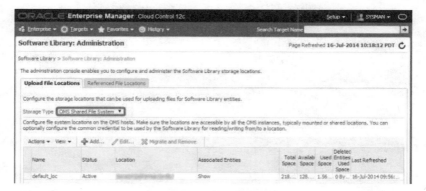

Figure 5.1   Software Library setup

Defining Roles and Assigning Users

Roles are named groups of related system and object privileges. You can create roles and then assign them to users and to other roles. You can assign any of the existing roles and the associated privileges to a new role.

When creating database zones and service templates, selective access can be granted only to custom roles. The self-service portal is intended for end users to be able to provision and manage their own cloud services. As such, end users need access only to the self-service portal and the resources they are assigned. Such capabilities are inherent in the predefined EM_SSA_USER role. Since predefined roles cannot be assigned to database zones and service templates, you need to create a custom cloud user role based on the standard EM_SSA_USER role. To do this, follow the path Setup → Security → Roles. You can use either the Create or Create Like button to create a new role.

> **Tip**
>
> If you use Create Like, it maps the underlying roles and privileges for you. For example, the EM_USER_SSA role is composed of the EM_USER_SSA_BASE role and additional privileges. If you select the EM_USER_SSA role and do a Create Like, the role that will be mapped to your new role is the underlying EM_USER_SSA_BASE role, *not* the EM_USER_SSA role, as you might expect. Roles can be granted recursively, of course (but not circularly), so what the user interface has done is to unravel that recursive role until it gets to the underlying EM_USER_SSA_BASE role and added that to your new role.

In the example that follows, we create a role from scratch.

1. Click on the Create button (see Figure 5.2).

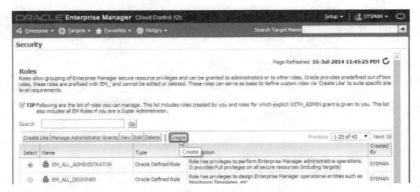

Figure 5.2   Creating a new role, step 1

2. Provide a name, such as DBaaS_Cloud_Users, and a description, and click Next (see Figure 5.3).

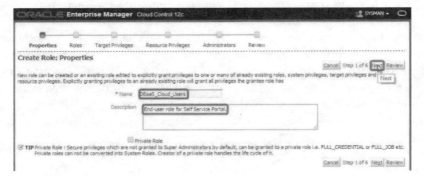

Figure 5.3   Creating a new role, step 2

3. Select the EM_SSA_USER role, then click the Move button to move the role to the list of Selected Roles, and then click Review, as in Figure 5.4. We don't need the remaining wizard steps, so they can be skipped.

Figure 5.4 Creating a new role, step 3

4. Check that all the details are correct, and click Finish to create the role. You should then see a confirmation that the role has been created successfully.

It is highly recommended that each end user have his or her own cloud user credentials, which enables effective monitoring of services and resource utilization, so the next step is to create an end user and grant that end user the DBaaS_Cloud_Users role.

1. Follow the path Setup → Security → Administrators. You can either select another administrator and click Create Like or just click Create (see Figure 5.5). I find it easier to do the latter, as you don't need to remove any extraneous privileges that Create Like can bring with it.

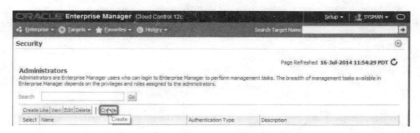

Figure 5.5 Creating a cloud administrator, step 1

2. Provide a username (I used DBAAS in this example) and password, and click Next (see Figure 5.6).

Figure 5.6   Creating a cloud administrator, step 2

3. Select the DBAAS_CLOUD_USERS role you just created, click the Move button to add it to the Selected Roles list, and click Review (see Figure 5.7). The remaining wizard steps are not needed.

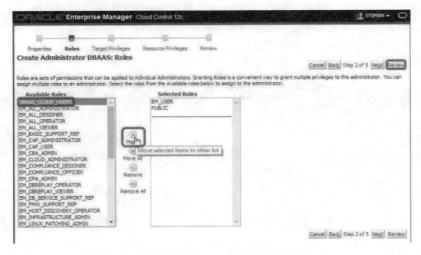

Figure 5.7   Creating a cloud administrator, step 3

4. Review the details to make sure they are correct, and then click Finish to create the DBAAS administrator. You should see a confirmation message that the administrator was created successfully

Creating a PaaS Infrastructure Zone

Before you enable or set up DBaaS or middleware as a service (MWaaS), you must create a PaaS infrastructure zone that enables you to define the placement policy constraints for a specified set of targets and the users to whom this zone will be available.

1. To create a PaaS infrastructure zone, you must log in using an account that has been granted the EM_CLOUD_ADMINISTRATOR role. Once you've done that, follow the path Setup → Cloud → PaaS Infrastructure Zone. On the PaaS Infrastructure Zone page, click the Create button (see Figure 5.8).

Figure 5.8   Creating a PaaS infrastructure zone, step 1

2. Provide a name and, optionally, a description for the zone, determine placement policy constraints per host (i.e., maximum CPU utilization and maximum memory allocation allowed), and click Next (see Figure 5.9).

Figure 5.9   Creating a PaaS infrastructure zone, step 2

3. If you already have a named credential defined for the hosts you are about to add, select it from the Named Credential dropdown list, or click the + sign to create a new named credential (see Figure 5.10).

Figure 5.10 Creating a PaaS infrastructure zone, step 3

4. Enter the username and password for the named credential, optionally provide Run Privilege (such as sudo), give the named credential a meaningful name, and click OK (see Figure 5.11).

Figure 5.11 Creating a PaaS infrastructure zone, step 4

5. Add the host (or hosts) you will be putting in this PaaS infrastructure zone by clicking Add (see Figure 5.12).

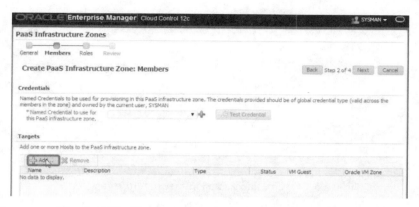

Figure 5.12   Creating a PaaS infrastructure zone, step 5

6. You can either search for the host names or just select them from the list. This is a multiselect screen, so you can select multiple rows by holding down the Shift key as you select, then click Select (see Figure 5.13).

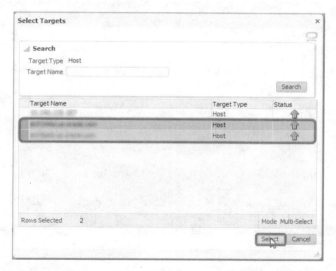

Figure 5.13   Creating a PaaS infrastructure zone, step 6

7. Now that you've added one or more hosts, you can select the named credential you defined earlier and click Test Credential (see Figure 5.14) to check that it works. (I think this screen should be redesigned and the Credentials part put *after* the Targets part, but let's just work with what we have!)

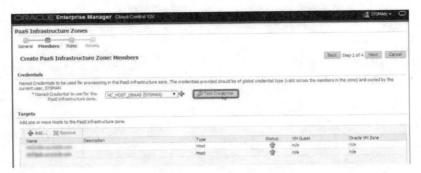

Figure 5.14   Creating a PaaS infrastructure zone, step 7

8. You should get an informational message that the credential test succeeded (if not, you will need to exit the Create PaaS Infrastructure Zone wizard and follow the path Setup → Security → Named Credentials to fix it, so it's best to get it right the first time!). Click OK to acknowledge the message (see Figure 5.15).

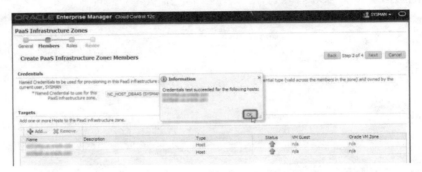

Figure 5.15   Creating a PaaS infrastructure zone, step 8

9. Click Next to move to step 3 of the wizard (see Figure 5.16).

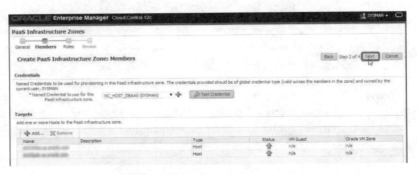

Figure 5.16   Creating a PaaS infrastructure zone, step 9

10. The zone can be made available to a restricted set of users by selecting the role (or roles) that can access it. We need to add the role we created earlier, so click the Add button (see Figure 5.17).

Figure 5.17 Creating a PaaS infrastructure zone, step 10

11. Select the DBAAS_CLOUD_USERS role, and then click Select (see Figure 5.18).

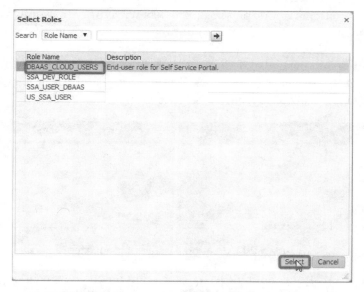

Figure 5.18 Creating a PaaS infrastructure zone, step 11

12. Click the Next button (see Figure 5.19).

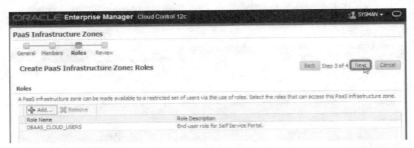

Figure 5.19   Creating a PaaS infrastructure zone, step 12

Finally, review the details and click Submit to create the PaaS infrastructure zone. You should now see a message that the PaaS infrastructure zone was created successfully.

Creating a Database Pool

A database pool is a collection of servers or clusters with preinstalled database software. Each server in a database zone has identical platform and database versions. For servers that support multiple ORACLE_HOMEs with different versions, a separate database zone must be created for each database version.

1. To create a database pool, follow the path Setup → Cloud → Database to go to the Database Cloud Self Service Portal Setup page. From here, select For Pluggable Database from the Create dropdown (see Figure 5.20).

Figure 5.20   Creating a database pool, step 1

2. Provide a name and, optionally, a description for the new pool. If you already have named credentials defined for this environment, you can simply select

them from the dropdown lists to the right, but if not, click the + sign to create a named credential for the host (see Figure 5.21).

Figure 5.21 Creating a database pool, step 2

3. Enter a username and password for the credential, optionally provide the run privilege (e.g., sudo), give the credential a meaningful name, and click OK (see Figure 5.22).

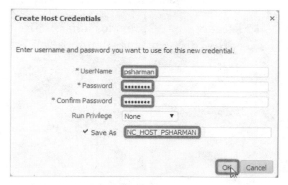

Figure 5.22 Creating a database pool, step 3

4. Likewise, you can provide a named credential for the grid infrastructure (if you are going to use it) and for the database. You can also specify a container database wallet password if you want to support encryption for the pluggable database that will be created (I normally provide this regardless because it saves coming back to redo this later if you change your mind). Next, we need to add one or more container databases to the pool from a single PaaS infrastructure zone. The filters we select here cannot be changed once the pool is created, so select these carefully. Choose the East Coast Zone we just created, a target type of database instance (the other choice is a Real Application Cluster [RAC] environment, but this example is being built in non-clustered

configurations), and set the platform and database version correctly. Then click Add (see Figure 5.23).

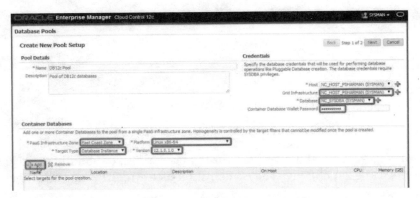

Figure 5.23   Creating a database pool, step 4

5. The Select and Add Targets pop-up provides a list of already existing databases, so simply select the cdb1 container database, and click Select (see Figure 5.24).

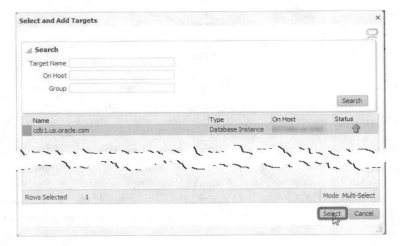

Figure 5.24   Creating a database pool, step 5

6. Click the Next button. If you want to set maximum ceilings for resource utilization, you can do it on this screen. I'm going to leave it at the defaults in this example and select Submit (see Figure 5.25). You should see a message saying the pool has been created successfully.

Figure 5.25 Creating a database pool, step 6

Configuring Request Settings

Next, we add some settings to restrict the scope for database requests.

1. Click Request Settings (see Figure 5.26).

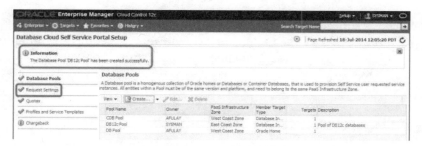

Figure 5.26 Configuring request settings, step 1

2. In this case, we want to change the request purging duration (the period of time after which completed creation requests will be purged from the repository) to 3 days, so change that and click Apply (see Figure 5.27). Again, you should see a confirmation message.

Figure 5.27 Configuring request settings, step 2

Setting Quotas

Next, we add a quota—the aggregate amount of resources that can be granted to each self-service user belonging to a certain role. This quota applies only to databases provisioned through the self-service portal.

1. To do this, click Quotas, then click on the Create button to create a new quota (or use an already existing one) (see Figure 5.28).

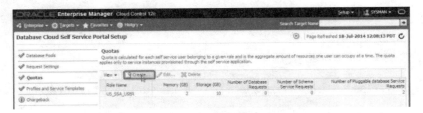

Figure 5.28   Adding a quota, step 1

2. Provide a role name and quota for the amount of memory and storage, as well as the number of database requests, schema service requests, and pluggable database service requests, then click OK (see Figure 5.29).

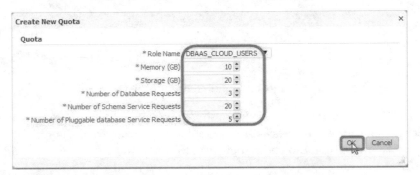

Figure 5.29   Adding a quota, step 2

Profiles and Service Templates

Next, we want to configure profile and service template definitions that can be used by self-service users to provision databases in selected zones.

1. Click Profiles and Service Templates. A database provisioning profile is not needed when creating an empty pluggable database, but we will walk quickly through the steps anyway. Click the Create button to create a database provisioning profile (see Figure 5.30).

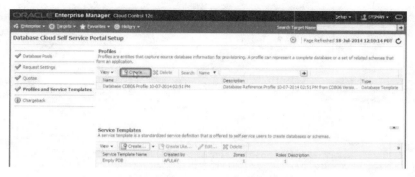

Figure 5.30 Creating a profile, step 1

2. Click the magnifying glass to search for a reference target (see Figure 5.31).

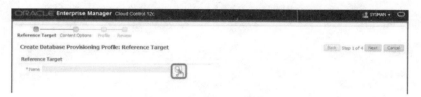

Figure 5.31 Creating a profile, step 2

3. Select the cdb1 container database, and click Select (see Figure 5.32).

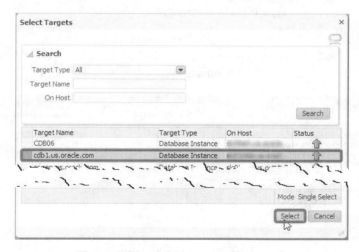

Figure 5.32 Creating a profile, step 3

4. Provide the relevant named credentials, and click Next (see Figure 5.33).

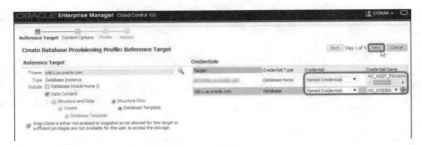

Figure 5.33   Creating a profile, step 4

5. Since we are creating a profile with structure only, step 2 of the wizard is skipped. On step 3, you can change the profile name, path, and scheduling, but for now, just click Next (see Figure 5.34).

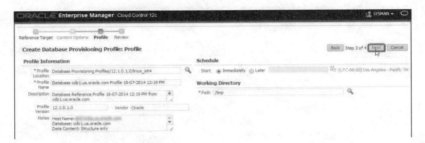

Figure 5.34   Creating a profile, step 5

6. Review the information, and click Submit to create the profile. You can change the page to refresh every 30 seconds on the right, and you should fairly quickly see that the profile has been created successfully (see Figure 5.35).

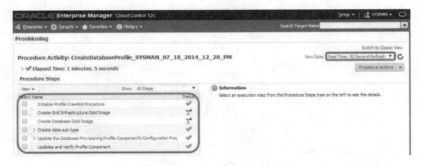

Figure 5.35   Creating a profile, step 6

Now we need to create a service template:

1. Follow the path Setup → Cloud → Database to go to the Database Cloud Self Service Portal Setup page again, click Profiles and Service Templates, and then click For Pluggable Database from the Create dropdown (see Figure 5.36).

Figure 5.36 Creating a service template, step 1

2. We're going to create a new service template to provision an empty pluggable database, so provide a name and, optionally, a description, select Create Empty Pluggable Database if not already selected, and then click Add (see Figure 5.37).

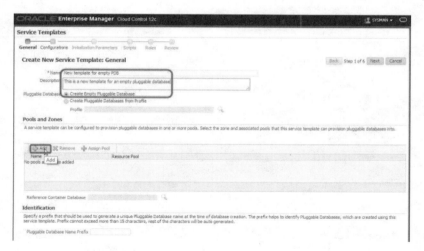

Figure 5.37 Creating a service template, step 2

3. In this case, we want to use the East Coast PaaS Infrastructure Zone created earlier, so select that row, and then click Select (see Figure 5.38).

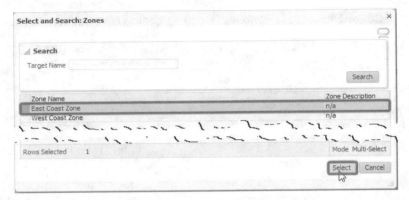

Figure 5.38   Creating a service template, step 3

4. Now that the zone is added, we want to assign a pool to the template. Click Assign Pool (see Figure 5.39).

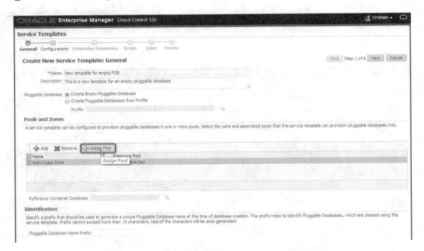

Figure 5.39   Creating a service template, step 4

5. Select the DB12c Pool created earlier, then click Select (see Figure 5.40).

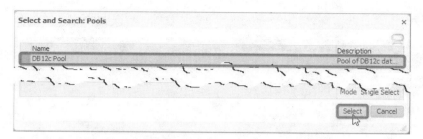

Figure 5.40 Creating a service template, step 5

6. Now we want to add a prefix to the pluggable database name, so enter a prefix, and click Next (see Figure 5.41).

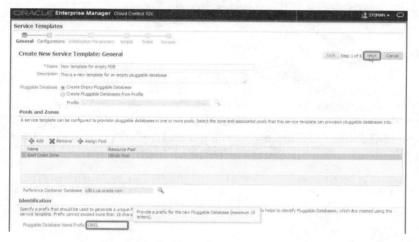

Figure 5.41 Creating a service template, step 6

7. On the Configurations page, you can set up the following parameters for the pluggable database service template:

   ■ **Workload**: Here you can set up different workload sizes (e.g., small, medium, and large) based on the CPU, memory, number of sessions, and storage requirements of a particular pluggable database service. These workload sizes can be chosen by the self-service user at request time.

   ■ **Role**: This is the database role that will be associated with the pluggable database for the service that will give it control over the service.

   ■ **Storage**: A number of tablespaces can be created for each pluggable database. This is where you set up the storage requirements, such as initial size, for those tablespaces.

First, let's create a workload. Click Create (see Figure 5.42).

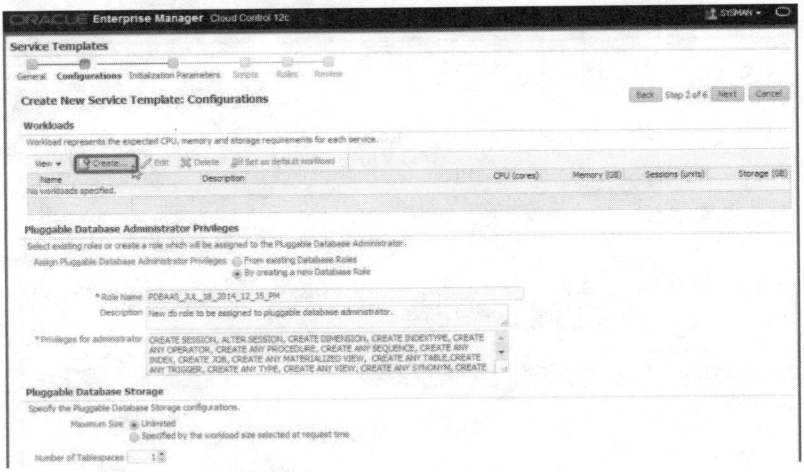

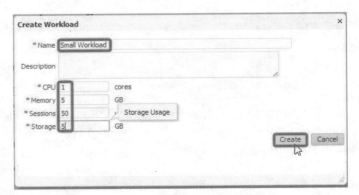

Figure 5.42 Creating a service template, step 7

8. In this case, we are creating a small workload, so name the workload appropriately; optionally add a description; set values for the number of CPU cores, amount of memory, number of sessions, and amount of storage allowed for the workload; and click Create (see Figure 5.43).

Figure 5.43 Creating a service template, step 8

9. Back on the Configurations page, provide a more meaningful name for the role that will be created, leave the other values at their default, and click Next (see Figure 5.44).

Figure 5.44 Creating a service template, step 9

10. On the next screen, you can set specific initialization parameters for databases created using this template. For now, leave that alone, and click Next (see Figure 5.45).

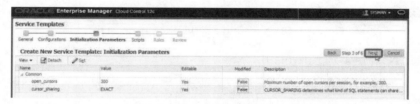

Figure 5.45 Creating a service template, step 10

11. On the next page, you can specify custom scripts that will be executed either before and after creating the pluggable database or before and after deleting it. Again, leave that at the defaults, and click Next (see Figure 5.46).

Figure 5.46 Creating a service template, step 11

12. On the Roles step, click the Add button (see Figure 5.47).

Figure 5.47   Creating a service template, step 12

13. Select the DBAAS_CLOUD_USERS role, then click Select (see Figure 5.48).

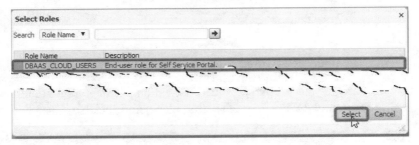

Figure 5.48   Creating a service template, step 13

14. Click Next (see Figure 5.49).

Figure 5.49   Creating a service template step, 14

15. Review the template details, and click Create (see Figure 5.50).

Figure 5.50 Creating a service template, step 15

16. You should get a message confirming the template was created successfully (see Figure 5.51). You'll notice that Chargeback can be configured next. We'll leave Chargeback for now, as it is covered in Chapter 6, "Metering and Chargeback in Enterprise Manager 12*c*."

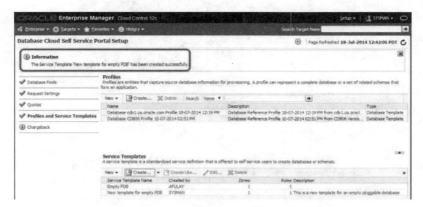

Figure 5.51 Creating a service template, step 16

So there you have it. Now we have PDBaaS set up. Let's look now at how you use all of this in the self-service portal.

Using the Self-Service Portal with PDBaaS in Enterprise Manager 12.1.0.4

Now let's cover how you actually use the self-service portal to create on demand an empty pluggable database. The main reason we want to do this, of course, is to automate the more mundane database administration tasks associated with creating a database. If we can leave these sorts of tasks more to the end users, while ensuring they do not have free reign to go about willy-nilly creating databases, it removes these boring tasks from our hands, and at the same time, automates the tasks to ensure correct configuration, performance, and so on.

The first step is to log in as a self-service user. Provide the username and password of the user you created earlier, and click Login. This takes you to the standard Welcome screen. The first thing to do from here is make it easier for this user to get to the right place. EM12*c* allows you to define home pages on a per-user basis, so we need to get to the self-service portal first.

1. Go to Enterprise → Cloud → Self Service Portal (see Figure 5.52).

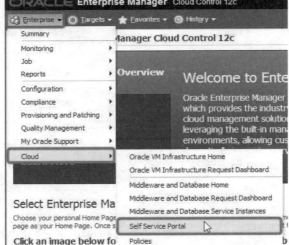

Figure 5.52   Accessing the Database Cloud Self Service Portal, step 1

2. Now you can select Set Current Page as My Home from the user menu on the top right of the screen next to Setup so that next time you log in, you see this page immediately (see Figure 5.53).

Figure 5.53   Accessing the Database Cloud Self Service Portal, step 2

3. You will see a confirmation message that the Home Page has been updated. Note that the default item to manage on this Infrastructure Cloud Self Service Portal is still set to Infrastructure - Oracle VM, so we need to swap that to Databases from the Manage dropdown list (unfortunately, this selection can't be set as a default) (see Figure 5.54).

Figure 5.54   Accessing the Database Cloud Self Service Portal, step 3

Now you are on the Database Cloud Self Service Portal page, which is where you can see all the information about requests that have already been made. In this case, of course, there are none, so the first thing you need to do is request a pluggable database. Note that this is the only request you have available to you at this stage because of the way we defined the DBaaS user in the setup.

1. From the Request dropdown list choose Pluggable Database (see Figure 5.55).

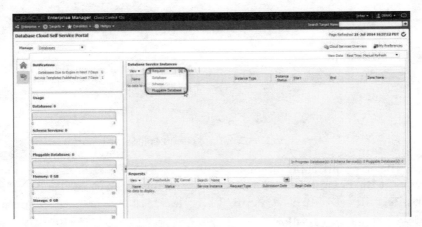

Figure 5.55   Requesting a pluggable database from the self-service portal, step 1

2. You are asked to select a service template from a list of those that have already been defined. Again, the user has been granted access to only one, so choose that, and click Select (see Figure 5.56).

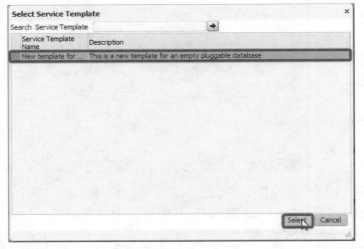

Figure 5.56   Requesting a pluggable database from the self-service portal, step 2

3. Next, you are presented with the Create Pluggable Database screen. There are a number of options to populate here:

- **Request Name**: The name given to the self-service request. This is populated with a default value, but you can, of course, change that to something more meaningful if you like.

- **Zone**: The PaaS infrastructure zone where the pluggable databases for this request will reside. Again, this will be populated by default, based on the zones the user has been given access to. In this case, the user can only use the East Coast Zone I created in my earlier post.

- **PDB Name**: Obviously, the name for the pluggable database that will be created. Make this something recognizable rather than something generic such as PDB6.

- **Database Service Name**: Again, use a meaningful service name because it will be used as the service name part of the connect string.

- **Workload Size**: Defines the resources allocated to the database service name and is also used to derive the database resource management plan. Again, in this example only one workload is defined.

- **Schedule Request**: The date and time that the request will be scheduled to be created (if not being created immediately), as well as the duration for its lifespan.

- **Administrator Credentials**: The pluggable database administrator account that will be created by the request for this pluggable database.

- **Tablespace name**: The name of the tablespace to be created as part of this request.

You can enter values for all of these fields (or accept the defaults) and then click Submit (see Figure 5.57).

Figure 5.57 Requesting a pluggable database from the self-service portal, step 3

4. Now you are returned to the Database Cloud Self Service Portal page, and the request you just created should be running (see Figure 5.58).

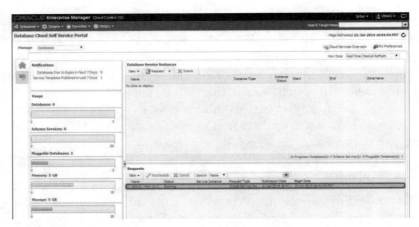

Figure 5.58   Requesting a pluggable database from the self-service portal, step 4

5. The default for this page is manual refresh, so you can change that by clicking the View Data dropdown list on the right side of the page. After a few minutes, you'll see the new service instance listed in the Database Service Instances region of the Database Cloud Self Service Portal page (see Figure 5.59).

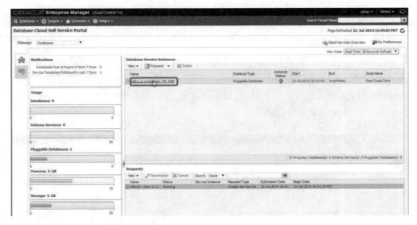

Figure 5.59   Requesting a pluggable database from the self-service portal, step 5

6. Notice on the left of the screen, there is additional information pertaining to notification, as well as usage values that will now have changed. EM12*c* uses green, yellow, and red to indicate usage that is at normal, warning, or critical levels. The notification section is designed to alert and notify the self-service users of pending expirations, as well as any new service templates that have been recently published and are available for use. The Usage section provides information regarding current utilization in relationship to the quotas (seen

on the right end of each bar) defined by the cloud administrator. If you click on the service instance name, it takes you to the pluggable database page where you can see the connection details that can be used to connect to the database to perform application development tasks (see Figure 5.60).

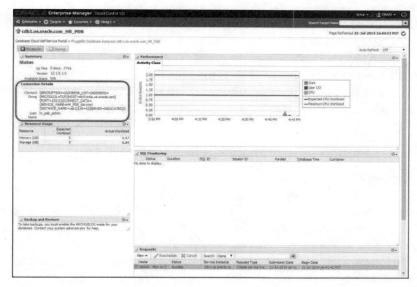

Figure 5.60   Requesting a pluggable database from the self-service portal, step 6

And that's it! Now you can concentrate on the more interesting parts of database administration life, like performance management, configuring high availability, eating donuts—okay, so maybe not eating donuts.

Deployment Issues

Chapter 4 introduced six deployment issues that need to be addressed in any consolidation exercise: security isolation, operational isolation, resource isolation, fault isolation, scalability, and high availability. Now that we've walked through the setup and use of PDBaaS, let's look at how it addresses each of these deployment issues.

Security Isolation when Using PDBaaS

In any consolidated environment, taking the "least privilege" approach will provide the maximum benefit in tightening security. In the pluggable database environment, the effect of granting a privilege or role is contained to the pluggable database where the grant was made, thus ensuring greater security.

At the user level, administrators can be defined in two ways:

- **PDB administrators**: Pluggable database administrators have the ability to administer just the pluggable databases to which they have been granted access.
- **CDB administrators**: Container database administrators can administer all databases within the container database.

By defining most administrators as pluggable database administrators, security is again tightened. The end result is that PDBaaS provides a very high level of security isolation.

Operational Isolation when Using PDBaaS

Operational isolation requires that any maintenance being performed on either a database or the environment it operates in affects the smallest number of other databases in the same pool. As more databases are consolidated as pluggable databases into a single container database, it follows that operations that affect an ORACLE_HOME will affect more databases. This drawback can be offset to a certain extent by the ease with which a pluggable database can be unplugged and moved to a different container database. The administrator can move databases very easily in the situation where a container database is being patched and some pluggable databases will not be supported yet in the new release (this can happen when certain applications are only certified against specific database versions, for example).

Pluggable databases can also be both backed up and recovered individually and even recovered to different points in time. This advantage increases the operational isolation significantly.

Further enhancements were provided in the January 2015 version of the database plugin:

- Out-of-place patching for DBaaS enables administrators to standardize and maintain the cloud infrastructure by applying both major and minor updates seamlessly.
- A pool patching mechanism allows process pools to subscribe to database and grid infrastructure images.
- New images are automatically deployed to service in the pool, and self-service users or administrators can choose to migrate databases to the new home.
- Subscription-based, mass scale, out-of-place patching and upgrades with reduced downtime are enabled.

Resource Isolation when Using PDBaaS

Resource Manager has the ability to create a container database–level plan to determine how resources are shared among the pluggable databases in a specific container database. In particular, this container database–level plan can control the

- CPU consumed by the pluggable database
- Number of concurrent sessions
- Amount of parallelization via the use of parallel server processes
- File I/O, but only in the case of Exadata

The system global area, program global area, and network I/O are not controlled by container database–level plans.

Fault Isolation when Using PDBaaS

Fault isolation is very straightforward in the pluggable database world. When an individual pluggable database experiences some sort of problem that may impact other pluggable databases in the same container database, the administrator can easily unplug the suspect pluggable database and plug it into another container database where the problem can be resolved in isolation. This solution would be much more complex in the traditional database architecture.

Once a fault has been isolated and resolved, fast recoverability and thus smaller mean time to recover (MTTR) can be improved using Flashback Database or point-in-time recoverability:

- **Flashback Database**: In the first release of the multitenant architecture, Flashback Database is an operation at the container database–level only. Future releases will enable Flashback Database as an operation at the individual pluggable database level.
- **Point-in-time recoverability**: Because point-in-time recovery can be performed at the individual pluggable database level, if you have multiple pluggable databases affected by an issue, you can issue parallel point-in-time recovery commands to improve MTTR.

Scalability when Using PDBaaS

All databases compete for the limited hardware resources (CPU, memory, and I/O) within a database pool, so you should ensure that a database is guaranteed sufficient resources and also doesn't have a detrimental impact on other databases within the pool. There are a variety of ways to ensure customers in a PDBaaS environment are getting the services or resources they are paying for, including

- Separation of resources at the pool level
- Quotas defining the amount of memory and storage and the number of database, schema service, and pluggable database service requests that can be allocated
- Workload definitions, based on the CPU, memory, number of sessions, and storage requirements, that can be chosen by the self-service user at request time

High Availability when Using PDBaaS

The topology of a complete database system architecture (e.g., a primary database along with multiple physical standby databases) is defined in the service template by the self-service administrator. If the "Enable Standby Locking" option is selected, self-service administrators can use this template to provision a primary database and then later submit a request to add or remove one or more standby databases to the existing service instance.

Alternatively, to enforce deployment standardization, locking the option will ensure that any provisioning performed using this service template will create (and delete, if selected) the primary database as well as all the standby databases at once.

Summary

PDBaaS provides the greatest level of database consolidation available, but of course it does require the use of the multitenant option in Oracle Database 12*c*. It also provides ways to address the common deployment issues that need to be faced by any consolidation exercise. The next step to look at is how we can measure the costs of using a database consolidation methodology and how we can either show the costs of those consolidated environments or charge those costs to the business owners of those environments. That's done via the concepts of metering and chargeback. The next chapter explains how metering and chargeback is implemented in Oracle Enterprise Manager Cloud Control 12*c*.

## 6

Metering and Chargeback in Enterprise Manager 12*c*

The previous two chapters covered setting up schema as a service, using the self-service portal with schema as a service, setting up Pluggable Database as a Service (PDBaaS), and using the self-service portal with PDBaaS, all of these using Oracle Enterprise Manager Cloud Control 12*c*. Now let's move on to an area where you start to get more back from all of this work—metering and chargeback.

Metering is something that Enterprise Manager has done since its very first release. It's a measurement of some form of resource—obviously in the case of Enterprise Manager, it's a measurement of how much computing resources, such as CPU, I/O, memory, and storage, have been used by an object. When I think way back to the very first release of Enterprise Manager I ever saw—the 0.76 release, whenever that was!—the thing that comes to mind most is that it had this remarkably pretty tablespace map that showed you diagrammatically just where every block in an object was in a particular tablespace. Remarkably pretty, as I said—but virtually useless because all you could do was look at the pretty colors!

Clearly, metering has come a long, long way since that time, and if you have had Enterprise Manager up and running for some time, you now have at your fingertips metrics on so many different things that you may be lost trying to work out what you can do with it all. Well, that's where chargeback comes into play. In simple terms, chargeback is (as the name implies) an accounting tool. In Enterprise Manager terms, it has three main functions:

- It provides a way of aggregating the enormous amount of metrics data that Enterprise Manager collects.
- It provides reports to the consumers of those metrics of how much they have used of those particular metrics.
- If you have set it up to do so, it provides a way for the IT department to charge those consumers for the resources they have used.

Let's expand on that last point a little further. Within the Chargeback application, the cloud administrator can set specific charges for specific resources. As an example, you might decide to charge $1 a month per gigabyte of memory used for a database. Those charges can be transferred to some form of billing application, such as Oracle's Self-Service E-Billing application, and end up being charged as a real cost to the end user. However, only a small number of people are actually using it to charge a cost to the end user. There are two reasons for that:

- First, most end users are still not in the mindset of paying for computing power in the same way as they pay for other utilities—that is, paying for the amount of computing power that is actually consumed, as we do with our gas, electricity, and phone bills.
- Second, most people have difficulty deciding just how much to charge for a "unit" (whatever that might be) of computing power. In fact, arguments over just what to charge for a unit of computing power have been known to last much longer than any meetings held to decide to actually implement chargeback!

The end result is that customers often choose to implement *show*back rather than chargeback. Showback is in many ways similar to chargeback. It's the ability to provide reports to end users that show how much computing resource they have used and to show them how much it would have cost the end users if the IT department had decided to actually charge for it. In some ways, this information is just as beneficial to the IT department as to the end users because it allows them to have a much better grasp on what they need to know for budgeting purposes, and it avoids the endless arguments about whether end users are being charged too much.

Terminology

Okay, let's talk about some of the new terminology you need to understand before we implement chargeback (from now on, we use the term *chargeback* to cover both *chargeback* and *showback* for simplicity's sake, and because the feature is actually called Chargeback in the Enterprise Manager Cloud Control product).

Chargeback Entities

The first concept you need to understand is that of a *chargeback entity*. In Enterprise Manager terms, a target typically uses some form of resource, and the chargeback application calculates the cost of that resource usage. In releases prior to Enterprise Manager 12.1.0.4, the chargeback application collected configuration information and metrics for a subset of Enterprise Manager targets. In the 12.1.0.4 release, you can add chargeback support for Enterprise Manager target types for which there is no current out-of-the-box chargeback support via the use of Enterprise Manager command-line interface (EMCLI) verbs. These chargeback targets, both out-of-the-box and custom types, are collectively known as *entities*.

You can get a complete list of all the items that we can set up chargeback for by clicking on Charge Plans, then Charge Item Library (see Figure 6.1).

You will then see a list of all the charge items, including a brief description of each item (see Figure 6.2).

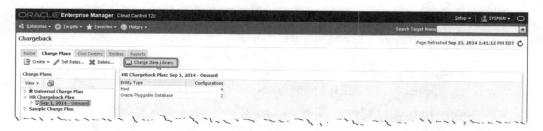

Figure 6.1 Accessing the charge item library

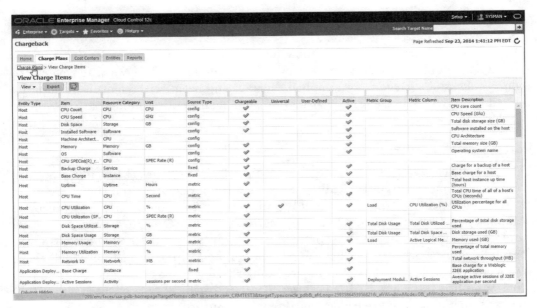

Figure 6.2   Available charge items

Charge Plans

A charge plan is what Enterprise Manager uses to associate the resources being charged for and the rates at which they are charged. Two types of charge plans are available:

- **Universal charge plan**: The universal charge plan contains the rates for CPU, storage, and memory. Although it is called the "universal" charge plan, it isn't really universal because it doesn't apply to all entity types. For example, it is not applicable to J2EE applications.

- **Extended charge plans**: The universal charge plan is an obvious starting point, but there are many situations where entity-specific charges are required. Let's say you have a lot of people who understand Linux, but there is a new environment being added to your data center that requires Windows knowledge. If you had to pay a contractor to come in to look after that environment because it was outside your knowledge zone, it would be fair to charge usage of the Windows environment at a higher rate. As another example, let's say your standard environments did not use Real Application

Clusters (RAC), and a new environment has come in that requires the high availability you can get from a RAC environment. RAC is, of course, a database option that you need to pay an additional license fee for, so that should be charged at a higher rate. An extended charge plan can be used to meet these sorts of requirements, as it provides greater flexibility to chargeback administrators. Extended charge plans allow you to do the following:

- Set up specific charges for specific entities
- Define rates based on configuration and usage
- Assign a flat rate regardless of configuration or usage
- Override the rates set for the universal plan

An out-of-the-box extended plan is provided that you can use as a basis for creating your own extended plans. This plan defines charges based on machine sizes for the Oracle Virtual Machine Guest entity.

Cost Centers

Obviously, when charges for resource usage are implemented, these charges must be assigned to something. In the chargeback application, the costs are assigned to a cost center. Cost centers are typically organized in a hierarchy and may correspond to different parts of an organization—for example, sales, development, human resources, and so forth—or they may correspond to different customers—for example, where you are a hosting company and host multiple customer environments. In either case, cost centers are defined as a hierarchy within the chargeback application. You can also import cost centers that have been implemented in your Lightweight Directory Access Protocol (LDAP) server if you want to use those.

Reports

The main benefit you get from using chargeback is the vast amount of information it puts at your fingertips. This information can be reported on by administrators in a variety of formats available via the Oracle BI Publisher tool, including pie charts and bar graphs, and you can drill down to charges based on a specific cost center, entity type, or resource. You can also make use of trending reports over time and can use this information to aid you in your IT budget planning. Outside the chargeback application itself, self-service users can view chargeback information related to the resources they have used within the self-service portal.

Setting Up Chargeback

Now you have an understanding of the capabilities of the chargeback application in the Enterprise Manager product suite. The next step, of course, is to set it up. Chargeback can be set up in Enterprise Manager 12*c* by any user with the EM_CBA_ADMIN role or, of course, as SYSMAN.

1. Once you are logged in as a user with the relevant privileges, follow the path Enterprise → Chargeback (see Figure 6.3).

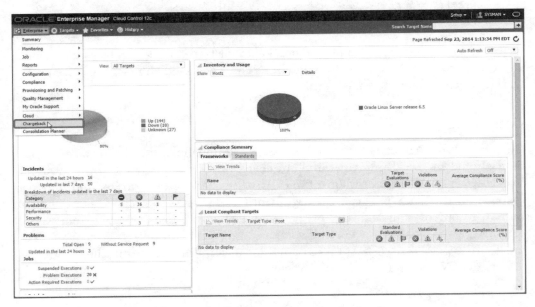

Figure 6.3   Setting up chargeback, step 1

2. The default currency symbol displayed in the chargeback application is the dollar sign ($). Note that this is just a symbol and does not have any impact on chargeback calculations, but you can change it if you want by clicking on the Settings tab (see Figure 6.4).

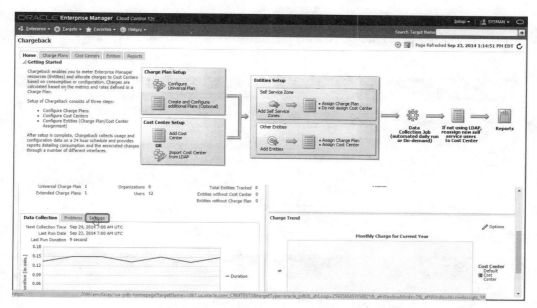

Figure 6.4 Setting up chargeback, step 2

3. You can enter a new currency symbol here, but for this environment, leave it at the default and click Change Plans (see Figure 6.5).

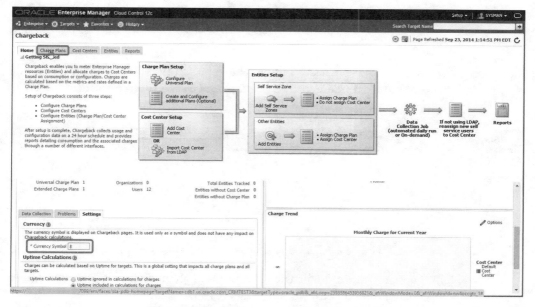

Figure 6.5 Setting up chargeback, step 3

4. The first thing to do is set rates for the universal charge plan, which covers the CPU usage, memory allocation, and storage allocation metrics. Click Set Rates (see Figure 6.6).

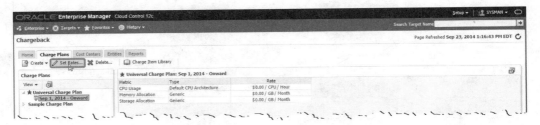

Figure 6.6   Setting up chargeback, step 4

5. Set the rates appropriately, and click Save (see Figure 6.7).

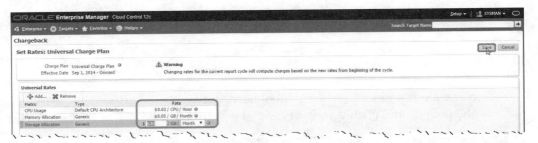

Figure 6.7   Setting up chargeback, step 5

6. The universal charge plan is useful, but in some situations, you may want to apply charges on other entities. That's where an extended charge plan can be used. To create an extended charge plan, click Create, then click Plan (see Figure 6.8).

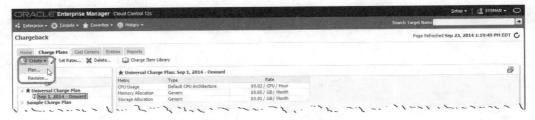

Figure 6.8   Setting up chargeback, step 6

7. Provide a meaningful name for the charge plan, then click Add to select an entity type for which you can set rates (see Figure 6.9).

Figure 6.9 Setting up chargeback, step 7

8. You can add multiple entity types to the charge plan at once, so choose Host and Oracle Pluggable Database, then click OK (see Figure 6.10).

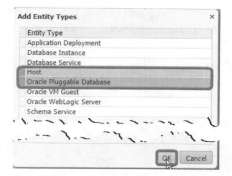

Figure 6.10 Setting up chargeback, step 8

9. You can now set up specific configurations for each entity type by selecting the entity and then clicking Setup Configurations (see Figure 6.11).

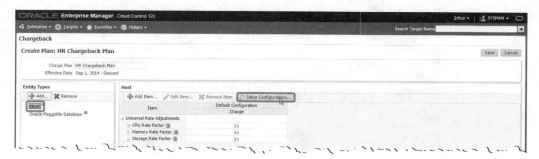

Figure 6.11 Setting up chargeback, step 9

10. Click the Add button (see Figure 6.12).

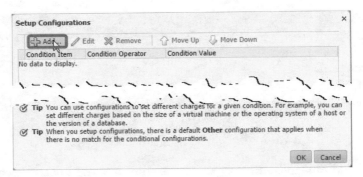

Figure 6.12   Setting up chargeback, step 10

11. In this example, different rates are charged for different machine architectures. This is the sort of thing you would do if you wanted to charge more for maintaining machines that are either outdated or for which you have less skill and may need to bring in consultants. To do this, you can set the Condition Item to Machine Architecture, then click the Search button to search for different values you can choose (see Figure 6.13).

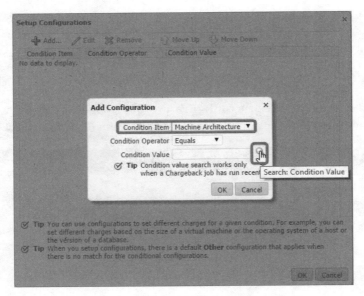

Figure 6.13   Setting up chargeback, step 11

12. In this scenario, we want to set up three different configurations:

   - Intel x86_64 as our default
   - Intel i686 as more expensive because it's outdated
   - PA-RISC 64-bit as more expensive because we have less skills in that area

You can select each in turn from the list, and click OK, as in Figure 6.14.

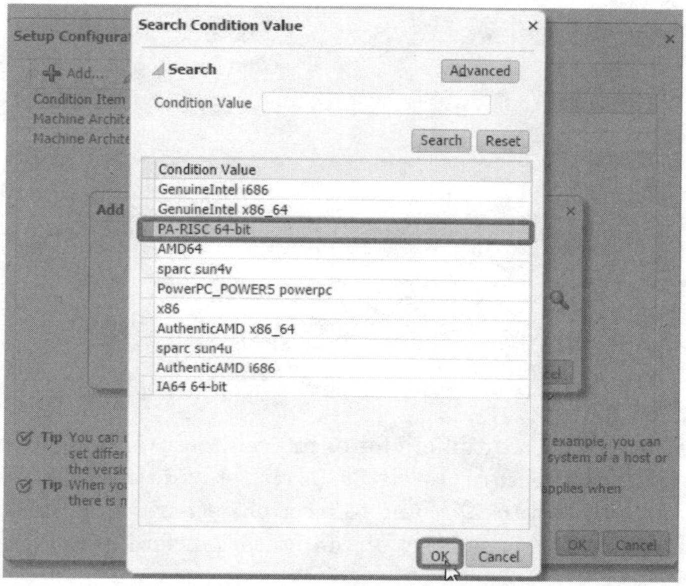

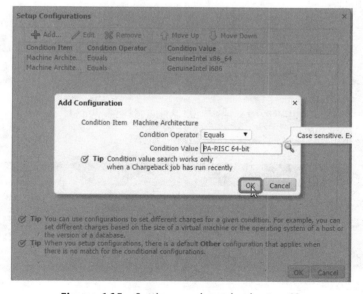

Figure 6.14   Setting up chargeback, step 12

13. Click OK (see Figure 6.15).

Figure 6.15   Setting up chargeback, step 13

14. On the Setup Configurations pop-up, click OK again (see Figure 6.16).

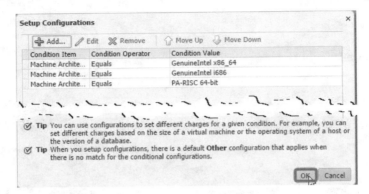

Figure 6.16   Setting up chargeback, step 14

15. You can now specify multipliers for each architecture. In this example, the preferred architecture (Intel x86-64) is set at 1, Intel i686 is set to 2x, PA-RISC 64 bit is set to 1.5x, and other architectures is set to 3x. Next, click Oracle Pluggable Database to set up configurations for it (see Figure 6.17).

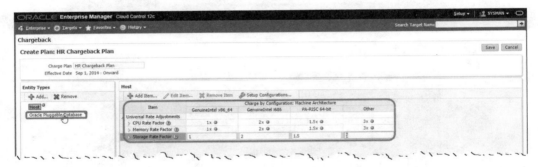

Figure 6.17   Setting up chargeback, step 15

16. Click Setup Configurations (see Figure 6.18).

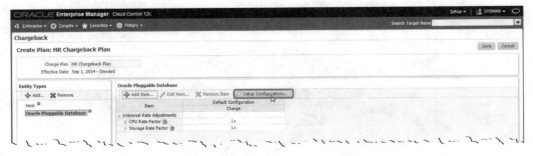

Figure 6.18   Setting up chargeback, step 16

17. Click Add (see Figure 6.19).

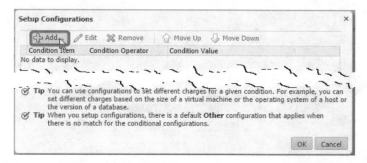

Figure 6.19   Setting up chargeback, step 17

18. On the Add Configuration pop-up, select Version for the Condition Item (see Figure 6.20).

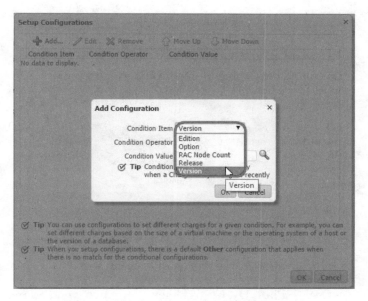

Figure 6.20   Setting up chargeback, step 18

19. In this scenario, clients who have not switched to the latest version of the database are charged more as a way of encouraging migration, so the Condition Operator and Condition Value are set to validate that. The option to charge more when using paid options such as partitioning and so on is also available. Click OK (see Figure 6.21).

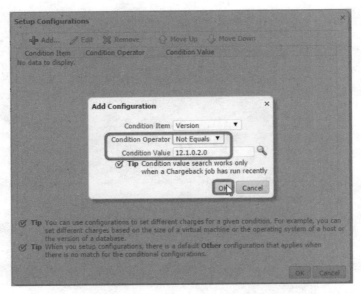

Figure 6.21   Setting up chargeback, step 19

20. On the Setup Configurations pop-up, click OK (see Figure 6.22).

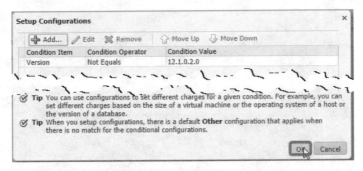

Figure 6.22   Setting up chargeback, step 20

21. Back on the Create Plan: HR Chargeback Plan page, you can increase the multiplier for configurations that aren't on the latest version, and click Save (see Figure 6.23).

Figure 6.23 Setting up chargeback, step 21

22. Once the charge plans are configured satisfactorily, you can also define cost centers that the charges will be assigned to. Cost centers are normally configured in a business hierarchy, so let's walk through the process of building that. Start by clicking the Cost Centers tab (see Figure 6.24).

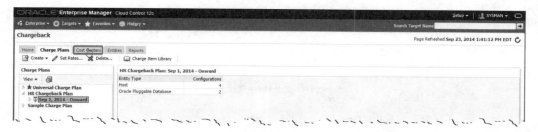

Figure 6.24 Setting up chargeback, step 22

23. Cost centers can either be imported from an existing LDAP configuration (done via the Action menu) or defined in the chargeback application. In this example, they are added to the chargeback application. To do this, click Add (see Figure 6.25).

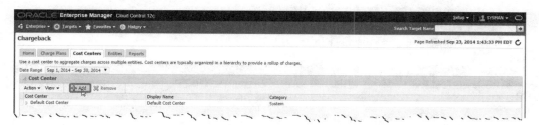

Figure 6.25 Setting up chargeback, step 23

24. On the New Cost Center pop-up, enter a cost center name and display name, then click OK (see Figure 6.26).

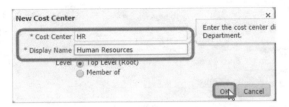

Figure 6.26   Setting up chargeback, step 24

25. You can do this as many times as you like. To add a cost center in a business hierarchy, first create a cost center at the top level (as shown previously), then create a cost center using the Member of radio button, and select the relevant top-level cost center, as shown here (see Figure 6.27).

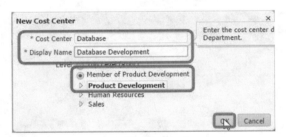

Figure 6.27   Setting up chargeback, step 25

26. Once you have defined all the cost centers you need, the next step is to add the relevant entities. An entity is either a target in Enterprise Manager or a custom resource that has been added to Enterprise Manager. Custom resources can include target types for which there is no current out-of-the-box chargeback support (covered in more detail in the documentation). To add entities, click the Entities tab (see Figure 6.28).

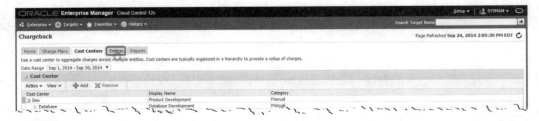

Figure 6.28   Setting up chargeback, step 26

27. Click Add Entities (see Figure 6.29).

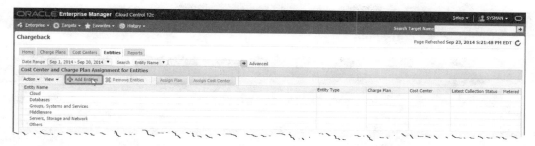

Figure 6.29 Setting up chargeback, step 27

28. This will start the Add Entities wizard. Click Add to select targets for charge-back (see Figure 6.30).

Figure 6.30 Setting up chargeback, step 28

29. Now it is time to add hosts. To search for hosts to add, deselect All, and select Host from the Target Type dropdown (see Figure 6.31).

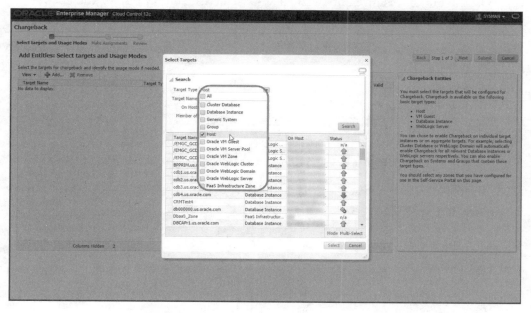

Figure 6.31 Setting up chargeback, step 29

30. From the list of hosts, select one or more hosts to add as an entity, and click Select (see Figure 6.32).

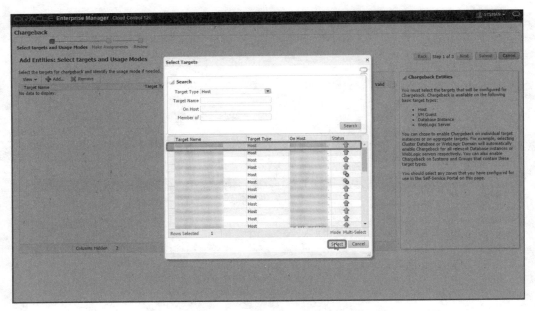

Figure 6.32   Setting up chargeback, step 30

31. On the Make Assignments wizard step, select the entity name, and click Assign Plan (see Figure 6.33).

Figure 6.33   Setting up chargeback, step 31

32. Select HR Chargeback Plan, and click OK to add the chargeback plan to this host (see Figure 6.34).

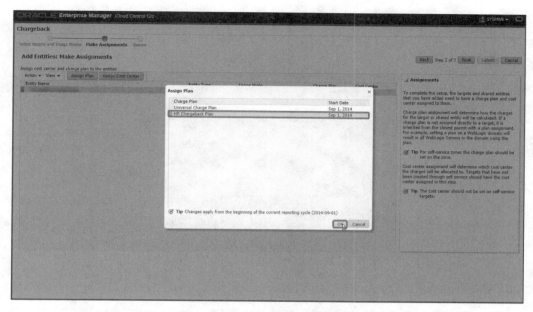

Figure 6.34 Setting up chargeback, step 32

33. To add a cost center to this host, click Assign Cost Center (see Figure 6.35).

Figure 6.35 Setting up chargeback, step 33

34. Select the relevant cost center, and click OK (see Figure 6.36).

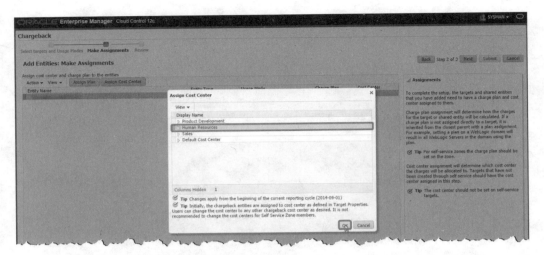

Figure 6.36   Setting up chargeback, step 34

35. Back on the Make Assignments step, click Next (see Figure 6.37).

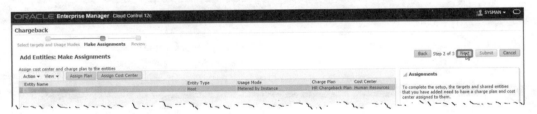

Figure 6.37   Setting up chargeback, step 35

36. Review the settings, and if they are correct, click Submit (see Figure 6.38).

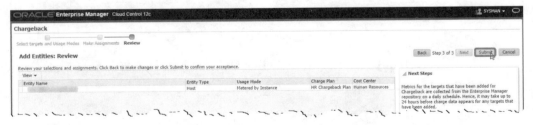

Figure 6.38   Setting up chargeback, step 36

37. You can walk through the same process to add one of the container databases and a platform as a service (PaaS) infrastructure zone as well. Once that has been done, you can schedule an on-demand data collection to start seeing the information for these entities in the chargeback application. To do that, select On-demand data collection from the Action dropdown menu (see Figure 6.39).

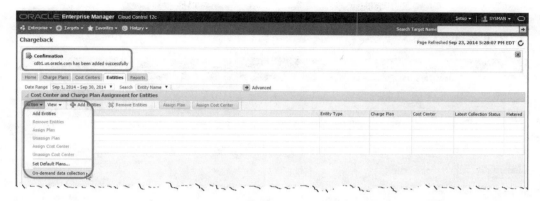

Figure 6.39 Setting up chargeback, step 37

38. Click Yes on the Confirmation pop-up (see Figure 6.40).

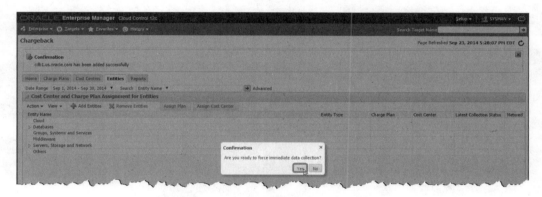

Figure 6.40 Setting up chargeback, step 38

39. In the Information message, click here to view the job status (see Figure 6.41).

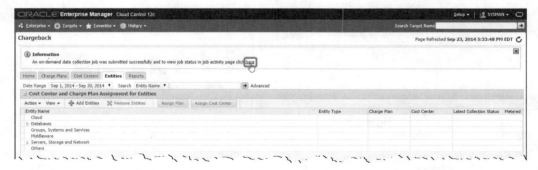

Figure 6.41 Setting up chargeback, step 39

40. Once the job status changes to 1 Succeeded, click Enterprise, then Charge-back (see Figure 6.42).

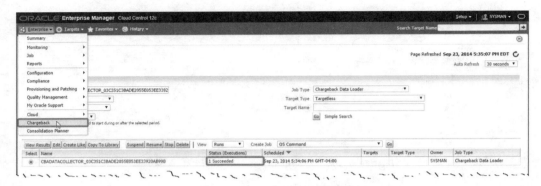

Figure 6.42   Setting up chargeback, step 40

41. You should see information being collected both in the Summary and Usage Trends regions (see Figure 6.43).

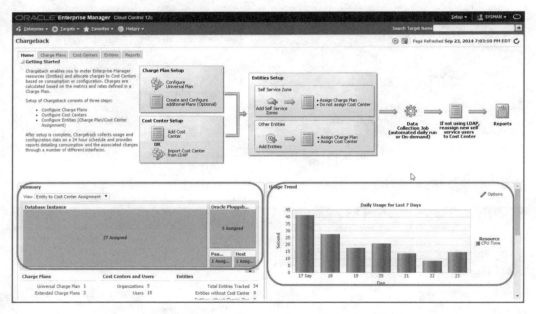

Figure 6.43   Setting up chargeback, step 41

It might seem like a very long-winded setup, but in reality, chargeback takes only a short time to configure. Of course, once it's configured, you then have all the joys of getting money out of the end clients for their resource usage—good luck with that one, I can't help you there!

Summary

The metering functionality that has been part of the Enterprise Manager product since its very early days allows us to both collate and report on the resource usage of particular targets within the Enterprise Manager environment. In combination with the chargeback application that was introduced with the 12c version of Enterprise Manager, you can now show business units the real cost of providing computing power. You can even charge the end users for the costs of their resource usage.

## 7

Manage and Administer the Database Cloud in Enterprise Manager 12c

Now that we've covered in some detail how to set up and configure the various database cloud models in Enterprise Manager Cloud Control 12c, you may be thinking that there really is no need for a database administrator (DBA) in the cloud world. After all, once the pools, zones, profiles, and templates are set up, database creation (and even destruction) is now in the hands of the self-service user. Depending on whether you are using a public or private cloud model, many of the time-consuming tasks such as installation, setup, and configuration may now be in the hands of cloud providers rather than DBAs.

In fact, nothing could be further from the truth. DBAs are still very much in demand in cloud environments. Moving to a cloud environment may remove much of the tactical work that DBAs have had to manage for so many years, but that simply frees them up to move to a more strategic position where they can focus on areas that are of more value to the business.

Although the creation and destruction of databases may now lie in the hands of self-service users, it will be a long time before users take on some of the other roles of the DBA, such as performance tuning (if indeed they ever take it on!). Old habits die hard, and it has long been the habit of users to reach out immediately to the DBA when they run into a performance problem. "The database is slow!" has been the catch cry for many years, even though it is often *not* the fault of the database. With so many technology layers between the end user and the database, one of the main reasons that users will still turn to the DBA for performance problems is that they simply lack the knowledge and skills to identify where the problem lies, let alone to understand and address the problem.

It may be more difficult in the cloud environment for the DBA to identify what sorts of performance issues are occurring. The reason for this added difficulty will largely be that DBAs are more remote from the day-to-day running of these databases than they may have been previously. One of the main roles of the DBA in the non-cloud world is to ensure databases are up and running, available to end users, and performing well. To that end, many DBAs have developed their own scripts that they run as cron jobs in the *nix world (or batch jobs in the Windows world), or they use tools such as Enterprise Manager to perform similar sorts of functionality. Of course, DBAs traditionally have had some form of access to the databases they are looking after, either by directly logging onto the machines that hold the databases or by accessing the databases across the network. In the cloud world, self-service users can create databases (up to the quotas that they have been provided with, of course) without the DBA even knowing the databases exist, let alone where they are. Thankfully, there is a straightforward answer to this issue—the Cloud Home page.

The Cloud Home Page

Once you have completed the setup of your cloud services and self-service users have started submitting requests, the Cloud Home page is useful for getting a cohesive view of all the different service types. To access the Cloud Home page, follow the path Enterprise → Cloud → Cloud Home, and you will see a screen like that shown in Figure 7.1.

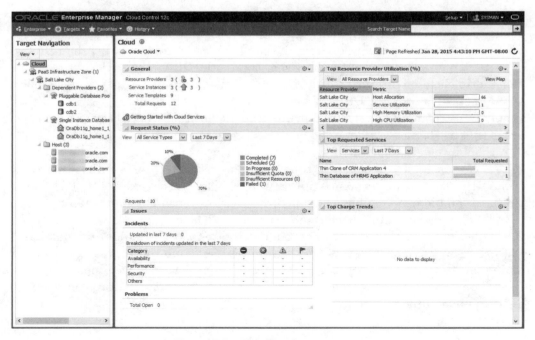

Figure 7.1   The Cloud Home page

From here you can see a number of regions—General, Request Status, Incidents, Top Resource Providers, Top Requested Services, and Top Charge Trends (data is displayed in the Charge Trends region only if you have enabled chargeback), so you get a good overview of the health of your cloud infrastructure. If you want to drill down to look at more details of what service instances you have available, you can click on the number to the right of Service Instances. This link will show you exactly what service instances are defined in your cloud environment, their status, the service type, the resource provider, the service template, and even who owns it (see Figure 7.2).

From here you can also click on the name of the service instance (for example, crm00001) to drill into the home page for that particular target, or you can simply select the row containing that target to do the following tasks:

- Start or stop the instance. Which one of these options is available depends on the status the instance is currently in. For example, if the service instance is already started, the Start option will remain grayed out.

- Examine the history of the service instance by clicking the History icon. This feature shows all the operations that have taken place against this particular service instance since it was created.

- Delete the service instance if it is no longer required. Obviously, caution should be taken before deciding to perform this operation.

You may find that the two most important links are the ones that show failed requests (the red slice of the pie chart in Figure 7.1) and the heat map (which you get to by clicking View Map on the top right of the screen shown in Figure 7.1). The failed request statuses are ones you'll want to investigate further to see what went wrong. Sometimes, this task is as simple as an attempt to start a database that's already started, but at other times, you'll find more complex issues that need further investigation and follow-up. You should also check here for requests that failed due to insufficient quota or resources and investigate whether more quota or resources need to be allocated.

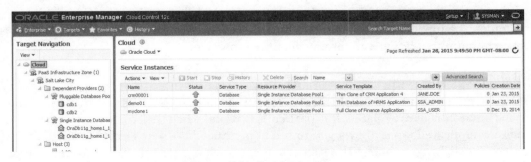

Figure 7.2 Service instances

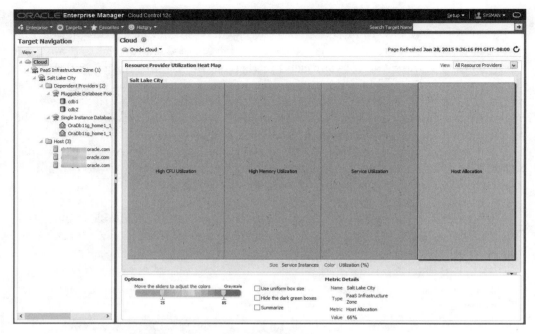

Figure 7.3   Heat map from a simple cloud environment

The heat map is a way to graphically view which resource providers (such as platform as a service [PaaS] infrastructure zones and database pools) are using the most resources. Even in the relatively simple environment we're using as a demonstration, the heat map (see Figure 7.3) shows that the host allocation for the Salt Lake City PaaS infrastructure zone, at 66 percent utilization, is starting to reach a level that may require adding more PaaS infrastructure zones. In more complex environments, you may see resource providers that show up as red. If you select that resource provider, you'll see what the problem is in the Metric Details region shown below the heat map, and you can drill into the Value link to discover more details.

There is also a menu of items that you can select from using the Oracle Cloud menu on the top left of the Cloud Home page. Several items in this menu are useful from an administration and management perspective.

Members → Topology

This menu item shows a graphical representation of how the different items in your cloud environment are related. It is particularly useful when the environment becomes more complicated, as it allows you to see at a glance how items are related to each other. By clicking on one of the items, you can see specific details listed under the Metric History region on the bottom right (see Figure 7.4 for an example).

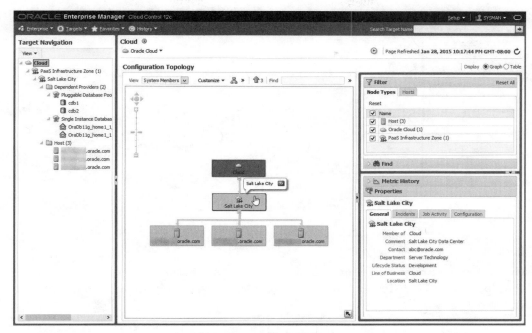

Figure 7.4 Configuration Topology

Resource Providers, Service Templates, Service Instances

Each of these menu items takes you to a list of the different entities. From here, it is easy to select and edit each particular entity. You can also get to each of these pages by clicking the links next to each one in the General region of the Cloud Home page. From each page, you are also able to create new items or delete existing ones. Figure 7.5 shows an example from the Resource Providers page.

Figure 7.5 The Resource Providers page

Figure 7.6   The Requests page

Requests

If you click on Show All under Requests, you can see a complete list of the requests that have been made in your cloud environment, as shown in Figure 7.6. From here you can

- Select an individual request and look at the details for it
- Reschedule the request if it hasn't already been executed
- Delete the request

If you click on Requests: → Dashboard, you'll be taken to a more graphical representation of the request trends over the past seven days, as shown in Figure 7.7. Note that you can click on the Settings spanner on the top left to change this time period to one more suitable to you (Figure 7.7, for example, shows the last 31 days' worth of requests). This page is particularly useful for showing request trends to management.

The Cloud Adviser

The information we've covered so far in this chapter is really the bread and butter, the day-to-day life of a cloud administrator. However, one of the main advantages of moving to a cloud environment is that it frees up a lot of the DBA's time. No longer do you need to focus on the mundane tasks of creating databases, looking after backups, and so on. The time that you used to spend working on these tasks is now available for you to take on a much more important role—the cloud adviser.

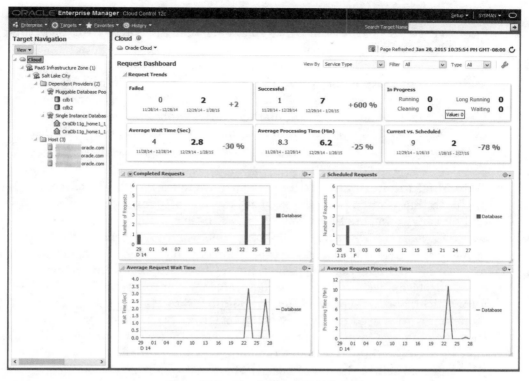

Figure 7.7   The Request Dashboard

What is the cloud adviser's role? Well, it's a role that many of us have been per-forming for years—the senior DBA role—expanded into the cloud environment. Since most of our business users do not have the technical background to be able to make informed decisions on technical issues, they still come to the DBA to provide that advice. Those technical issues fall into a variety of broad topics, which the rest of this chapter examines.

Security

Security is of paramount importance in the cloud world, because if you get the security model wrong in the cloud environment, you may not have an environment to administer and manage for very long! We've all no doubt heard of the security breaches that seem to be increasingly common in the cloud environment. Security breaches might involve stolen usernames and passwords from cloud providers and, more seriously, stolen data. Oracle database technology is used the world over to secure large volumes of confidential data—financial data, employee data, customer information, and so much more. Securing that data, and ensuring it remains secure, is an essential part of the DBA's role. Following are some of the tools that can be used to assist with this task:

- **Transparent Data Encryption (TDE)**: TDE is a way to stop would-be attackers from bypassing the database and reading sensitive information directly from the files that make up the Oracle database. This protection is extended to any backups that have been made of the database as well. TDE allows encryption of individual columns right up to entire tablespaces, so you can choose how much of your data to secure.

- **Data Masking and Subsetting**: As you move to the cloud environment, one approach that is often taken for security reasons is to migrate development and test environments to the cloud first, as these environments are often seen as lower risk. However, at the same time, you want to ensure that your developers and quality assurance (QA) engineers have environments that are as close to production as possible so they have a realistic environment to test performance on. Those two requirements may at first glance seem antithetical, but Enterprise Manager contains Data Masking and Subsetting tools that can be used to address the issue. Oracle Data Masking and Subsetting allows you to sanitize copies of production data for development and QA environments so that your production data is not compromised. It also allows you to use subsets of the data in cases where you simply do not have enough storage to take a full copy of your production data into these environments.

Of course, you need to secure your data against more than just external attacks. Most studies of security breaches indicate that these breaches are more often the work of insiders than of external hackers (regardless of the fact that the most reported-on breaches are external). So from a security perspective, you must have tools and technologies that can be used to both track and secure against internal attacks as well. Some of the Oracle products that help to address this space include Transparent Data Encryption, Oracle Audit Vault, and Oracle Database Vault.

Server and Database Sizing

In theory, scaling a database in the cloud world is as simple as requesting more processing capability. In reality, we all know that service providers, be they an internal IT department or an external hosting provider, will have limitations as far as the hardware they have available to them. One of the value-add roles that a DBA can perform is to determine the amount of resources required now to meet current needs as well as to scale to meet future requirements. Enterprise Manager 12*c* has a number of tools that can be used to assist the DBA in this arena, including the following:

- **Consolidation Planner**: Consolidation Planner is a tool that can be used to plan a cloud architecture for server consolidation or for any other consolidation model. It allows you to identify source and destination targets and applicable technical and functional constraints, such as where the application can reside. You can also use Consolidation Planner to determine whether source environments can be consolidated onto hardware that you have not yet purchased, providing greater confidence that machines you are looking at purchasing will be suitable for the workloads you plan to put on them.

- **Chargeback**: As we covered in Chapter 6, "Metering and Chargeback in Enterprise Manager 12c," chargeback is an accounting tool that provides a way to aggregate the enormous amount of metrics data that Enterprise Manager collects, a way to report to consumers of those metrics how much they have used of those particular resources, and, if you have set it up to do so, a way for the IT department to charge those consumers for the resources they have used. However, its usefulness is not restricted to these functions. Once the chargeback application is configured and running, you accumulate a history of how many resources have been used by specific applications or databases, which in turn allows you to project some form of capacity planning figures for future growth. Obviously, you still need to talk to the application owners to get an idea of whether any new functionality may impact those figures, but at the very least, you have a starting point that can be used to predict future resource requirements.

Performance Tuning

As mentioned at the beginning of this chapter, contacting the DBA is all too often the first port of call for users complaining about performance, even before they can identify the database as the source of the performance issue. Of course, if we've ensured server and database sizing has been done correctly, we shouldn't see too much in the way of performance issues. Nevertheless, we all know that server and database sizing is far too often a reactive rather than proactive exercise, so we still need to undertake the same sorts of performance problem identification and resolution exercises that we are familiar with from the non-cloud environment. This topic is far too large to cover here—indeed, whole books have been written about Oracle performance tuning—so we won't go into more detail now. Suffice it to say, you will still need to perform this role but with the added complexity of not necessarily knowing beforehand what other environments may be directly impacting yours.

Consequently, you should become familiar with the pages covered at the beginning of this chapter, particularly the Cloud Home. It's there that you can get an overview of what cloud instances have been created and can drill down to see all the different service entities that have been created and removed.

Summary

Oracle Enterprise Manager Cloud Control 12*c* should be your tool of choice when monitoring, administering, and managing the Oracle database cloud environment. As you've seen over the past few chapters, it provides the capability to set up both schema as a service and DBaaS as well as to configure the chargeback application. Additionally, as we've seen in this chapter, Enterprise Manager 12*c* allows you to perform the ongoing management and administration of the cloud environment you have set up. One final step remains as an often undertaken task in the cloud environment: cloning of databases from one environment to another. That's the subject of our next chapter.

## 8

Cloning Databases in Enterprise Manager 12*c*

Cloning databases has been a part of the role of a database administrator (DBA) since data was first chiseled onto stone tablets. DBAs are frequently called on to both clone and refresh database copies for all sorts of business reasons. As the Oracle product set has broadened over the years, more and more ways to clone data have been introduced. This chapter restricts the discussion to the two main types of clones built in a cloud environment using EM12*c*—*full* clones and *snap* (or thin) clones. Also, since the thrust of this entire book is on building databases in a cloud environment, the details covered here are specific to using EM12*c* in the cloud environment.

Full Clones

A full clone, as the name implies, involves taking a complete or full copy of an existing database. This can be done in one of two ways—by taking a Recovery Manager (RMAN) backup or by issuing an RMAN DUPLICATE command—so let's take a look at each of those options.

RMAN Backups

Oracle's Recovery Manager utility, more commonly known as RMAN, has been around since Oracle 8.0, so you probably need no introduction to it. RMAN backups, which are created using either backup sets or image copies, can be used to create profiles, which in turn can be used to create full database clones.

Creating a full database clone using an RMAN backup in the cloud environment requires a number of steps:

1. Enabling the DBaaS cloud. This involves some common setup tasks required for setting up a private database cloud. These tasks are covered in Chapter 5, "Database Consolidation in Enterprise Manager 12*c*," so if you need to, refresh your memory by rereading that chapter. In summary, the tasks are

   a. Defining roles and assigning users

   b. Creating a platform as a service (PaaS) infrastructure zone

   c. Creating a database pool

   d. Configuring request settings

   e. Setting quotas

2. Creating a profile either by taking an RMAN backup or using an existing RMAN backup.

3. Creating a service template based on the profile just created.

Let's walk through the last two steps in more detail.

Creating a Profile by Taking an RMAN Backup

To create a profile by taking an RMAN backup, start on the Getting Started: Databases page.

1. Go to Setup → Cloud → Database. From here, click on the Data Sources link and ensure the Data Profiles tab is active, and then click Create, as shown in Figure 8.1.

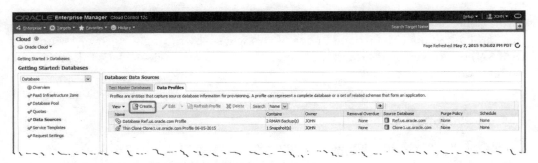

Figure 8.1 Creating a data profile

2. The Create Database Provisioning Profile wizard starts, which has only four steps. Step 1 looks pretty bland when you first see it, as it simply asks you to select a reference target. This is the entity that the backup will be taken from, so in many ways, "reference source" would be a better description. When you select your reference target, the rest of the screen is populated on the basis of that target. You can create a profile based on either an ORACLE_ HOME target type or a database target type. In our case, we want to create a profile based on a database, so select the specific database by clicking the magnifying glass on the first page of the wizard. That opens the screen shown in Figure 8.2, where you select the Ref database as the reference target.

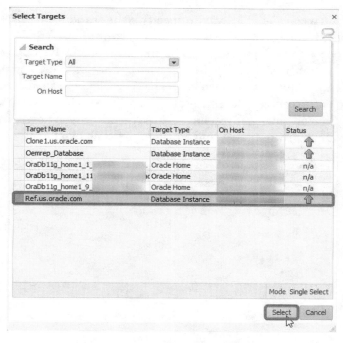

Figure 8.2   Selecting the reference target

3. Once you click the Select button, it takes you back to a much more populated version of step 1 of the wizard. Here, you can click on the Structure and Data radio button (the Create and RMAN Backup radio buttons are selected by default), and also specify credentials. In the example shown in Figure 8.3, preferred credentials for both the host containing the database and the database itself are already created, so you can just use those and click Next.

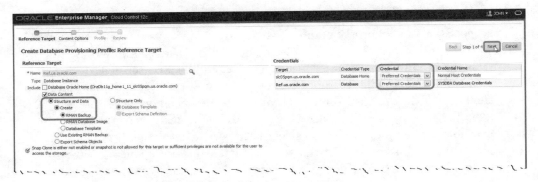

Figure 8.3   Step 1 of the Create Profile wizard

4. Step 2 of the wizard enables you to specify some standard RMAN configuration options. If the database you are using is running in ARCHIVELOG mode, you can choose to perform either an online or an offline backup. You can also choose the number of channels to use, whether or not to use compression, the backup location, and details such as the backup filename format, backup file tag, and name of the control file. In Figure 8.4, all the settings have been left at their defaults (obviously, if you have RMAN settings you normally would use, you can change any of them), and you can just click Next.

Figure 8.4   Step 2 of the Create Profile wizard

5. On step 3 of the wizard, you are prompted for Profile Information (see Figure 8.5):

- **Profile Location (mandatory)**: This is the location in the software library where the database profile will be created.
- **Profile Name (mandatory)**: This is a unique name for the profile.
- **Description (optional)**: Provide a description for the profile that identifies the information you want to see in the description.
- **Profile Version and Vendor (optional)**: These fields should be prepopulated. There is no need to change them.
- **Notes (optional)**: Again, this field will be prepopulated. You can add or delete anything you need here.
- **Schedule**: In the Schedule section, you can start the profile creation immediately or schedule it for some later time. You can also set a repeat policy to repeat the profile creation regularly. If you are scheduling a repeat creation, you need to place the backup on a Network File System (NFS) directory that is shared among all pool members.
- **Purge Policy**: The Purge Policy region allows you to either not purge any data that's been collected or to purge it after a certain number of days or snapshots.
- **Working Directory**: This field allows you to specify a directory for any temporary files to be kept as part of the profile creation. It defaults to /tmp.

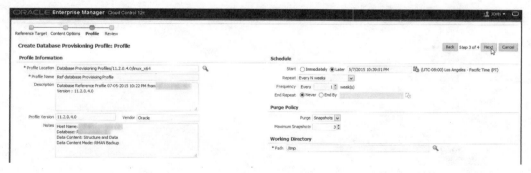

Figure 8.5   Step 3 of the Create Profile wizard

6. Step 4 of the wizard, the Review step, enables you to review all of the inputs you have made. If you are satisfied that you have made all the right choices, you can click on the Submit button to create the profile, as shown in Figure 8.6.

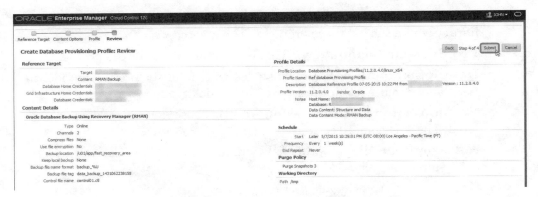

Figure 8.6   Step 4 of the Create Profile wizard

You are taken to the Procedure Activity page where you can watch the profile being created. Normally, I change the View Data value on the far right to refresh every 30 seconds, and choose Select All under the View menu to watch all the steps automatically refresh. If there are any problems with the profile creation, you can select the checkbox to the left of the step that fails to see more information displayed on the right of the screen. In the example we've walked through here, you can see in Figure 8.7 that there were no problems and the profile was created in just under 2 minutes.

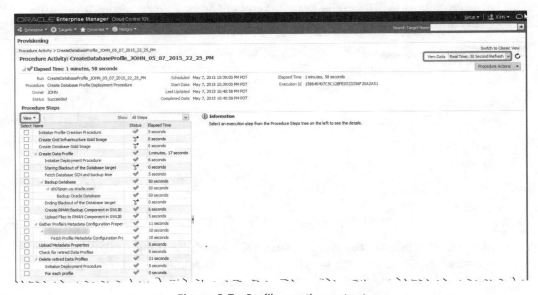

Figure 8.7   Profile creation output

Creating a Profile Using an Existing RMAN Backup

Now let's look at how to create a database profile using an existing RMAN backup. In most cases, using an existing backup is a more common scenario than using a new backup because most people already have RMAN backups of their databases.

The steps for creating a profile using an existing RMAN backup start in exactly the same way as creating a profile by taking an RMAN backup. Start on the Getting Started: Databases page (you can reach it by following the path Setup → Cloud → Database). From here, click on the Data Sources link and ensure the Data Profiles tab is active, then click Create, as shown in Figure 8.8.

Figure 8.8 Creating a data profile

Again, this starts the Create Database Provisioning Profile wizard. When you select your reference target, the rest of the screen is populated on the basis of that target. In our case, we want to create a profile based on an existing RMAN backup of a database, so you can select the specific database by clicking the magnifying glass on the first page of the wizard. That opens the screen shown in Figure 8.9, where the Ref database has been selected as our reference target.

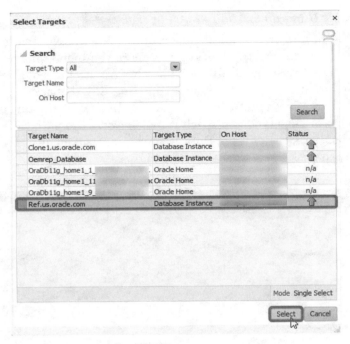

Figure 8.9   Selecting the Reference Target

Once you click the Select button, it takes you back to a much more populated version of step 1 of the wizard.

1. Here, you can click on the Structure and Data radio button but this time also specify credentials. In the example in Figure 8.10, preferred credentials for both the host containing the database and the database itself are already created, so just use those, and click Next. You will also notice a third option here (Export Schema Objects) that isn't covered so far because it's used for schema as a service, not complete clones.

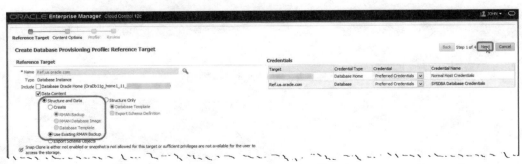

Figure 8.10   Step 1 of the Create Profile wizard

2. This step takes you to a screen that shows a list of all the existing backups you can use to create the profile. You need to be a little careful when selecting the backup you want to use here, as unfortunately they're not listed in any logical order. When you select the backup you want to use to create the profile, the backup set pieces for that backup are listed below in a master detail form. Click the Next button to move to the next screen, as shown in Figure 8.11.

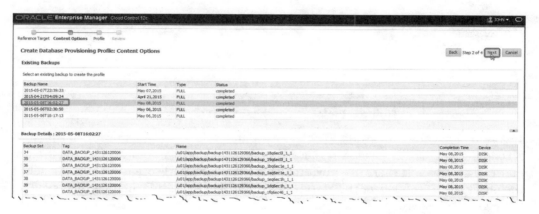

Figure 8.11   Step 2 of the Create Profile wizard

3. On the next screen, you are again prompted for profile information, schedule, and working directory. In this case, because we are working off a single existing RMAN backup, it makes no sense to set a repeat policy, so the options we had to do that when creating a profile based on a new RMAN backup are not available to us. It is useful to include the fact that this profile is taken from an existing RMAN backup in the description field, as shown in Figure 8.12, but doing so is totally optional. Once you have made any changes you want on this page, click the Next button.

Figure 8.12   Step 3 of the Create Profile wizard

4. You are taken to the review screen where you can click the Submit button again, as shown in Figure 8.13.

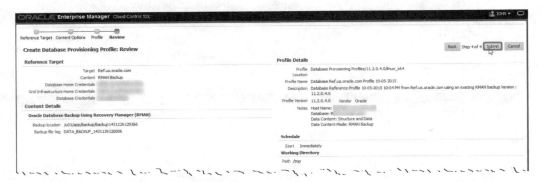

Figure 8.13   Step 4 of the Create Profile wizard

Again, you can change the View Data value on the far right to refresh every 30 seconds, and choose Select All under the View menu to watch all the steps automatically refresh. If there are any problems with the profile creation, you can select the checkbox to the left of the step that fails to see more information displayed on the right of the screen. In the example we've walked through here, you can see in Figure 8.14 that there were no problems, and the profile was created in just under 1 minute.

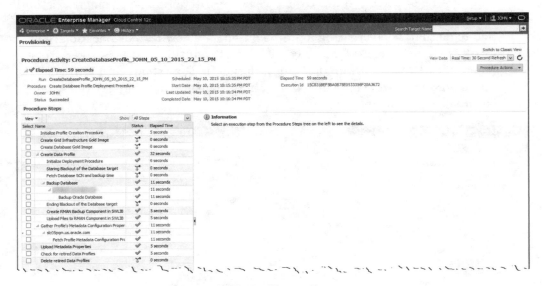

Figure 8.14   Profile creation output

Creating a Service Template from a Database Profile

Once you have created a database profile, either by taking an RMAN backup or using an existing RMAN backup, the next step in making this profile available to the self-service user is to create a service template. It is these service templates that will populate the catalog that the self-service user can select from, which is why creating a service template is such an important step.

To create a service template using either of the profiles we've just discussed, you must be logged into EM12*c* as a user who has been granted the EM_SSA_ ADMINISTRATOR role.

1. To create a template, follow the same path as you did previously to get to Data Sources (Setup → Cloud → Database), only in this case you select the next option in the list, Service Templates, as shown in Figure 8.15.

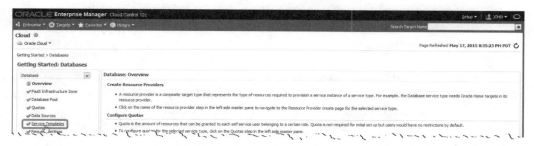

Figure 8.15 Accessing service templates

2. This takes you to the Database: Service Templates page, where you will see a list of the service templates that already exist (provided other service templates have already been created, of course!). Probably the most useful thing you can see on this screen is the number of service instances. This will tell you how many times the service template has been used to provision a database. To start the service template creation wizard, simply click the Create button, as shown in Figure 8.16.

Figure 8.16 Starting the Service Template wizard

3. The first step of the wizard, the General page, enables you to specify the following information:

   ▪ **Name**: The name of the service template will be selected by the self-service user from the self-service catalog, so it is wise to make it a recognizable name and to minimize the amount of technical information in the name. The reason for this second point is that self-service users are generally business users, so a name such as "3-node RAC Cluster using 11.2.0.3 with Data Guard" is completely meaningless to them.

   ▪ **Description**: Expand on the name a little more here. You might include the database name the clone is taken from, for example, as self-service users will normally recognize that name.

   ▪ **Source Identification**: This region is where you specify to create the database using a profile (or to use an existing database if you haven't created profiles). If you are creating a database using a profile, here is also where you specify which profile you are using as well as the profile version (you can either specify the latest version or allow the user to select the version at request time). Once you specify a profile, the Shared Location field at the bottom of the page will be auto-populated. (Note that if you do not have an NFS mount or similar for the shared location, you will need to manually copy the files to this location before moving to step 2 of the wizard.)

   ▪ **Database Definition**: You can either create a single-instance or RAC database using this wizard. The Database Definition region is where you specify this option along with the number of nodes if this is a RAC database. You can also specify the database SID here (or allow the user to select one at request time), as well as the domain name. In addition, you can allow the user to create standby databases, along with the main database being created, by clicking the Enable Standby Database checkbox.

   ▪ **Pools and Zones**: Service templates can be configured to provision databases in more than one zone. This region is where you specify one or more zones and associated resource pools that the service template can provision databases into. Once you have selected the zone and pool, the host target will be populated for you in the Reference Host field.

   Figure 8.17 shows a completed example of this General page using one of the templates we created previously. You can simply click Next to move to the next step of the wizard.

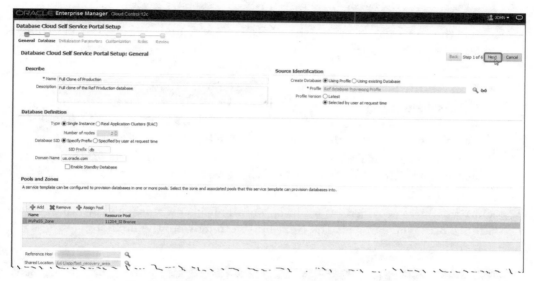

Figure 8.17   Step 2 of the Template Creation wizard

4. On the next screen, the reference host information is prepopulated for you according to the information you supplied in step 2 of the wizard. You need to make selections for the following regions:

- **Storage type**: You can use either Automatic Storage Management (ASM) or file system–based storage. If you choose ASM, you need to specify the disk group. (Note that this is a mandatory field as you would expect, even though the user interface doesn't indicate that by having an asterisk next to the Disk Group field. If you attempt to use ASM for the storage group but do not specify a disk group, you'll receive an error when you click the Next button.) If you choose File System, you will need to either specify a location or accept the default of $ORACLE_BASE/oradata.

- **Fast Recovery**: The Fast Recovery region is not mandatory, but if you want your self-service users to schedule backups and be able to restore their databases to a previous point in time, you should enable the fast recovery area, specify a location (either ASM or file system based), specify a size for the fast recovery area, and select the Enable Archiving checkbox.

- **Listener Port**: This is again a mandatory field. You can click on the magnifying glass, and the listener port number will be populated on the basis of the host that was chosen from step 2 of the wizard.

- **Administrator Credentials**: In this mandatory field, you must either use the same password for the SYS, SYSTEM, and DBSNMP users that will be created in the new database or specify different passwords for each user.

- **Non Administrator Credentials**: If you want to restrict access to the other schemas that are normally in an Oracle database, you can select those here and specify a password for them. These schemas will then be locked down so they can't be accessed by self-service users.

- **Master Account Privileges**: Here you can specify a name for the master account and either add or remove privileges that will be granted to this account.

Once you have provided information for all of these areas, as shown in Figure 8.18, you can click the Next button to move to the next step of the wizard.

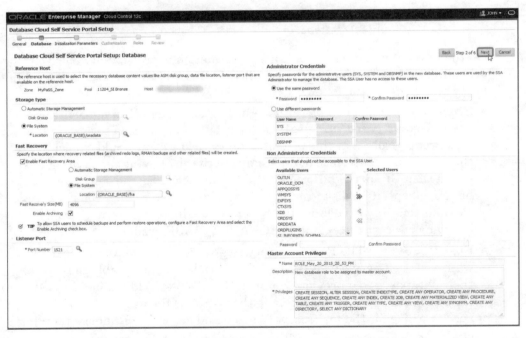

Figure 8.18   Step 3 of the Template Creation wizard

5. On the Initialization Parameters screen (shown in Figure 8.19), you can edit any of a range of initialization parameters for the database. Note that not all parameters can be changed here—just the subset that Oracle Corporation believes you may want to change.

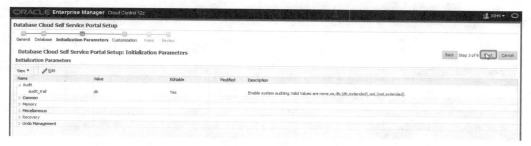

Figure 8.19   Step 4 of the Template Creation wizard

6. On the fifth screen of the Template Creation wizard, you can specify the following:

- **Custom Scripts for Create**: These are scripts that are stored as directives in the Software Library. You can execute scripts before and after creating the service instance and can also specify a SQL script to run after the service instance creation (obviously, executing a SQL script before service instance creation doesn't make sense). You can specify which user the SQL script will run as, too. These scripts allow you to do a lot of customization work, even to perform your own data masking routines as SQL scripts if you want.

- **Custom Scripts for Delete**: Just as you can specify the scripts to run before and after service instance creation, you can specify scripts to run before and after deleting a service instance.

- **Target Properties**: In the Target Properties region, you can specify global target properties, such as lifecycle status, department, and so on. If you do specify a global target property, you can then make it mandatory by clicking the Required checkbox. You can also lock the value you have entered for the property by clicking the padlock icon. Locking will prevent self-service users from modifying the value of the property. In the example shown in Figure 8.20, the LifeCycle Status property is set to Test, but it is left as both optional and changeable by the self-service user.

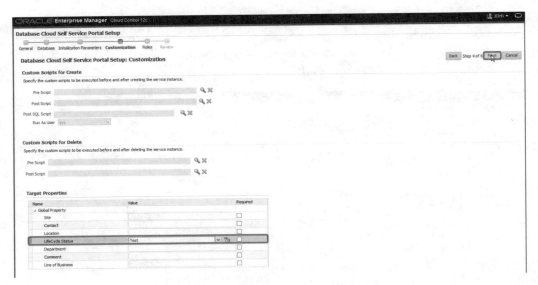

Figure 8.20   Step 5 of the Template Creation wizard

7. On the next screen, Roles, you need to add the roles that will be able to use this template. Enterprise Manager users assigned this role (or roles) will then have access to the template, and it will appear in the Self-Service Catalog for those users. To add a role, you simply click the Add button and select the relevant roles. In the example shown in Figure 8.21, the Developer role is added.

Figure 8.21   Step 6 of the Template Creation wizard

8. The final step of the Template Creation wizard allows you to review all the inputs you have made thus far. If you want to make any changes, you can use the Back button to go back to the step where you need to make corrections. Otherwise, you can simply click Create, as shown in Figure 8.22, to create the service template.

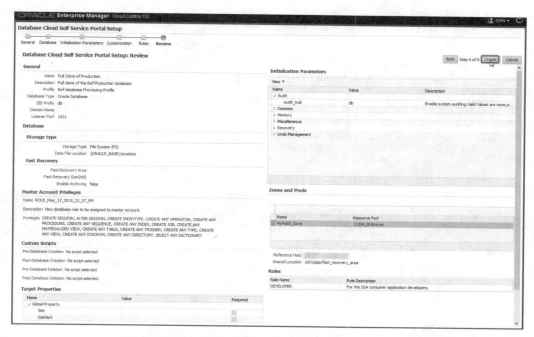

Figure 8.22 Step 7 of the Template Creation wizard

9. Once you have created the service template, you will see a message saying the template was created successfully, as shown in Figure 8.23.

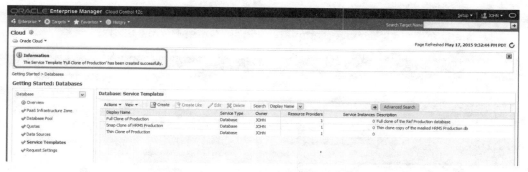

Figure 8.23 Confirmation that the service template was created

RMAN DUPLICATE

In the previous sections, we covered creating a full database clone using an RMAN backup, either a new backup done as part of the cloning procedure or an existing RMAN backup that was done for another purpose (usually your normal backup routines). There is another way to create a full database clone that does not require the use of a backup. This feature, also known as *live cloning*, uses an RMAN DUPLICATE command to duplicate your live database. Just as when using an RMAN backup to create a full database clone, there are a number of steps to creating a live clone:

1. Enabling the DBaaS cloud. This involves some common setup tasks required for setting up a private database cloud. These tasks are covered in Chapter 5, so if you need to, refresh your memory by rereading that chapter. In summary, the tasks are

   a. Defining roles and assigning users

   b. Creating a PaaS infrastructure zone

   c. Creating a database pool

   d. Configuring request settings

   e. Setting quotas

2. Creating a service template using Live Clone.

Let's look at the details of this last step.

1. Go to the Database Cloud page by following the path Setup → Cloud → Database. From there, click Service Templates, as shown in Figure 8.24.

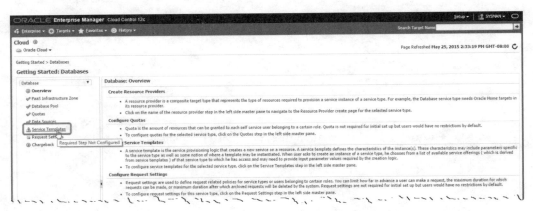

Figure 8.24   Accessing the Service Templates page

2. Once you are on the Service Templates page, click the Create button, as shown in Figure 8.25.

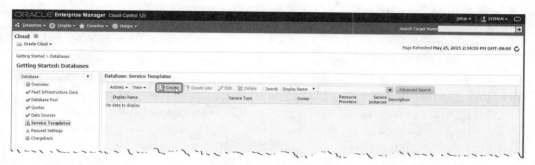

Figure 8.25   Starting the Create Template wizard

3. On this next screen, you choose to use live cloning. As you can see on the right side of Figure 8.26, instead of using a profile that was created earlier, I've select Using existing Database and specified the name of the database I'm cloning from.

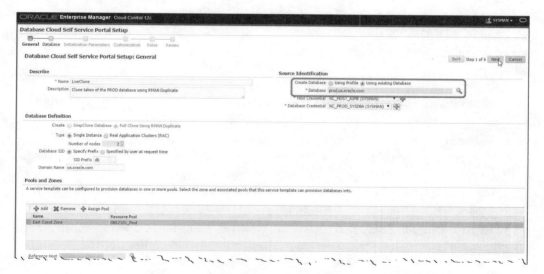

Figure 8.26   Step 1 of the Create Template wizard

The remaining screens are the same as they were for creating a service template using an RMAN backup, so they are not reproduced here—just look back to the section "Creating a Service Template from a Database Profile."

There are two points that you need to keep in mind when using RMAN DUPLICATE to take a live clone:

- Because (generally) we are cloning off of the production environment, the clone command will generate load on that environment. This may be different from using an RMAN backup, as the backup can be placed on another machine, thus moving the load to that machine.

- Because we are doing this task directly from a service template, and thus bypassing the creation of a data profile, there is no opportunity to have this cloning performed as a scheduled operation unless the self-service user changes the default start time. If immediate cloning is not desirable from a load perspective, you will need to educate the self-service user to change the start date and time.

Snap Clones

In simple terms, Snap Clone is a storage-agnostic self-service approach to rapidly creating space-efficient clones of large databases (and by and large, we're talking terabytes or more). Now that's probably more buzzwords in one sentence than anyone's brain can deal with without exploding, so let's look at some of those terms more closely:

- **Storage agnostic**: Snap Clone supports all storage vendors, both network attached storage (NAS) and storage area network (SAN).

- **Self-service**: In the XaaS world—where X can be any of infrastructure (I), middleware (MW), platform (P), or database (DB)—one of the key features is empowering the end user to do the work rather than waiting on some techie to find time in her or his otherwise busy schedule. So it's the end user who makes the ad hoc clones here, not the storage admin.

- **Rapid**: People simply don't have the time anymore to wait weeks for provisioning to happen (for that matter, they probably never did, but that's another discussion), so you have to support the functionality to clone databases in minutes rather than the days or weeks it used to take.

- **Space efficient**: When you're working with terabyte or larger databases, you may not have the storage to create full-sized clones, so you have to significantly reduce the storage footprint to start with.

The Challenges Snap Clone Addresses

Snap Clone can be used to address number of major challenges:

- **Lack of automation**: Manual tasks such as provisioning and cloning of new databases (e.g., for test or development systems) is one area that many DBAs complain is too time consuming. It can take days to weeks, often because of the need to coordinate the involvement of different groups, as shown in Figure 8.27.

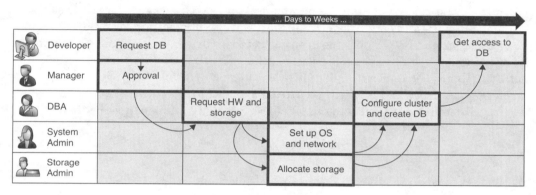

Figure 8.27   The standard cloning workflow

When an end user, whether a developer or a QA engineer, needs a database, he or she typically has to go through an approval process like that shown in the figure, which then translates into a series of tasks for the DBA, the sysadmin, and the storage admin. The sysadmin has to provide the compute capacity, and the storage admin has to provide the space on a filer. Finally, the DBA has to install the bits, create the database (optionally on Real Application Clusters), and deliver the database to the user. Clearly, this is a cumbersome and time-consuming process that needs to be improved.

- **Database unfriendly solutions**: Obviously, when there is a need looking for a solution, different people take different approaches to resolving that need. There are a variety of point solutions and storage solutions out there, but the vast bulk of them are not database aware. They tend to clone storage volumes rather than databases and have no visibility into the database stack, which of course makes it hard to triage performance issues as a DBA. They also lack the ability to track configuration, compliance, and data security issues, and they have limited or no lifecycle capabilities.

- **Storage issues and archaic processes**: One of the main issues DBAs face is storage. Data volumes are ever increasing, particularly in these Big Data days, and the growth can often outpace your storage capacity. You can throw more disks at the problem, but it never seems to be enough, and you can end up with degraded performance if you take the route of sharing clones between users. There can also be different processes and different priorities between the storage team and the DBA team, and you may still have fixed refresh cycles, making it difficult to clone on an ad hoc basis.

In the latest release of Snap Clone, you can provide thin clones via either software solutions (Solaris ZFS and CloneDB) or hardware solutions (Sun ZFS Storage Appliance, NetApp, and EMC). Let's touch on each of these in a bit more detail. The examples presented here use Enterprise Manager 12.1.0.4.3 with the latest plugins (specifically for Snap Clone, the important plugin is the Enterprise Manager for Storage Management plugin release 12.1.0.5.0). If you are on a slightly different version, you may see a slightly different look and feel to the user interface and available functionality.

Software Solutions

Let's start by looking at the software-based solutions.

Snap Clone using Solaris ZFS

Snap Clone using ZFS uses a single stock Solaris 11.1+ image, which can be either physical or virtual (note that it doesn't use the Sun ZS3 appliance). It supports both NAS and SAN. If you are using SAN, then mount the logical unit numbers (LUNs) as raw disk and format with the ZFS filesystem. It's important to note here that this does *not* require any snapshot or cloning licenses from the storage vendor, as these features are available for free.

Additional features provided with this solution include compression, de-duplication, I/O caching, and so on. If you also need high availability in this configuration, that can be handled externally either via Solaris Clusters or by using the high-availability features of the underlying hypervisor.

Figure 8.28 shows what the configuration looks like diagrammatically.

CloneDB Using dNFS

With CloneDB using direct network file storage (dNFS), you get the capability to create thin copies of a database from RMAN image copies. This approach uses the NFS v3 client that's embedded in the database technology since 11.2.0.3. Currently, this is supported for single-instance databases, but only on filesystems (i.e., ASM is not yet supported).

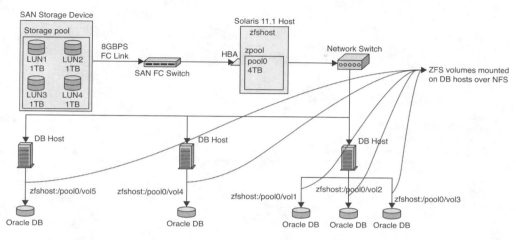

Figure 8.28   Snap Clone using ZFS

The advantages of this approach include the following:

- It's easy to set up.
- No special storage software is needed.
- It works on all platforms.
- It's both time efficient (instantaneous cloning) and space efficient (you can create multiple clones based on one backup).
- It uses dNFS to improve the performance, high availability, and scalability of NFS storage.

Hardware Solution

As mentioned previously, the hardware solution for Snap Clone is available on a range of hardware, including Sun ZFS Storage Appliance, NetApp, and EMC. The EMC configuration is the most interesting one, as Snap Clone on EMC includes support for databases on ASM, so let's look at that example in more detail.

Using Snap Clone on ASM and EMC storage provides the ability to create "live" thin clones of databases that are on ASM. A live clone is *not* snapshot based but rather a live clone of the database that can be within the same cluster or in a different one. Both single-instance and RAC are supported—supported versions are 10.2.0.5 and higher of the database and 11.2 and higher of the grid infrastructure code. This functionality works on both EMC VMAX (with Time Finder VPSnap) and VNX storage appliances. Figure 8.29 shows what this configuration looks like diagrammatically.

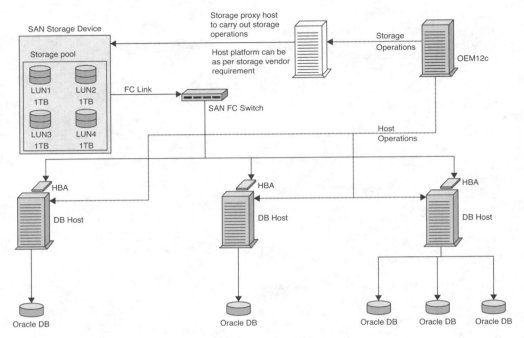

Figure 8.29   Snap Clone using ASM on EMC storage

Snap Clone Setup

Now that we've looked at the different setups architecturally, let's walk through the setup for Snap Clone. In this example, we use CloneDB because it requires the most straightforward setup. Refer to the Cloud Administration Guide (found under Private Cloud Setup and Administration in the EM12*c* documentation) for more details on the other setups.

The steps to set up Snap Clone are as follows:

1. Update the relevant plugins (or install them if you don't already have them). You will need the following plugins (the versions mentioned here are for the 12.1.0.4.3 environment used in this example):

    ▪ Enterprise Manager for Cloud version 12.1.0.9.0

    ▪ Enterprise Manager for Oracle Cloud Framework version 12.1.0.2.0

    ▪ Enterprise Manager for Storage Management version 12.1.0.5.0

    ▪ Enterprise Manager for Oracle Database version 12.1.0.7.0

2. Set up the relevant roles, users, PaaS infrastructure zones, and database pools, as described in Chapter 5.

3. Create a database profile and service template so that self-service users can create thin clones as they require.

Let's look at the details of step 3.

Creating a Database Profile

Creating a database profile to use Snap Clone is a little bit different from creating the profiles we looked at earlier.

1. Start from the same place (Setup → Cloud → Database → Data Sources → Data Profiles, and then click Create). In this case, we are going to create the profile using an RMAN Database Image, as shown in Figure 8.30. Note the message that also appears on this screen (at the bottom) that says Snap Clone is not enabled. This rather spurious message occurs because we don't have any relevant hardware installed that we can use to create Snap Clone. However, it can be safely ignored because we are using CloneDB in this example.

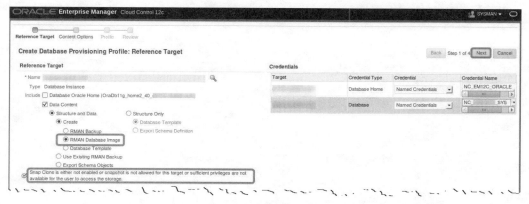

Figure 8.30 Creating a database profile for Snap Clone, step 1

2. In this example, the database from which the profile is created is running in ARCHIVELOG mode. That means that on the next screen, shown in Figure 8.31, the backup can be done in online mode. A directory for the backup to take place in must also be specified.

Figure 8.31   Creating a database profile for Snap Clone, step 2

Steps 3 and 4 of the wizard are the same as in previous database profile creations in this chapter, so for brevity, they are omitted here. Now we can look at using that profile in the service template creation.

1. Again, we start that from Setup → Cloud → Database → Service Templates, and then click the Create button. The main difference here is that once we select the database profile we just created, there will now be a Create CLONEDB option, as you can see in Figure 8.32.

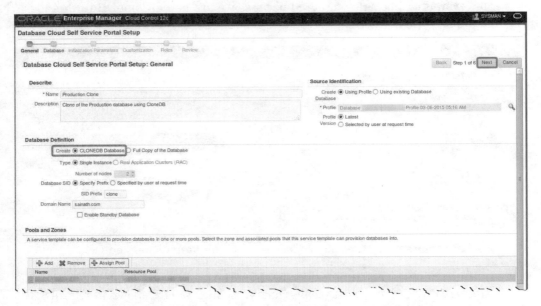

Figure 8.32   Creating a service template for Snap Clone, step 1

2. The important information we need to provide to use Snap Clone with CloneDB is on the next screen. We need to tell the wizard a location that is shared using NFS—in this example, that the location is set up using /u02/copy-on-write as an NFS share, as shown in Figure 8.33.

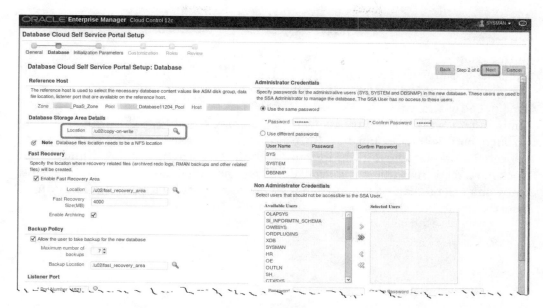

Figure 8.33 Creating a service template for Snap Clone, step 2

3. Again the remaining steps of the wizard are the same as in the previous service template examples, they are omitted here. At the end, however, you should see a message that the service template has been created successfully, as shown in Figure 8.34. Once that is complete, the self-service user can select this template from the Self Service Catalog, just as shown in previous examples in earlier chapters.

Figure 8.34 Creating a service template for Snap Clone, step 3

Summary

In this chapter, we looked at the two main types of clones built in a cloud environment using Enterprise Manager 12*c*—full clones and snap (or thin) clones. A full clone involves taking a complete or full copy of an existing database, which can be done in one of two ways: by taking an RMAN backup or issuing an RMAN DUPLICATE command. A snap clone takes advantage of copy-on-write technology, available through both software and hardware solutions, to rapidly create space-efficient clones of large databases. These clones contain only changed blocks; unchanged blocks are read from the test master database the clone is built from. As a result, many snap clones can be taken from a single test master without using anywhere near the amount of storage the test master takes up.

## 9

Virtualizing RAC 12*c* (DB Clouds) on Oracle VM— Grid Infrastructure

Cloud computing promises to usher in a new era for the corporate IT universe. Every day, we hear that the cloud within the typical IT organization is inevitable, if not already present in some form; it is reasonable to conclude that cloud computing is only a matter of when, not if.

The cloud computing winds of change have been blowing for quite a few years now, recently picking up momentum at Oracle Corporation—almost every key Oracle product focuses on cloud computing as a paradigm. This focus is evident in the *c* (for "cloud") that is appended to the current release number of Oracle products. Real Application Clusters (RAC) is no exception to Oracle's turn toward cloud computing.

Virtualization is the foundation of cloud computing because it is widely implemented today. What is virtualization, and what part does it play in the cloud universe? This chapter and the next offer insights, recommendations, and step-by-step instructions on setting up virtualized RACs, with an emphasis on virtualization, cloud computing, Oracle Virtual Machine (OVM) for x86, and Oracle Enterprise Manager Cloud Control 12*c* (EM12*c*). These virtualized RACs can then be utilized within the framework of database as a service (DBaaS) for rapid and easy deployment as database cloud services.

The overlap between the material in this and other chapters is intended to reiterate important concepts as well as to present the topics in the proper context.

Following is a list of the sections in this chapter:

- Database Clouds Based on RAC—The Necessary Ingredients
- Virtualization—360 Degrees

- What Are VM Monitors (Hypervisors)?
- Types of Hypervisors
- Types of Virtualization
- OVM for x86—360 degrees
- Xen—Synopsis and Overview
- OVM—Overview and Architecture
- What Are OVM Templates?
- OVM 3.x—A Brief Introduction
- Virtualized RAC Using OVM Templates—Approach 1
- Set Up and Configure a Virtualized RAC Database Cloud—Approach 2

This chapter guides you, step by step, through installing, setting up, and configuring a virtualized RAC 12*c* using OVM for x86. The next chapter takes a similar approach, with one major difference—the underlying virtualization technology (hypervisor) is Oracle VirtualBox instead of OVM for x86. This information gives you the choice of using either virtualization technology or both technologies to set up virtualized Oracle RAC 12*c* database clouds. An overview of cloud computing and the role and relevance of virtualization from the perspective of cloud computing are also covered in both chapters. All versions of the hypervisors used are the latest and greatest at the time of the publication of this book.

Database Clouds Based on RAC—The Necessary Ingredients

Cloud computing can be described as "fill-in-the-blank as a service": for example, infrastructure as a service (IaaS), platform as a service (PaaS), and database as a service (DBaaS). A more detailed overview of cloud computing, its various flavors, paradigms, prevalent trends, and a whole lot more are presented in the next chapter.

How do we plan for, set up, build, and configure Oracle database clouds? The short answer is OVM for x86, EM12*c*, and RAC. Together they make up the true database cloud solution from Oracle, especially if you are planning your own private database clouds behind your corporate firewalls. *OVM for x86* is used interchangeably with *OVM* in this chapter and the next.

An overview of virtualization is presented in this chapter with a follow-up section on cloud computing in the next chapter.

Virtualization—360 Degrees

Virtualization is the opposite of a physical entity in the IT universe. Here are some salient features and key points about virtualization:

- Virtualization is the foundation stone in the cloud computing era.
- Virtualization is an inevitability in the IT universe: the sooner you embrace it, the better off you are.
- Virtualization can be summarized as an abstraction layer.
- Virtualization has proved to be a game-changer, resulting in unprecedented server utilization.
- Virtualization enables agile availability of resources to the end user, thereby shaving considerable time from the IT provisioning life cycle.
- Virtualization in the modern day can be characterized as the gateway and roadmap to secure and elastic corporate IT scalability.
- Virtualization implies a fantastic alternative to physical reality—the possibilities are endless.
- The alternative to virtualization consists of physical hosts with a lot of useless spare capacity, resulting in many resources being underutilized.
- Although Oracle database administrators (DBAs) were slow to virtualize their databases, the trend has finally gained momentum and reached critical mass.

What Are VM Monitors (Hypervisors)?

A VM monitor, also known as a *hypervisor*, enables OS kernels to run and coexist as guests, thereby enabling virtualization at the OS level. Hypervisors are responsible for allocation and coordination of CPU, memory, I/O, peripheral resources, and so on, to the guest VMs.

Types of Hypervisors

There are two types of hypervisor:

- **Type 1:** This type is known as a *native*, or more commonly, *bare-metal* hypervisor. It installs on bare-metal hardware and does not require an OS on which to be installed. Examples are VMware ESX/vSphere, Microsoft

HyperV, Xen, and OVM. Bare-metal hypervisors are enterprise-grade hypervisors that enable cloud computing as it is widely known and understood today.

- **Type 2:** This type is known as a *hosted hypervisor* and is installed on an already existing OS on the system: examples are OVM VirtualBox, VMware Server, and VMware Workstation. Hosted hypervisors are mostly for personal use; for example, learning new technologies and colocating various OS families on your laptop.

Here are some key points and salient features about hypervisors:

- A hypervisor is at the lowest level of the stack from a technology standpoint.
- A hypervisor enables agility and rapid deployment of resources within the IT space.
- Hypervisors result in increased efficiency by merit of elastic resource consolidation.

Following are some benefits and advantages of implementing hypervisors:

- Increased resource utilization
- Fault tolerance and high availability
- Isolation and multitenant support
- Support for a wide range of popular OS families

Types of Virtualization

There are three types of virtualization prevalent in the industry today (only the first two categories are explained in the following sections, as they are relevant to this chapter):

- Paravirtualization
- Hardware-assisted/full virtualization
- Partial virtualization

What Is Paravirtualization?

In paravirtualization, guest VMs use a special hypercall application binary interface (ABI) in a modified OS for performance and simplicity. The modified OS communicates with the hypervisor, and tasks are relocated from the virtual domain to the host domain.

OVM implements this type of virtualization. The Oracle/Red Hat Enterprise Linux family of paravirtualized guests are supported with OVM as paravirtualized guests.

Paravirtualization is generally *relatively* faster than hardware virtualization. This is not to imply that either type of virtualization is either slow or not fast enough.

What Is Hardware-Assisted/Full Virtualization?

Hardware-assisted virtualization is also known as *full* or *native* virtualization and requires CPU support.

This type of virtualization enables unmodified guest OS kernels to run within a simulated hardware infrastructure but generally is relatively slower than paravirtualization.

Microsoft Windows and Oracle Solaris families of hardware/full virtualized guests are supported with paravirtualized drivers on OVM.

OVM for x86—360 Degrees

OVM for x86 is a type 1 hypervisor based on Xen, the de facto nth-generation open-source hypervisor. Xen is a mainstream technology, widely used by dominant cloud computing providers such as Amazon and Rackspace, as well as by Oracle's own public cloud. OVM provides both server virtualization and management components. OVM 3.x is based on Xen 4.x and has been significantly enhanced to be an industrial-grade product capable of configuring, administering, managing, and supporting thousands of servers hosting both Oracle and non-Oracle applications. Some of the advances in this relatively new version include dynamic resource scheduling (DRS), high availability–enabled server pools (clusters), and dynamic power management. OVM is augmented with the Virtual Assembly Builder and Template Builder components, which combine to form a complete virtualization picture within the OVM family.

Following are some of the key points about OVM's capabilities and some of its advantages (as with any technology, OVM has its fair share of nuances, most of which can be taken care of by proper configuration and by following implementation best practices):

- Server load-balancing
- Centralized network and storage management
- Physical to virtual (P2V) and virtual to virtual (V2V) conversion
- Web services API

- Support for Windows, Linux, and Solaris as guest OS families
- Agility and fast deployment with OVM templates and Oracle Virtual Assembly Builder
- Web-based GUI management
- OVM zones—multiple server and storage pools
- High availability and live migration with OVM server pools
- Running mixed heterogeneous workloads within a single consolidated machine
- Very *fast*—delivers near-native performance
- Simple and easy installation—low learning curve

Another nice point is that OVM is *free*—you pay only for support.

Note
OVM is the only virtualization offering for the x86 architecture that is certified with all major Oracle products.

Xen—Synopsis and Overview

Xen originated at Cambridge University and is the leading open-source, industry-standard hypervisor. Ian Pratt founded XenSource, the company behind Xen, which was acquired by Citrix in 2007. Xen 4.x is the latest version as well as the underlying version for OVM 3.x.

The Xen hypervisor is the virtualization base of Amazon EC2, the market leader in the cloud computing IaaS service model. Oracle is part of the Xen Advisory Board and contributes to its development. Other members of the Xen Advisory Board include Citrix, Hewlett Packard, IBM, Intel, Novell, Oracle, and Red Hat.

OVM—Overview and Architecture

OVM is made up of two components:

- OVM Server, the Xen-based open-source hypervisor component
- OVM Manager, the Java-based thin-client GUI management component

OVM Server

OVM server is the actual hypervisor component based on Xen. It installs on bare-metal x86 hardware and does not require a preinstalled OS.

OVM boots a small 64-bit domain called DOM0, which is used for assigning, distributing, and coordinating CPU, I/O, and other resources. Guest VMs are created and configured as in DOMus.

OVM Manager

Based on WebLogic server, OVM Manager is a Java-based management server component with a Web-based UI. It utilizes Oracle Database as a management repository and comes prepackaged with a free XE version of Oracle Database, which can be converted to all other flavors of the Oracle Database server family.

Recently, with OVM 3.2.x, MySQL is now also supported as a repository database option. OVM agent processes are used on each OVM server for communication and management purposes. OVM uses *server pools* (or clusters) to group virtualization resources: each server pool encompasses one or more OVM servers.

What Are OVM Templates?

OVM templates, or Golden Images, are factory-packaged, preinstalled, and pre-configured images of preconfigured VMs containing software products that are complete with built-in best practices and are ready to go. They provide reusability and full-stack implementation. All major Oracle products—for example, Oracle Database server, Fusion Middleware, Enterprise Linux, and RAC—are available as OVM templates.

OVM templates are the vehicles to significant reduction of installation and configuration costs in the IT landscape.

Methods of Creating OVM Templates

The following methods can be employed/deployed to create OVM templates:

- P2V conversion
- Create VM templates from existing VM images
- Create VM templates from just enough operating system (JeOS)

OVM Builder

OVM Assembly Builder gives you the capability of a structured process for appliance consolidation into cohesive and reusable assemblies by rapidly creating and configuring full-stack topologies and provisioning them onto virtualized appliances.

OVM Builder is used for creating dedicated VMs called *software appliances* and facilitates deployment of the entire application as a single, automatically configured unit. This tool can facilitate the building of private clouds significantly by building VM assemblies and deploying OVM templates.

OVM 3.x—A Brief Introduction

OVM 3.x, the latest release, takes scalability to a whole new level. With tons of new features, OVM 3.3 is based on Xen 4.x.

Being highly scalable, this latest version of OVM includes many enhancements:

- A feature-rich Web-based UI with improved backup and recovery capability
- Simplified VM deployment, administration, and management with 64-bit DOM0
- Application-driven virtualization, up to 128 virtual CPUs, and 1 TB memory per guest VM
- Jobs-based VM operations
- Dynamic resource management
- Dynamic power management
- Comprehensive network and storage management
- Multiple-template cloning in a single step
- Over 100 factory-packaged best-practices built into OVM templates
- A centralized configuration and management solution in the form of OVM Manager.

In other words, 3.x is truly an enterprise-grade, groundbreaking release. OVM 3.x is completely and fully managed by a browser-based UI provided by OVM Manager.

If you haven't already embarked on this journey, now is a great time to upgrade and migrate your OVM infrastructures from 2.x to 3.x.

OVM 3.x: High Availability–Enabled OVM Ecosystem

OVM provides broad-based high availability across the virtualization ecosystem in the form of high availability–enabled server pools (or clusters) on shared storage. Salient features include

- Live migration of guest VMs
- Automatic failover/restart of guest VMs in case of server failure
- Oracle Cluster File System 2 (OCFS2), with high availability on a cluster file system
- Server pool load balancing, which uses a best-fit algorithm to place guest VMs on the most appropriately loaded VM server
- Clustered OVM Manager

Virtualized RAC Using OVM Templates—Approach 1

This approach is the easiest and fastest way to set up your own virtualized RAC database clusters as part of virtualized Oracle RAC database clouds. Simply download the OVM for x86 templates for RAC, install them, and in less than an hour, you have your own virtualized RAC up and running. This methodology is truly revolutionary and illustrates the beauty and power of agile provisioning of complex infrastructures and applications in cloud environments using virtualized templates.

While this approach is not covered in complete detail, the main utility used to set up, configure, and deploy a virtualized RAC from OVM templates, DeployCluster, is presented in the following section.

Use DeployCluster to Configure and Deploy the Virtualized RAC

This section walks you through using the DeployCluster tool to rapidly configure and deploy a virtualized RAC database cluster. Listing 9.1 shows the example run.

Listing 9.1   DeployCluster Tool

```
[root@bsfmgr01 deploycluster]# ./deploycluster.py -u admin -p password -M bsfracovm1,bsfracovm2 -N
bsfrac64.ini
Oracle RAC OneCommand (v1.1.2) for Oracle VM - deploy cluster -
   (c) 2011-2012 Oracle Corporation
 (com: 26700:v1.1.0, lib: 126247:v1.1.0, var: 1200:v1.1.2) - v2.6.6 -
   bsfmgr01.bsflocal.com (x86_64)
Invoked as root at Sat Sep 22 20:10:04 2012  (size: 37600, mtime: Sun Aug  5 12:37:58 2012)
Using: ./deploycluster.py -u admin -p **** -M bsfracovm1,bsfracovm2 -N bsfrac64.ini

INFO: Attempting to connect to Oracle VM Manager...

INFO: Oracle VM Client  (3.1.1.399) protocol (1.8) CONNECTED (tcp) to
     Oracle VM Manager (3.1.1.305) protocol (1.8) IP (192.168.1.51) UUID
(0004fb0000010000da73c3bcce15ca2e)
```

```
INFO: Inspecting /home/oracle/ovm3/deploycluster/bsfrac64.ini for number of nodes defined....
INFO: Detected 2 nodes in: /home/oracle/ovm3/deploycluster/bsfrac64.ini
INFO: Located a total of (2) VMs;
      2 VMs with a simple name of: ['bsfracovm1', 'bsfracovm2']
INFO: Verifying all (2) VMs are in Running state
INFO: VM with a simple name of "bsfracovm1" is in Running state...
INFO: VM with a simple name of "bsfracovm2" is in Running state...
INFO: Detected that all (2) VMs specified on command have (5) common shared disks
between them (ASM_MIN_DISKS=5)

INFO: The (2) VMs passed basic sanity checks and in Running state, sending cluster details
as follows:
      netconfig.ini (Network setup): /home/oracle/ovm3/deploycluster/bsfrac64.ini
      buildcluster: yes
INFO: Starting to send cluster details to all (2) VM(s).....
INFO: Sending to VM with a simple name of "bsfracovm1"....
INFO: Sending to VM with a simple name of "bsfracovm2"......
INFO: Cluster details sent to (2) VMs...
      Check log (default location /u01/racovm/buildcluster.log) on build VM (bsfracovm1)...
INFO: deploycluster.py completed successfully at 20:10:19 in 15.7 seconds (00m:15s)
Logfile at: /home/oracle/ovm3/deploycluster/deploycluster2.log
```

Figures 9.1 and 9.2 each show parts of a sample run of the DeployCluster tool. On your monitor display, INFO: (Figure 9.1) and [OK   ] (Figure 9.2) should be green: all green means all good to go!

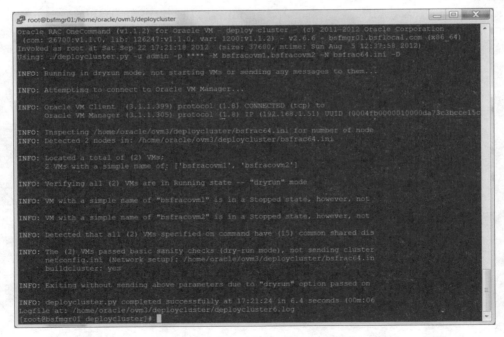

Figure 9.1   An example run of the DeployCluster tool for setting up RAC using Oracle VM for x86 templates

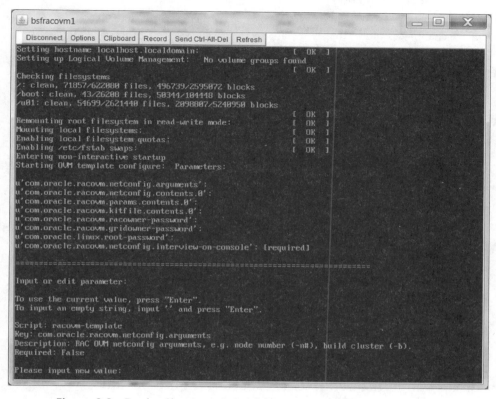

Figure 9.2   DeployCluster tool: Configuring and setting up RAC using
Oracle VM for x86 templates

Note

At the time of writing, OVM for x86 templates for RAC were only available for up
to version 11gR2 and *not* for 12c. This is the recommended approach for setting up
Oracle RAC as database clouds; however, because of the absence of OVM templates
for 12c, we have included the longer alternative approach outlined in the next section. The other rationale for including this approach is that it enables you to learn
the specific actions required to set up and configure RAC 12c from scratch.

Set Up and Configure a Virtualized RAC Database Cloud—
Approach 2

This section takes you through an alternative, step-by-step approach to setting up
your own virtualized RAC 12c in OVM for x86.

Note

This chapter assumes that you already have an OVM 3.x server pool in an up-and-running state. If this is not the case, please refer to the OVM documentation to set up OVM 3.x. The following sections assume that you are familiar with basic RAC concepts (presented in earlier chapters). Also, this chapter and the next chapter are structured in a way that enables you to set up RAC database clouds in the comfort of your own home for learning purposes. Please note that the steps are identical to corporate RAC setups; however, the infrastructure is pared down to enable you to make use of hardware available at home.

The following hardware and software were used for setting up the OVM server pool for this example:

- OVM Manager and EM12c:
  - (Qty: 1) 64-bit Intel x86 machine with 8 GB RAM
- OVM servers for server pool:
  - (Qty: 3) 64-bit Intel x86 machines with 16 GB RAM each
- Shared storage:
  - (Qty: 1) 64-bit Intel x86 machine with 8 GB RAM
  - Openfiler with 1 TB disk space available on iSCSI

Roadmap to a Virtualized RAC 12c Cluster: High-Level Steps

Following are the high-level steps to build your own virtualized RAC–based database cloud:

1. Set up and configure the required hardware and software for an OVM server pool on shared storage.
2. Prepare and plan: Do your homework.
3. Install and set up grid infrastructure.
4. Install and set up non-shared database home(s).
5. Create a RAC database.
6. Configure and set up the RAC database as a monitored target in EM12c.

All of the preceding steps are detailed, elaborated on, and/or executed in the following sections of this chapter and the next one, with several alternative options presented for some of the involved steps.

While all of the following steps apply equally to corporate environments, they are written in such a way that you can set up a virtualized database cloud environment in your home, thereby learning how to install, set up, configure, and monitor RAC with minimal hardware.

OVM: Prerequisites, Preparation, and Planning

Ensure that the following virtual infrastructure is available and ready for deployment in a brand-new RAC setup.

Step 9.1—Set Up a Server Pool in OVM for x86

This chapter assumes that you already have a basic server pool in OVM for x86 complete with OVM Manager 3.x and EM12c release 2 set up, configured, and ready to go for deploying an Oracle RAC 12c cluster. (The hardware/software configuration used in this chapter and the next one is outlined in the preceding section.) In case you need help with this process, be assured that this is a simple and easy process with a minimum, low, and intuitive learning curve if you follow the appropriate OVM for x86 installation and setup documentation manuals.

The following sections detail the steps involved in configuring OVM for RAC 12c.

Step 9.2—Configure Network Time Protocol

Press the Push to All Servers button for Network Time Protocol (NTP).

Step 9.3—Create the Required Network for RAC 12c

Continue with the following steps:

1. Choose OVM Manager → Networking → Networks → Create (+) Button.
2. Select the Create a Hybrid Network with Bonds/Ports and VLANS option.
3. Enter the name and description of the OVM network. Select the Virtual Machine option.
4. Select the relevant ports.
5. Select the relevant VLAN segments.
6. Select the appropriate IP addressing scheme. Enter the IP addresses, net masks, and bonding options if applicable.

As shown in Figure 9.3, the new OVM network has been successfully created and is ready to be deployed and used.

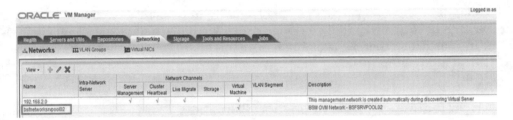

Figure 9.3   Oracle VM 3.x: Dedicated network for Oracle RAC 12*c*

Step 9.4—Create the Required Shared Virtual Disks for the GRID1 ASM Disk Group

To create the disks, follow these steps:

1. Choose OVM Manager → Repositories → Select OVS Repository → Virtual Disks → Create (+) Button:

2. Create a virtual disk with the following options:

   - Size: 15 GB

   - Allocation type: Sparse allocation

   - Shareable: Yes

3. Repeat the preceding process for all five GRID1 Automatic Storage Management (ASM) disks.

Note

For production environments, it is highly recommended to have physical block devices presented as virtual disks for the various ASM disk groups.

As shown in Figure 9.4, all of the virtualized shareable ASM disks for the GRID1 disk groups have been created and are now ready for use.

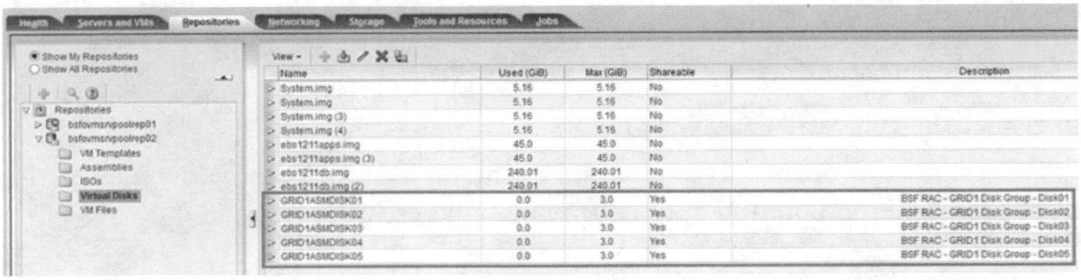

Figure 9.4   Oracle VM 3.x: Virtualized disks for GRID1 ASM disk group for RAC 12*c*

Note

Step 9.5 has two alternative approaches, both of which are explained in quite a bit of detail next. Each step has further substeps, which are illustrated as well.

Step 9.5, Approach 1

Step 9.5, Approach 1, is illustrated in the following substeps.

Step 9.5, Approach 1a—Create the VM for RAC Server Node 1 from Scratch Using an ISO Boot Image to Install OEL 6.x

To create the Oracle Enterprise Linux (OEL) 6.x VM for RAC using an ISO boot image, follow these steps (as shown in Figure 9.5):

1. Choose OVM Manager → Servers and VMs → Select Server Pool → Create Virtual Machine Button.

2. Select the Create a New VM option.

3. As shown in Figure 9.5, select and enter the following options for the RAC-Node-01 VM:

   - Server pool
   - Server pool repository
   - VM description
   - High Availability: Unchecked
   - Operating system: Oracle Linux 6
   - Domain type: Xen PVM
   - Start policy: Start on best server
   - Memory (MB): 2,048 (The minimum required is 4,096. However, in cases where you are short on physical memory and are building the RAC for learning purposes, this can suffice.)
   - Max memory (MB): 8,192
   - Processors: 2
   - Max processors: 4
   - Priority: 50
   - Processor cap %: 100

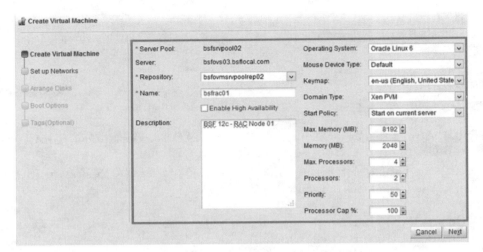

Figure 9.5   Oracle VM 3.x: Creating a VM for RAC-Node-01

4. Select Network and then press the Add VNIC button twice to create two virtual network interface cards (VNICs) for the RAC-Node-01 VM (see Figure 9.6).

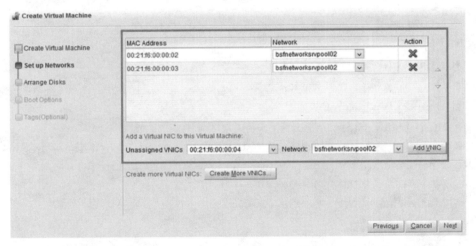

Figure 9.6   Oracle VM 3.x: Specifying virtual network interface cards for the public and private cluster interconnect networks required for the RAC

5. Choose Next to move on to Setup Networks and Arrange Disks.

6. Select and enter the following options for the VM disks (see Figure 9.7):

   ▪ CD/DVD

   ▪ Virtual disk

   Press the Create (+) button.

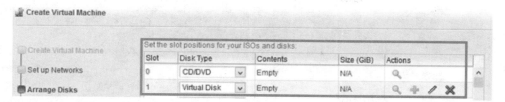

Figure 9.7   Oracle VM 3.x: Specifying virtualized disk/optical media for RAC-Node-01

7. Select the imported ISO for Linux 6.x.

8. Select and enter the following options:

   ▪ Repository

   ▪ Virtual disk name

   ▪ Description

   ▪ Shareable: Unchecked

   ▪ Size: 25 GB

   ▪ Allocation type: sparse allocation

9. Select the ISO for OEL 6.x (see Figure 9.8).

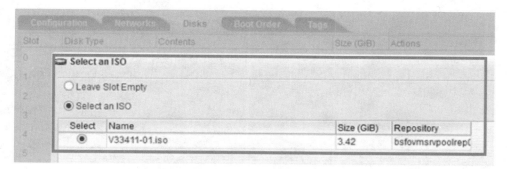

Figure 9.8   Oracle VM 3.x: Specify the ISO for Oracle Enterprise Linux 6.x 64-bit x86

10. As shown in Figure 9.9, repeat the preceding process to add/select the following disks:

   ▪ ISODATA1 ASM disk group:

      ▫ Qty: 6

      ▫ Individual disk size: 50 GB

   ▪ RECO1 ASM disk group:

      ▫ Qty: 1

      ▫ Individual disk size: 50 GB

   Select the Disk boot option. Press the Finish button to create the RAC-Node-01 VM.

Figure 9.9   Oracle VM 3.x: Guest VM for RAC-Node-01

Step 9.5, Approach 1b—Import the OEL 6.x x86-64 ISO into the OVM Repository

To import the OEL 6.x x86-64 ISO image into the OVM repository, follow these steps:

1. Go to OVM Manager → Repositories → Select OVM Repository → ISOs → Import ISO Button.

2. Select and enter the following (see Figure 9.10):

   - Server

   - ISO download location: ftp://oracle:password@192.168.2.20/software/ OEL63_x86_64/V33411-01.iso (Replace the IP address, username, and password with your own.)

Note

Ensure that the Very Secure File Transfer Protocol Daemon (VSFTPD) server (FTP service) is set up correctly and that the ISO is available at the desired location and has the correct permissions.

Figure 9.10   Oracle VM 3.x: Specify the FTP location for the OEL 6.x 64-bit x86 VM template

Note that the status of the import process shows as In Progress, with a message showing Download Virtual CDROM....

Monitor the progress of the ISO import process in an SSH session to one of the Oracle VM servers (OVS) to which the OVS repository is connected.

```
[root@bsfovs03 ISOs]# pwd
/OVS/Repositories/0004fb0000030000d0cb473db1b6a1ae/ISOs
[root@bsfovs03 ISOs]# ls -l
total 276480
-rw-r--r-- 1 root root 282066944 Feb 24 12:57 0004fb0000150000ba1fd09b4e2bd98c.iso
```

Keep checking periodically after brief intervals to monitor the progress of the ISO import process.

```
[root@bsfovs03 ISOs]# pwd
/OVS/Repositories/0004fb0000030000d0cb473db1b6a1ae/ISOs

[root@bsfovs03 ISOs]# ls -l
total 2890752
-rw-r--r-- 1 root root 2959081472 Feb 24 13:04 0004fb0000150000ba1fd09b4e2bd98c.iso
```

At this point, the OEL 6.x ISO has been successfully imported (see Figure 9.11). Start up the VM, boot it from the OEL 6.x ISO, and go through the steps of setting up and installing Oracle Enterprise Linux 6.x.

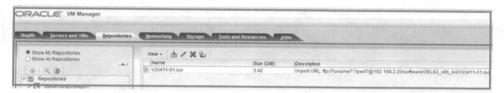

Figure 9.11   Oracle VM 3.x: Imported ISO for Oracle Enterprise Linux 6.x 64-bit x86 is now ready for use as a bootable virtual CD/DVD drive

Step 9.5, Approach 2

Step 9.5, Approach 2, is illustrated in the following sub-steps.

Step 9.5, Approach 2a—Create the VM for RAC Server Node 1 Using an OVM OEL 6.x Template

To create the VM for RAC Server Node using an OVM OEL 6.x template, follow these steps:

1. Download the OEL 6.x OVM 3.x template from https://edelivery.oracle.com/linux.

2. Unzip the ISO and make it available via FTP.

3. Go to OVM Manager → Repositories → Select OVM Repository → Assemblies → Import VM Assembly Button (see Figure 9.12). Enter the following:

   - Server

   - VM assembly download location

   Note that the status of the VM assembly import process shows as In Progress with a message showing "Downloading Assembly..." and then another one showing "Unpacking Template...."

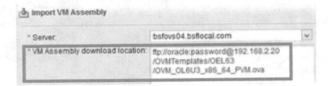

Figure 9.12 Oracle VM 3.x: Specify the FTP location of the Oracle VM assembly for Oracle Enterprise Linux 6.x 64-bit x86

Monitor the progress of the VM assembly import process within an SSH session to one of the OVS servers to which the OVS repository is connected.

```
[root@bsfovs03 11941bfbbc]# pwd
/OVS/Repositories/0004fb0000030000d0cb473db1b6a1ae/Assemblies/11941bfbbc

[root@bsfovs03 11941bfbbc]# ls -l
total 617472
drwxr-xr-x 2 root root      3896 Feb 24 15:20 imports
-rw-r--r-- 1 root root 631541760 Oct 10 16:17 package.ova
drwxr-xr-x 2 root root      3896 Feb 24 15:21 unpacked
```

Keep checking periodically after brief intervals.

As shown in Figure 9.13, the OVM assembly for OEL 6.3 x86-64 has been imported successfully and is now ready for use.

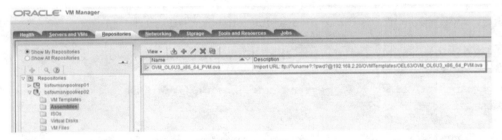

Figure 9.13 Oracle VM 3.x: Oracle VM assembly for Oracle Enterprise Linux 6.x 64-bit x86

Step 9.5, Approach 2b—Create the OEL 6.3 x86-64-PVM OVM Template from the Newly Created Assembly into the OVM Repository

To create the OEL 6.3 x86-64-PVM OVM template from the newly created assembly into the OVM repository, follow these steps:

1. Choose OVM Manager → Repositories → Select OVM Repository → VM Assemblies → Select VM Assembly → Create VM template.

2. Enter and select the following (see Figure 9.14):
   - Assembly VMs
   - VM template name
   - Description

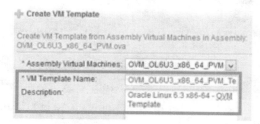

Figure 9.14　The VM template name and description

3. As shown in Figure 9.15, the OEL 6.3 x86_64 OVM template has been successfully created and is now ready for deployment.

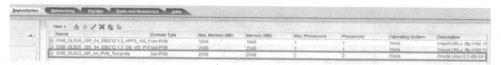

Figure 9.15　The OEL 6.3 x86_64 OVM template

Step 9.5, Approach 2c—Edit the Newly Created OEL 6.3 x86-64-PVM OVM Template

To edit the newly created OEL 6.3 x86-64-PVM OVM template, follow these steps:

1. Choose OVM Manager → Repositories → VM Templates → Select VM Template → Edit.
2. Modify the following options:
   - Max memory (MB): 8,192
   - Memory (MB): 4,096
   - Max processors: 8
   - Processors: 4
   - Enable High Availability: Unchecked (OVM HA is incompatible with Oracle RAC)
   - Networks: Add/specify the appropriate network(s)

- Boot order: Disk
- Virtual disks:
  - Add virtual disk for Oracle software binaries: 25 GB

Step 9.5, Approach 2d—Create Clone Customizer for the RAC Node OVM Template

To create a clone customizer for the RAC node OVM template, follow these steps:

1. Choose OVM Manager → Repositories → VM Templates → Select VM Template.
2. Press the Create Clone Customizer button.
3. Specify the name and description of the new clone customizer for the RAC 12*c* cluster node VMs.
4. Modify the Clone Type to Thin Clone (see Figure 9.16). This is a fast and efficient way to create new VM clone machines.

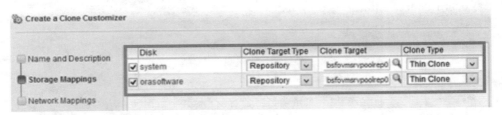

Figure 9.16   Oracle VM 3.x: Specify the virtual disks for RAC-Node-01

5. Specify the network settings for the clone customizer (if any custom modifications are required).

Step 9.5, Approach 2e—Create the RAC-Node-01 VM from the VM Template Using the Advanced Clone Customizer Method

To create the RAC-Node-01 VM from the VM template using the Advanced Clone Customizer method do the following:

1. Go to OVM Manager → Servers and VMs → Select Server Pool → Create Virtual Machine.
2. Select the Clone from an existing VM Template option (see Figure 9.17). Enter and select the following options:
   - Clone count: 1
   - Repository: Select OVS repository
   - VM template: Select the OEL 6.3 x86_64 template

- Server pool: Select the appropriate server pool
- Description

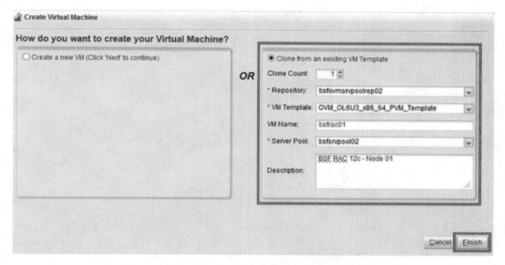

Figure 9.17   Cloning from the existing template

3. Press the Finish button to create the RAC-Node-01 VM. The finished product is shown in Figure 9.18.

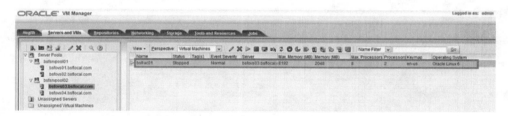

Figure 9.18   The VM for RAC-Node-01 created from the Oracle Enterprise Linux 6.x 64-bit x86 template

Step 9.6—Edit the Newly Created VM for RAC-Node-01

To edit the VM for RAC-Node-01 follow these steps:

1. Choose OVM Manager → Servers and VMs → Select Server Pool → Select Virtual Machine → Edit Virtual Machine.
2. Modify the following options as shown in the configuration tab (Figure 9.19):
   - Operating system: Oracle Linux 6
   - Max memory (MB): 8,192

- Max processors: 8
- Networks: Specify the appropriate network(s)
- High Availability: Unchecked (OVM HA is incompatible with Oracle RAC)
- Boot order: Disk
- Start policy: Start on best server
- Virtual disks:
  - System (virtual disk): Add another disk for Oracle binaries: 25 GB
  - GRID1 ASM disk group:
    Qty: 6 Disks
    Individual disk size: 15 GB
  - DATA1 ASM disk group:
    Qty: 6 Disks
    Individual disk size: 50 GB
  - RECO1 ASM disk group:
    Qty: 1 Disk
    Individual disk size: 50 GB

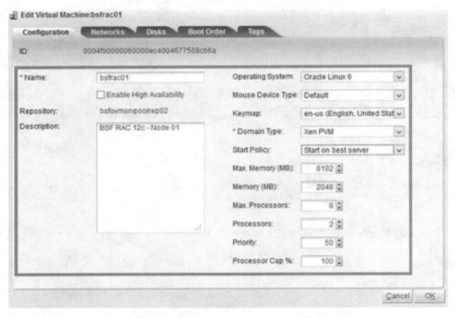

Figure 9.19   Configure the newly created VM

3. On the Network tab, add two VNICs (see Figure 9.20), one each for the public and private cluster interconnects.

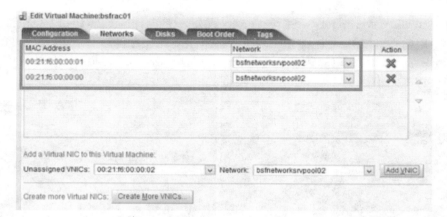

Figure 9.20   Add the required VNICs

4. Finally, on the Disks tab, attach the shared virtualized disks for the ASM disk groups (see Figure 9.21).

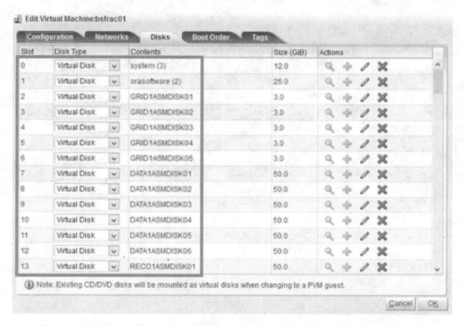

Figure 9.21   Oracle VM 3.x: Attach the shared virtualized disks for the GRID1, DATA1, and RECO1 ASM disk groups

Step 9.7—Start Up the RAC-Node-01 VM

To start up the RAC-Node-01 VM, follow these steps:

1. Go to OVM Manager → Servers and VMs → Select Server Pool → Select Virtual Machine → Start Virtual Machine.

2. Press the Launch Console button to start the VNC console window (see Figure 9.22).

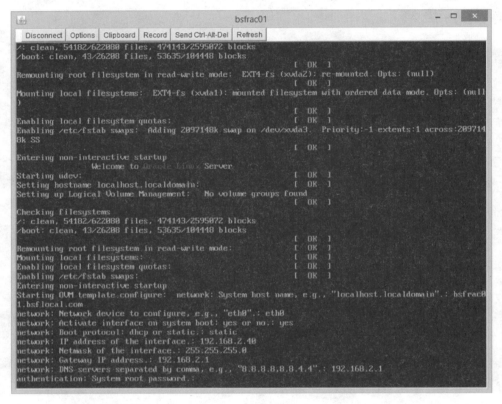

Figure 9.22 Oracle VM 3.x: Boot RAC node—First-boot interview/configuration process

3. Configure the various options in the new VM in the first-boot interview process:

   - System hostname: For example, bsfrac01.bsflocal.com (12c RAC-Node-01)
   - Specify VNIC device: For example, ETH0
   - Boot protocol (static/DHCP): Static
   - Activate VNIC on boot: YES

- IP address of the interface: For example, 192.168.2.41. (For the public network, ensure that this is an unused IP address. If you have a DNS server(s), register the IP address/hostname with it.)
- Netmask: For example, 255.255.255.0
- IP address of gateway: For example, 192.168.2.1
- IP addresses of DNS servers(s): For example, 255.255.255.0
- OS root password: *******

Set Up and Configure RAC-Node-01

The following sections explain how to set up and configure Node 01 for RAC 12*c*.

Step 9.8—Set the Network Configuration of the Private Cluster Interconnect VNIC

To set the network configuration of the private cluster interconnect VNIC, issue the following commands:

```
[root@bsfrac01 network-scripts]# pwd
/etc/sysconfig/network-scripts
[root@bsfrac01 network-scripts]# cp ifcfg-eth0 ifcfg-eth1
[root@bsfrac01 network-scripts]# vi ifcfg-eth1
You have new mail in /var/spool/mail/root
[root@bsfrac01 network-scripts]# cat ifcfg-eth1
DNS1=192.168.2.1
GATEWAY=192.168.2.1
NETMASK=255.255.255.0
IPADDR=192.168.3.40
BOOTPROTO=static
ONBOOT=yes
NM_CONTROLLED=no
DEVICE=eth1
```

Step 9.9—Modify /etc/hosts File to Include the Relevant Entries for RAC 12c

To modify the /etc/hosts file to include the relevant entries for RAC 12*c*, open the fie and edit it, as in the following:

```
[root@bsfrac01 network-scripts]# vi /etc/hosts

127.0.0.1 localhost.localdomain localhost localhost4
::1 localhost6.localdomain6 localhost6

# PUBLIC IP Addresses of 12c RAC Cluster
192.168.2.40          bsfrac01        bsfrac01.bsflocal.com
192.168.2.41          bsfrac02        bsfrac02.bsflocal.com
192.168.2.42          bsfrac03        bsfrac03.bsflocal.com
192.168.2.43          bsfrac04        bsfrac04.bsflocal.com
192.168.2.44          bsfrac05        bsfrac05.bsflocal.com

# SCAN IP Addresses of 12c RAC Cluster
192.168.2.70          bsfrac-scan     bsfrac-scan.bsflocal.com
192.168.2.71          bsfrac-scan     bsfrac-scan.bsflocal.com
192.168.2.72          bsfrac-scan     bsfrac-scan.bsflocal.com
```

```
# Virtual IP Addresses of 12c RAC Cluster
192.168.2.60            bsfrac-vip01   bsfrac-priv01.bsflocal.com
192.168.2.61            bsfrac-vip02   bsfrac-priv02.bsflocal.com
192.168.2.62            bsfrac-vip03   bsfrac-priv03.bsflocal.com
192.168.2.63            bsfrac-vip04   bsfrac-priv04.bsflocal.com
192.168.2.64            bsfrac-vip05   bsfrac-priv05.bsflocal.com

# Private Cluster Interconnect IP Addresses of 12c RAC Cluster
192.168.3.40            bsfrac-priv01  bsfrac-priv01.bsflocal.com
192.168.3.41            bsfrac-priv02  bsfrac-priv02.bsflocal.com
192.168.3.42            bsfrac-priv03  bsfrac-priv03.bsflocal.com
192.168.3.43            bsfrac-priv04  bsfrac-priv04.bsflocal.com
192.168.3.44            bsfrac-priv05  bsfrac-priv05.bsflocal.com
```

Note

Single Client Access Name (SCAN) listener IP information is included in the /etc/ hosts file. The SCAN IPs should be registered with the appropriate DNS server(s).

Step 9.10—Check for Space Requirements

Ensure that enough TMP space is available to support RAC12*c*:

```
[root@bsfracvx1 ~]# df -h /tmp
Filesystem              Size  Used Avail Use% Mounted on
/dev/mapper/vg_bsfracvx1-lv_root
                        26G   5.3G  20G  22% /
```

Step 9.11—Disable the Linux Software Firewall

Next, disable the Linux software firewall.

Note

This step is optional and should be exercised with caution. Only do it if you have ancillary hardware/software firewalls in place in the corporate landscape.

```
[root@bsfrac01 ~]# service iptables status
Table: filter
Chain INPUT (policy ACCEPT)
num  target     prot opt source              destination
1    ACCEPT     all  --  0.0.0.0/0           0.0.0.0/0           state RELATED,ESTABLISHED
2    ACCEPT     icmp --  0.0.0.0/0           0.0.0.0/0
3    ACCEPT     all  --  0.0.0.0/0           0.0.0.0/0
4    ACCEPT     tcp  --  0.0.0.0/0           0.0.0.0/0           state NEW tcp dpt:22
5    REJECT     all  --  0.0.0.0/0           0.0.0.0/0
reject-with icmp-host-prohibited

Chain FORWARD (policy ACCEPT)
num  target     prot opt source              destination
1    REJECT     all  --  0.0.0.0/0           0.0.0.0/0
 reject-with icmp-host-prohibited

Chain OUTPUT (policy ACCEPT)
num  target     prot opt source              destination

[root@bsfrac01 ~]# service iptables off
Usage: iptables {start|stop|restart|condrestart|status|panic|save}
[root@bsfrac01 ~]# service iptables stop
```

```
.iptables: Flushing firewall rules:                     [  OK  ]
iptables: Setting chains to policy ACCEPT: filter       [  OK  ]
iptables: Unloading modules: c                          [  OK  ]
[root@bsfrac01 ~]# chkconfig iptables off
[root@bsfrac01 ~]# service ip6tables status
Table: filter
Chain INPUT (policy ACCEPT)
num  target     prot opt source            destination
1    ACCEPT     all     ::/0               ::/0                        state RELATED,ESTABLISHED
2    ACCEPT     icmpv6  ::/0                ::/0
3    ACCEPT     all     ::/0               ::/0
4    ACCEPT     tcp     ::/0               ::/0                        state NEW tcp dpt:22
5    REJECT     all     ::/0               ::/0
reject-with icmp6-adm-prohibited

Chain FORWARD (policy ACCEPT)
num  target     prot opt source            destination
1    REJECT     all     ::/0               ::/0
reject-with icmp6-adm-prohibited

Chain OUTPUT (policy ACCEPT)
num  target     prot opt source            destination

[root@bsfrac01 ~]# service ip6tables stop
ip6tables: Flushing firewall rules:                     [  OK  ]
ip6tables: Setting chains to policy ACCEPT: filter      [  OK  ]
ip6tables: Unloading modules:                           [  OK  ]
[root@bsfrac01 ~]# chkconfig ip6tables off
```

Step 9.12—Configure and Restart NTPD Client

Edit/configure the /etc/ntp.conf file and restart the Network Time Protocol Daemon (NTPD) server on the RAC node VM.

```
$ vi /etc/ntp.conf
# Modify the following line to reflect the NTP servers with which the time
# will be synchronized
server 192.168.2.20
```

Step 9.13—Partition, Format, and Mount /u01 on the 25 GB Local Virtual Hard Disk

To partition, format, and mount /u01 on the 25 GB local virtual hard disk, start by doing the following:

```
[root@bsfrac01 /]# mkdir /u01
You have new mail in /var/spool/mail/root
[root@bsfrac01 /]# mount /dev/xvdb1 /u01
[root@bsfrac01 /]# df -m
Filesystem         1M-blocks     Used Available Use% Mounted on
/dev/xvda2              9985     8087      1392  86% /
tmpfs                   1940        1      1940   1% /dev/shm
/dev/xvda1                99       50        45  53% /boot
/dev/xvdb1             25195      172     23743   1% /u01
```

Make the mount point persistent by modifying the /etc/fstab file:

```
#
# /etc/fstab
# Created by anaconda on Fri Sep  7 08:14:40 2012
#
```

```
# Accessible filesystems, by reference, are maintained under '/dev/disk'
# See man pages fstab(5), findfs(8), mount(8) and/or blkid(8) for more info
#
LABEL=/                   /                    ext4      defaults      1 1
LABEL=/boot               /boot                ext4      defaults      1 2
/dev/xvda3                swap                 swap      defaults      0 0
tmpfs                     /dev/shm             tmpfs     defaults      0 0
devpts                    /dev/pts             devpts    gid=5,mode=620 0 0
sysfs                     /sys                 sysfs     defaults      0 0
proc                      /proc                proc      defaults      0 0
/dev/xvdb1                /u01                 ext4      defaults      0 0
```

Step 9.14—Disable the SELINUX Option

Disable the SELINUX option by modifying the following file:

```
[root@bsfrac01 /]# vi  /etc/selinux/config

# This file controls the state of SELinux on the system.
# SELINUX= can take one of these three values:
#     enforcing—SELinux security policy is enforced.
#     permissive—SELinux prints warnings instead of enforcing.
#     disabled—No SELinux policy is loaded.
SELINUX=disabled
# SELINUXTYPE—Can take one of these two values:
#     targeted—Targeted processes are protected,
#     mls—Multilevel security protection.
SELINUXTYPE—Targeted
```

Step 9.15—Install VSFTPD (FTP Server)

Install VSFTPD (FTP server) by performing the following:

```
[root@bsfrac01 ~]# yum install vsftpd
```

Note

This step is optional.

Step 9.16—Install X Window System Desktop

Install the X Window System desktop by performing the following steps:

```
[root@bsfrac01 /]# yum groupinstall "X Window System" desktop
Loaded plugins: security
Setting up Group Process
Package 1:xorg-x11-xauth-1.0.2-7.1.el6.x86_64 already installed and latest version
Package hal-0.5.14-11.el6.x86_64 already installed and latest version
Package 1:dbus-1.2.24-7.0.1.el6_3.x86_64 already installed and latest version
Resolving Dependencies
--> Running transaction check
---> Package NetworkManager.x86_64 1:0.8.1-34.el6_3 will be installed
.
.
.
openssh-server                              x86_64                    5.3p1-84.
1.el6
ol6_latest                  298 k
```

```
  rhn-check                                              noarch
1.0.0-87.0.6.el6
ol6_latest                        60 k
  rhn-client-tools                                       noarch
1.0.0-87.0.6.el6
ol6_latest                       492 k
  rhn-setup                                              noarch
1.0.0-87.0.6.el6
ol6_latest                        96 k

Transaction Summary
================================================================================================
================================================================================================
Install     265 Package(s)
Upgrade      19 Package(s)

Total download size: 123 M
Is this ok [y/N]: y
Downloading Packages:
(1/284): ConsoleKit-x11-0.4.1-3.el6.x86_64.rpm   |  20 kB      00:00
(2/284): DeviceKit-power-014-3.el6.x86_64.rpm    |  90 kB      00:00
.
.
.
Dependency Updated:
  libreport.x86_64 0:2.0.9-5.0.1.el6_3.2                      libreport-cli.x86_64 0:2.0.9-
5.0.1.el6_3.2                    libreport-plugin-kerneloops.x86_64 0:2.0.9-5.0.1.el6_3.2
  libreport-plugin-logger.x86_64 0:2.0.9-5.0.1.el6_3.2       libreport-plugin-
mailx.x86_64 0:2.0.9-5.0.1.el6_3.2        libreport-plugin-reportuploader.x86_64 0:2.0.9-
5.0.1.el6_3.2
  libreport-python.x86_64 0:2.0.9-5.0.1.el6_3.2              nspr.x86_64 0:4.9.2-
0.el6_3.1                         nss.x86_64 0:3.13.6-2.0.1.el6_3
  nss-sysinit.x86_64 0:3.13.6-2.0.1.el6_3                    nss-tools.x86_64 0:3.13.6-
2.0.1.el6_3                     nss-util.x86_64 0:3.13.6-1.el6_3
  openssh.x86_64 0:5.3p1-84.1.el6                            openssh-clients.x86_64
0:5.3p1-84.1.el6                openssh-server.x86_64 0:5.3p1-84.1.el6
  rhn-check.noarch 0:1.0.0-87.0.6.el6                        rhn-client-tools.noarch
0:1.0.0-87.0.6.el6               rhn-setup.noarch 0:1.0.0-87.0.6.el6
Complete!
```

Note

The output of the X Window System desktop installation is very long and has been abbreviated.

Modify the /etc/inittab file to start with a GUI login and reboot the system:

```
#id:3:initdefault: # Change Option 3 to 5 as shown in the following lineid:5:initdefault:
```

Step 9.17—Reboot RAC-Node-01 for All of the Preceding Setups/Configurations to Take Effect

To reboot, issue the following command:

```
[root@bsfrac01 network-scripts]# shutdown -r
```

After a successful reboot, you will arrive at the login screen (see Figure 9.23).

Figure 9.23   Oracle VM 3.x: RAC-Node-01—OS/Linux 6.x 64-bit x86 login screen

Step 9.18—Verify the Network Settings after the Node Reboots

To verify the network settings after the reboot, do the following:

```
[root@bsfrac01 /]# ifconfig -a
eth0    Link encap:Ethernet  HWaddr 00:21:F6:00:00:01
        inet addr:192.168.2.40  Bcast:192.168.2.255  Mask:255.255.255.0
        inet6 addr: fe80::221:f6ff:fe00:1/64 Scope:Link
        UP BROADCAST RUNNING MULTICAST  MTU:1500  Metric:1
        RX packets:49103 errors:0 dropped:117 overruns:0 frame:0
        TX packets:12982 errors:0 dropped:0 overruns:0 carrier:0
        collisions:0 txqueuelen:1000
        RX bytes:33876842 (32.3 MiB)  TX bytes:939705 (917.6 KiB)
        Interrupt:57

eth1    Link encap:Ethernet  HWaddr 00:21:F6:00:00:00
        inet addr:192.168.3.40  Bcast:192.168.3.255  Mask:255.255.255.0
        inet6 addr: fe80::221:f6ff:fe00:0/64 Scope:Link
        UP BROADCAST RUNNING MULTICAST  MTU:1500  Metric:1
        RX packets:25180 errors:0 dropped:117 overruns:0 frame:0
        TX packets:198 errors:0 dropped:0 overruns:0 carrier:0
        collisions:0 txqueuelen:1000
        RX bytes:1316336 (1.2 MiB)  TX bytes:12163 (11.8 KiB)
        Interrupt:58
```

```
lo          Link encap:Local Loopback
            inet addr:127.0.0.1  Mask:255.0.0.0
            inet6 addr: ::1/128 Scope:Host
            UP LOOPBACK RUNNING  MTU:16436  Metric:1
            RX packets:16 errors:0 dropped:0 overruns:0 frame:0
            TX packets:16 errors:0 dropped:0 overruns:0 carrier:0
            collisions:0 txqueuelen:0
            RX bytes:930 (930.0 b)  TX bytes:930 (930.0 b)
```

Oracle Software Preinstallation Steps on the RAC-Node-01 VM

Perform the following checks (steps 9.19–9.28) to satisfy the prerequisites for RAC 12*c* on Node 01.

Step 9.19—Check Space Requirement on /tmp

To check that the space requirement has been met, do the following (10 GB is recommended):

```
[oracle@bsfrac01 Database]$ df -h /tmp
Filesystem          Size  Used Avail Use% Mounted on
/dev/xvda2          9.8G  7.9G  1.4G  86% /
```

Step 9.20—Create the Required and Relevant OS Groups

Issue these commands to create the OS groups:

```
[root@bsfrac01 /]# groupadd -g 54327 asmadmin
[root@bsfrac01 /]# groupadd -g 54328 asmoper
[root@bsfrac01 /]# groupadd -g 54329 asmadmin
[root@bsfrac01 /]# groupadd -g 54324 asmdba
[root@bsfrac01 /]# groupadd -g 54324 backupdba
[root@bsfrac01 /]# groupadd -g 54325 dgdba
[root@bsfrac01 /]# groupadd -g 54326 kmdba
[root@bsfrac01 /]# groupadd -g 54321 oinstall
[root@bsfrac01 /]# groupadd -g 54322 dba
[root@bsfrac01 /]# groupadd -g 54323 oper
```

> **Note**
>
> Some of the preceding steps are optional, and whether they should be done depends on the user's job function; for example, DBA, DMA, storage/system administrator, or other role.

Step 9.21—Create the Oracle and Grid OS Users as the Oracle DB HOME Software Owners and Grid Infrastructure HOME Software Owners and Set Their Initial Passwords

To create the Oracle and Grid OS users as the Oracle DB HOME Software Owners and Grid Infrastructure HOME Software owners, respectively, and set their initial passwords, issue these commands:

```
[root@bsfrac01 /]# useradd -u 54321 -g oinstall -G dba,asmdba oracle
[root@bsfrac01 /]# useradd -u 54322 -g oinstall -G asmadmin,asmdba grid

[root@bsfrac01 /]# passwd grid
Changing password for user grid.
New password:
Retype new password:
passwd: all authentication tokens updated successfully.

[root@bsfrac01 /]# passwd oracle
Changing password for user oracle.
New password:
Retype new password:
passwd: all authentication tokens updated successfully.
```

Step 9.22—Create the Optimal Flexible Architecture (OFA) Directory Structure for RAC 12c

As the root OS user, run the following commands:

```
[root@bsfrac01 /]# mkdir -p  /u01/app/12.1.0/grid
[root@bsfrac01 /]# mkdir -p /u01/app/grid
[root@bsfrac01 /]# mkdir -p /u01/app/oracle
[root@bsfrac01 /]# chown -R grid:oinstall /u01
[root@bsfrac01 /]# chown oracle:oinstall /u01/app/oracle
[root@bsfrac01 /]# chmod -R 775 /u01/
```

Step 9.23—Observe/Verify the Required and Relevant Permissions of the Created OFA Directory Structure

Check the required and relevant permissions set for the OFA directory structure:

```
[root@bsfrac01 oracle]# ls -l /u01
total 4
drwxrwxr-x 5 grid oinstall 4096 Feb 25 23:29 app
[root@bsfrac01 oracle]# ls -l /u01/app/
total 12
drwxrwxr-x 3 grid    oinstall 4096 Feb 25 23:29 12.1.0
drwxrwxr-x 2 grid    oinstall 4096 Feb 25 23:29 grid
drwxrwxr-x 2 oracle oinstall 4096 Feb 25 23:29 oracle
```

Step 9.24—Set Up and Configure the NTPD

Configure the NTPD:

```
[root@bsfrac01 ~]# service ntpd start
Shutting down ntpd:                              [  OK  ]
[root@bsfrac01 ~]# chkconfig ntpd on
```

Step 9.25—Turn Off and Unconfigure the Avahi Daemon

Do the following to turn off and unconfigure the Avahi daemon:

```
[root@bsfrac01 ~]# service avahi-daemon stop
Shutting down Avahi daemon:                      [  OK  ]
[root@bsfrac01 ~]# chkconfig avahi-daemon off
```

Step 9.26—Install Packages/Options for Linux Kernel

Within OEL, using the GUI software installer (see Figure 9.24) *or* using the rpm command-line utility, ensure that the following packages for OEL 6.x x86_64 are installed with greater-than/equal-to versions. Additionally, download and install ancillary packages to aid with the performance of the RAC.

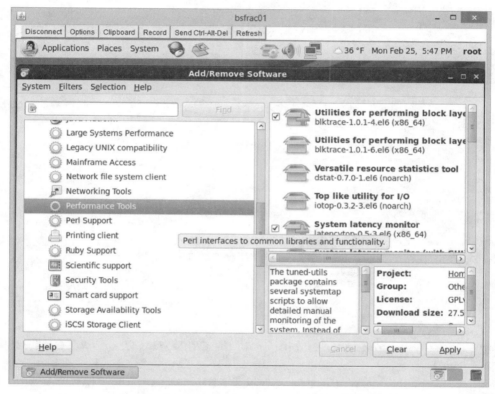

Figure 9.24　Oracle VM 3.x: RAC-Node-01—OS/Linux 6.x 64-bit x86 custom package/rpm installation

```
glibc-2.12-1.7.el6 (i686)
glibc-2.12-1.7.el6 (x86_64)
glibc-devel-2.12-1.7.el6 (x86_64)
glibc-devel-2.12-1.7.el6.i686
libstdc++-4.4.4-13.el6 (x86_64)
libstdc++-4.4.4-13.el6.i686
libstdc++-devel-4.4.4-13.el6 (x86_64)
libstdc++-devel-4.4.4-13.el6.i686
gcc-4.4.4-13.el6 (x86_64)
gcc-c++-4.4.4-13.el6 (x86_64)
ksh
make-3.81-19.el6
sysstat-9.0.4-11.el6 (x86_64)
```

```
libgcc-4.4.4-13.el6 (i686)
libgcc-4.4.4-13.el6 (x86_64)
libaio-0.3.107-10.el6 (x86_64)
libaio-0.3.107-10.el6.i686
libaio-devel-0.3.107-10.el6 (x86_64)
libaio-devel-0.3.107-10.el6.i686
binutils-2.20.51.0.2-5.11.el6 (x86_64)
compat-libcap1-1.10-1 (x86_64)
compat-libstdc++-33-3.2.3-69.el6 (x86_64)
compat-libstdc++-33-3.2.3-69.el6.i686

[root@bsfrac01 ~]# rpm -qa glibc*
glibc-common-2.12-1.80.el6_3.5.x86_64
glibc-devel-2.12-1.80.el6_3.5.x86_64
glibc-2.12-1.80.el6_3.5.x86_64
glibc-headers-2.12-1.80.el6_3.5.x86_64
[root@bsfrac01 ~]# rpm -qa libstdc++*
libstdc++-4.4.6-4.el6.x86_64
libstdc++-devel-4.4.6-4.el6.x86_64
[root@bsfrac01 ~]# rpm -qa gcc*
gcc-c++-4.4.6-4.el6.x86_64
gcc-4.4.6-4.el6.x86_64
[root@bsfrac01 ~]# rpm -qa ksh*
ksh-20100621-16.el6.x86_64
[root@bsfrac01 ~]# rpm -qa make*
make-3.81-20.el6.x86_64
[root@bsfrac01 ~]# rpm -qa sysstat*
sysstat-9.0.4-20.el6.x86_64
[root@bsfrac01 ~]# rpm -qa libgcc*
libgcc-4.4.6-4.el6.x86_64
[root@bsfrac01 ~]# rpm -qa libgcc*
libgcc-4.4.6-4.el6.x86_64
[root@bsfrac01 ~]# rpm -qa libaio*
libaio-devel-0.3.107-10.el6.x86_64
libaio-0.3.107-10.el6.x86_64
[root@bsfrac01 ~]# rpm -qa binutils*
binutils-2.20.51.0.2-5.34.el6.x86_64
[root@bsfrac01 ~]# rpm -qa compat-lib*
compat-libcap1-1.10-1.x86_64
compat-libstdc++-33-3.2.3-69.el6.x86_64
```

Step 9.27—Create Primary Partitions for All the GRID1, DATA1, and RECO1 ASM Disk Groups

Next, create primary partitions for all the GRID1, DATA1, and RECO1 ASM disk groups:

```
[root@bsfrac01 ~]# fdisk /dev/xvdc
device contains neither a valid DOS partition table, nor Sun, SGI, or OSF disklabel.
Building a new DOS disklabel with disk identifier 0x6a917f21.
Changes will remain in memory only, until you decide to write them.
After that, of course, the previous content won't be recoverable.

Command (m for help): n
Command action
   e   extended
   p   primary partition (1-4)
p
Partition number (1-4): 1
First cylinder (1-6527, default 1):
```

Using default value 1

```
Last cylinder, +cylinders or +size{K,M,G} (1-6527, default 6527):
```

Using default value 6527

```
Command (m for help): w
The partition table has been altered!
```

Note

Repeat the preceding steps for all the ASM disks, including grid infrastructure disks.

Step 9.28—Verify the Partition Structures for the Underlying Disks in the GRID1, DATA1, and RECO1 ASM Disk Groups

Verify the partition structures for the underlying disks:

```
[root@bsfrac01 /]# fdisk -l
```

Step 9.29—Configure ASM Library on RAC-Node-01

Configure the ASM library by performing the following steps:

```
[root@bsfrac01 dev]# /etc/init.d/oracleasm configure
Configuring the Oracle ASM library driver.

This will configure the on-boot properties of the Oracle ASM library
driver. The following questions will determine whether the driver is
loaded on boot and what permissions it will have. The current values
will be shown in brackets ('[]'). Hitting <ENTER> without typing an
answer will keep that current value. Ctrl+C will abort.

Default user to own the driver interface []: oracle
Default group to own the driver interface []: asmdba
Start Oracle ASM library driver on boot (y/n) [n]: y
Scan for Oracle ASM disks on boot (y/n) [y]: y
Writing Oracle ASM library driver configuration: done
Initializing the Oracle ASMLib driver:                 [  OK  ]
Scanning the system for Oracle ASMLib disks:           [  OK  ]

[root@bsfrac01 dev]# oracleasm createdisk GRID1DISK01 /dev/xvdc1
Writing disk header: done
Instantiating disk: done
[root@bsfrac01 dev]# oracleasm createdisk GRID1DISK02 /dev/xvdd1
Writing disk header: done
Instantiating disk: done
[root@bsfrac01 dev]# oracleasm createdisk GRID1DISK03 /dev/xvde1
Writing disk header: done
Instantiating disk: done
[root@bsfrac01 dev]# oracleasm createdisk GRID1DISK04 /dev/xvdf1
Writing disk header: done
Instantiating disk: done
```

```
[root@bsfrac01 dev]# oracleasm createdisk GRID1DISK05 /dev/xvdg1
Writing disk header: done
Instantiating disk: done
[root@bsfrac01 dev]# oracleasm createdisk DATA1DISK01 /dev/xvdh1
Writing disk header: done
Instantiating disk: done
[root@bsfrac01 dev]# oracleasm createdisk DATA1DISK02 /dev/xvdi1
Writing disk header: done
Instantiating disk: done
[root@bsfrac01 dev]# oracleasm createdisk DATA1DISK03 /dev/xvdj1
Writing disk header: done
Instantiating disk: done
[root@bsfrac01 dev]# oracleasm createdisk DATA1DISK04 /dev/xvdk1
Writing disk header: done
Instantiating disk: done
[root@bsfrac01 dev]# oracleasm createdisk DATA1DISK05 /dev/xvdl1
Writing disk header: done
Instantiating disk: done
[root@bsfrac01 dev]# oracleasm createdisk DATA1DISK06 /dev/xvdm1
Writing disk header: done
Instantiating disk: done
[root@bsfrac01 dev]# oracleasm createdisk RECO1DISK06 /dev/xvdn1
Writing disk header: done
Instantiating disk: done
```

Note

You can also choose to set up and configure UDEV rules for the ASM disks:

```
[root@bsfrac01 dev]# /etc/init.d/oracleasm listdisks
DATA1DISK01
DATA1DISK02
DATA1DISK03
DATA1DISK04
DATA1DISK05
DATA1DISK06
GRID1DISK01
GRID1DISK02
GRID1DISK03
GRID1DISK04
GRID1DISK05
RECO1DISK06
```

Step 9.30—Download and Stage the Oracle Software Binaries

Download, unzip, and stage the Oracle software grid and database software binaries:

```
[oracle@bsfrac01 Database]$ unzip -q linuxx64_database_12.1BETA_130131_1of2.zip
```

Repeat the unzip process for all the software binary zip files, and verify the unzipped and staged directory structure.

Step 9.31—Establish a Save Point: Make a Backup Copy of the Ready-to-Go OVM in the Form of an OVM Template

Go to OVM Manager → Servers and VMs → Select Server Pool → Select Oracle VM → Right-click → Clone or Move.

Step 9.32—Remove (Temporarily) the Shared Disks and Clone the Ready-to-Go OVM

Go to OVM Manager → Servers and VMs → Select Server Pool → Select Oracle VM, and click the Edit button.

As shown in Figure 9.25, this action temporarily removes all the shared ASM virtual disks. You need to do this; otherwise, clones of these disks will be created unnecessarily during the ensuing cloning process for all the RAC nodes.

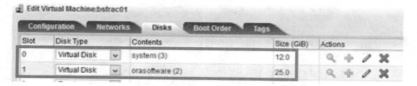

Figure 9.25   Oracle VM 3.x: RAC-Node-01—Local virtual disks after temporarily removing the virtualized shared disks for Automatic Storage Management

Step 9.33—Clone the Other Nodes of the RAC Cluster from the Ready-to-Go Node 01 VM

To clone the other nodes of the RAC, follow these steps:

1. Go to OVM Manager → Servers and VMs → Select Server Pool → Select Oracle VM and right-click. Choose Clone or Move (see Figure 9.26).

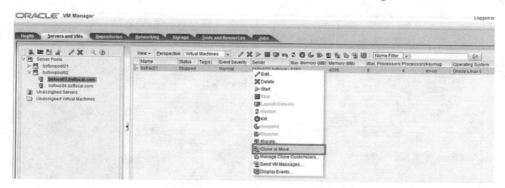

Figure 9.26   Oracle VM 3.x: Clone the other RAC nodes from the VM from Node 01

2. Select the Create a clone of this VM option.
3. Select and enter the following options:
   - Target server pool
   - Description
   - Clone to a: VM
   - Clone count: Specify the clone count for the RAC nodes

As shown in Figure 9.27, all the nodes for a five-node RAC have been successfully created and are ready for further configuration.

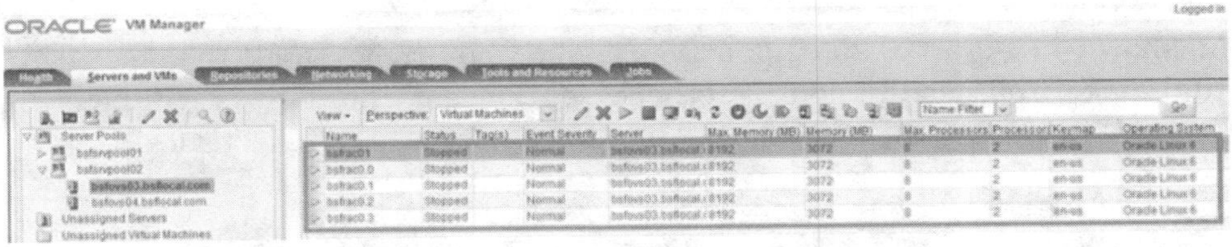

Figure 9.27   Oracle VM 3.x: VMs for all nodes of the RAC have been created and cloned

Step 9.34—Reattach the Shared Disks to the RAC Node OVMs

Next reattach the shared disks to the RAC node OVMs:

1. Go to OVM Manager → Servers and VMs → Select Server Pool → Select Oracle VM, and click the Edit button (see Figure 9.28).

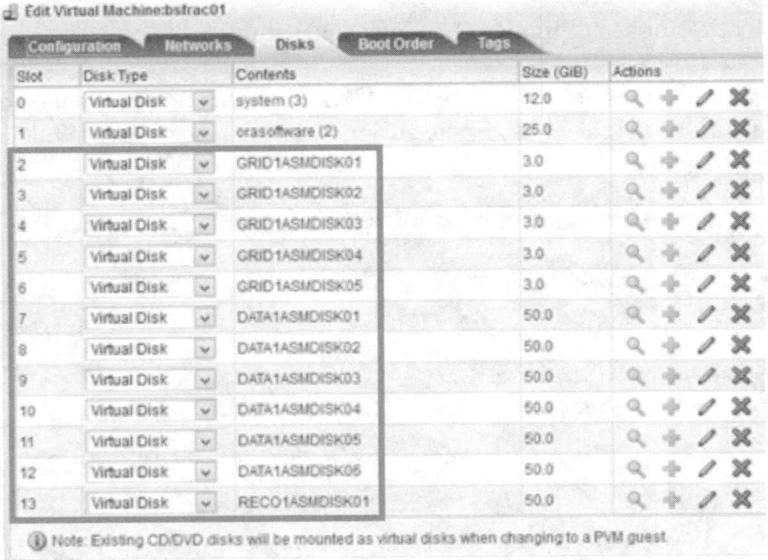

Figure 9.28   Oracle VM 3.x: RAC-Node-01—Reattach the virtualized shared disks for Automatic Storage Management

2. Select the shared disks.

3. Repeat the preceding steps for all the RAC node VMs.

Step 9.35—Start Each Guest VM and Edit the Network Settings

1. Go to System → Preferences → Network Settings → IPv4 Settings.
2. Modify the IP addresses of the eth0 (public) and eth1 (private cluster inter-connect) NICs, as shown in Figure 9.29.

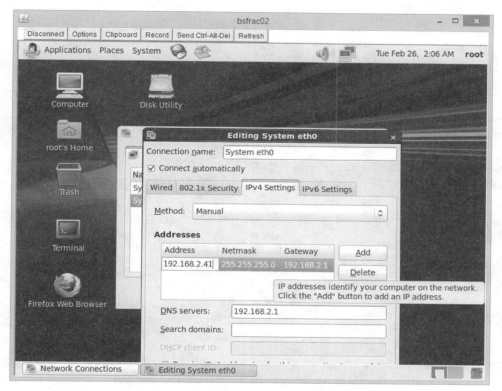

Figure 9.29 Oracle VM 3.x: RAC-Node-01—Network configuration for the RAC node VMs

3. Repeat for all of the RAC nodes.

Install and Set Up 12*c* Grid Infrastructure

As you can see from the preceding sections, setting up and installing Oracle RAC is all about doing an extensive amount of homework in the right way. To summarize the activity covered in the last few sections, ensure that the following virtual infrastructure is available and ready for deployment in a brand-new RAC setup:

- Dedicated virtual network for RAC has been created and configured.
- Virtualized shared ASM disks for the GRID1 ASM disk group are created and ready for use.
- VMs that will constitute the nodes of the RAC 12*c* have been created, set up, and configured.
    - OEL 6.x is set up and configured on RAC-Node-01 using two alternative approaches: installing it from scratch or using the downloadable templates for OVM for x86.
    - The VMs for the other nodes of the RAC 12*c* have been cloned from the RAC-Node-01 VM.

It's *now* time to set up Oracle grid infrastructure and get the RAC 12*c* bird off the ground and in the air.

Step 9.36—In OVM Manager for x86, Start All the VMs for the Oracle RAC 12c Cluster

As shown in Figure 9.30, at this point you want to start the VMs for the RAC 12*c* cluster.

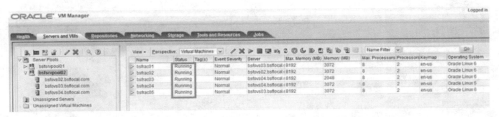

Figure 9.30   Oracle VM 3.x: Start up the VMs for the RAC 12*c* cluster

Step 9.37—In the Grid Infrastructure Staging Directory, Run the OUI to Set Up the Grid Infrastructure

Enter the information and make the selections in the Wizard Entry screens of the Oracle Universal Installer (OUI), as shown in Figures 9.31 through 9.45. In some cases, you will need to edit according to the specific needs of your organization.

1. Enter the My Oracle Support (MOS) credentials for support on software updates and patches (see Figure 9.31), or choose to skip them.

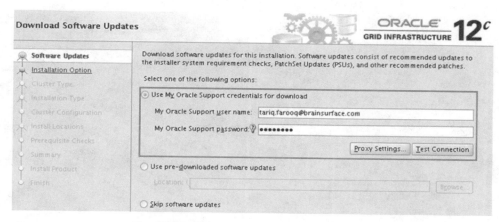

Figure 9.31   Enter your support credentials.

2. Select the Install and Configure Oracle Grid Infrastructure for a Cluster option (see Figure 9.32).

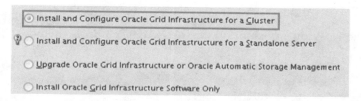

Figure 9.32   Select Install and Configure Oracle Grid Infrastructure for a Cluster.

3. Select the Configure a Flex Cluster option (see Figure 9.33).

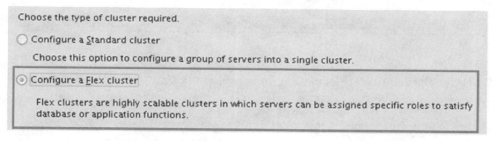

Figure 9.33   Select Configure a Flex Cluster.

4. Select the appropriate product language(s).

5. Enter the required information for Single Client Access Name (SCAN) and Grid Naming Service (GNS) (see Figure 9.34).

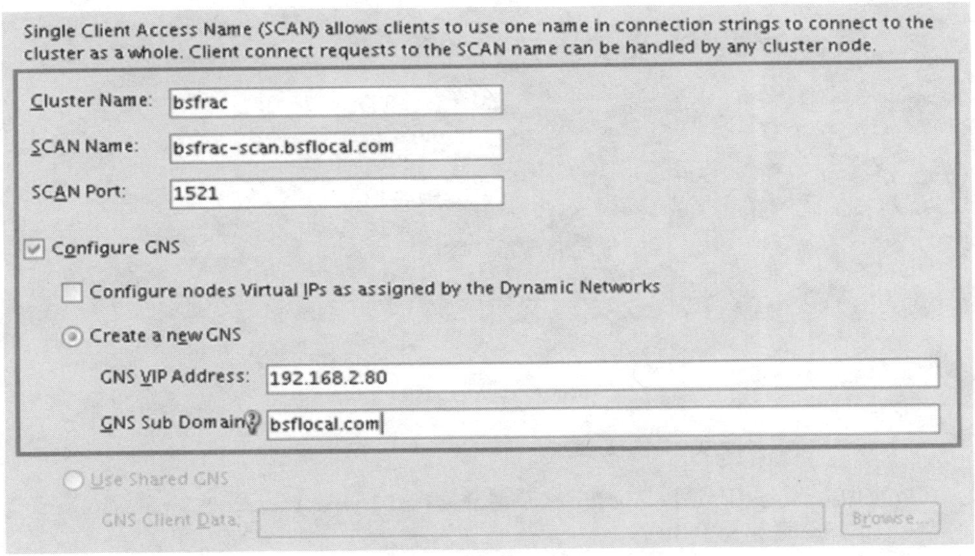

Single Client Access Name (SCAN) allows clients to use one name in connection strings to connect to the cluster as a whole. Client connect requests to the SCAN name can be handled by any cluster node.

Cluster Name: bsfrac

SCAN Name: bsfrac-scan.bsflocal.com

SCAN Port: 1521

☑ Configure GNS

　　☐ Configure nodes Virtual IPs as assigned by the Dynamic Networks

　　⦿ Create a new GNS

　　　　GNS VIP Address: 192.168.2.80

　　　　GNS Sub Domain: bsflocal.com

　　○ Use Shared GNS

　　　　GNS Client Data: [   ] [Browse...]

Figure 9.34   Enter SCAN and GNS information.

6. Enter the relevant information for the RAC 12*c* nodes, including for HUB and LEAF nodes (see Figure 9.35).

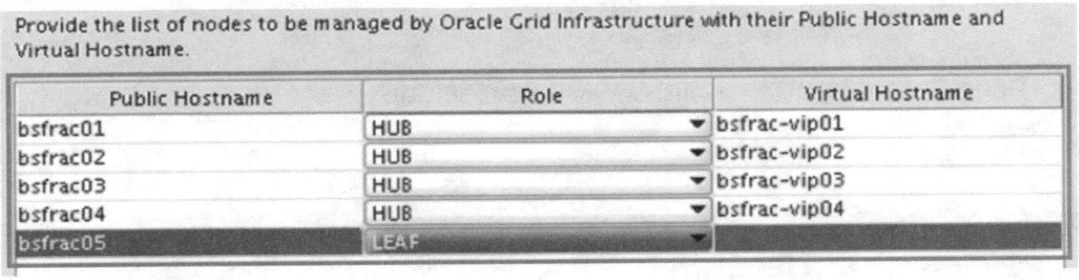

Provide the list of nodes to be managed by Oracle Grid Infrastructure with their Public Hostname and Virtual Hostname.

Public Hostname	Role	Virtual Hostname
bsfrac01	HUB ▼	bsfrac-vip01
bsfrac02	HUB ▼	bsfrac-vip02
bsfrac03	HUB ▼	bsfrac-vip03
bsfrac04	HUB ▼	bsfrac-vip04
bsfrac05	LEAF ▼	

Figure 9.35   Enter HUB and LEAF node information.

7. Enter the required information for establishing and testing SSH connectivity and user equivalence between all the RAC nodes, as in Figure 9.36.

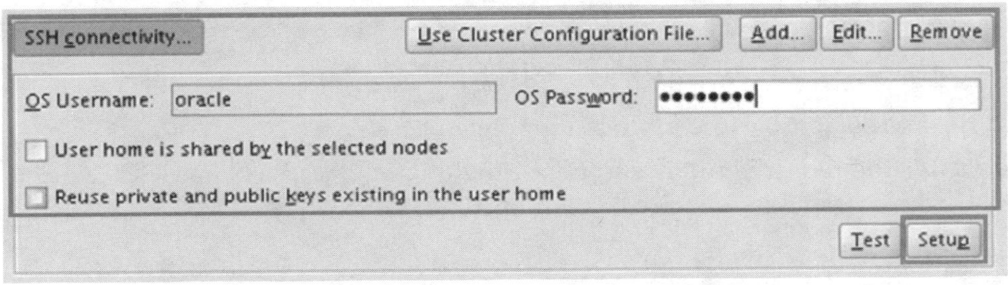

SSH connectivity...	Use Cluster Configuration File...	Add...	Edit...	Remove

OS Username: oracle   OS Password: ••••••••

☐ User home is shared by the selected nodes

☐ Reuse private and public keys existing in the user home

[Test] [Setup]

Figure 9.36   Enter credentials for SSH connectivity.

8. Once step 7 is done, the system tests the SSH connectivity between the nodes (see Figure 9.37).

> Testing passwordless SSH connectivity between the selected nodes. This may take several minutes, please wait...

Figure 9.37　Password-less connectivity testing in progress

9. Specify the network interfaces for public, private cluster interconnect, and ASM. The system will validate those as well (see Figure 9.38).

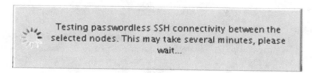

Private interfaces are used by Oracle Grid Infrastructure for internode traffic.

Interface Name	Subnet	Use for
eth0	192.168.2.0	Public
eth1	192.168.3.0	ASM & Private

Note: If you intend to store Oracle Cluster Registry (OCR) and voting disk files using Oracle Flex Automatic Storage Management (Oracle Flex ASM), then you must designate at least one of the private

> Validating Public And Private Interfaces Across Cluster Nodes

Figure 9.38　The system validates the public and private interfaces across the cluster nodes.

10. Select the Configure Grid Infrastructure Management Repository option (see Figure 9.39).

As part of setting up Grid Infrastructure software you can optionally configure Grid Infrastructure Management Repository which is a special type of database that will assist in the management operations of Oracle Grid Infrastructure.

Configure Grid Infrastructure Management Repository

⦿ Yes

○ No

Figure 9.39　Select the Configure Grid Infrastructure Management Repository option.

11. If you choose No, then the message in Figure 9.40 is displayed.

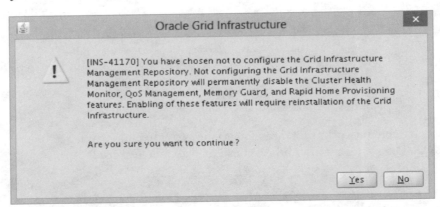

Figure 9.40   Grid Infrastructure Management Repository is not selected as an option.

12. Specify the ASM disks for the GRID1 ASM disk group with a HIGH redundancy level (see Figure 9.41).

Figure 9.41   Specify the ASM disks for the GRID1 ASM disk group.

13. Enter the passwords for the Oracle SYS and ASMSNMP DB users.

14. Select the Do Not Use Intelligent Platform Management Interface (IPMI) option.

15. Specify the OS groups for ASM.

16. Enter the Oracle BASE and HOME locations.

17. Enter the Oracle inventory location (see Figure 9.42).

You are starting your first installation on this host. Specify a directory for installation metadata files (for example, install log files). This directory is called the "inventory directory". The installer automatically sets up subdirectories for each product to contain inventory data. The subdirectory for each product typically requires 150 kilobytes of disk space.

Inventory Directory: `/u01/app/oraInventory`   Browse...

Members of the following operating system group (the primary group) will have write permission to the inventory directory (oraInventory).

oraInventory Group Name: oinstall

Figure 9.42   Enter the inventory location.

18. Enter the root OS password or sudo access credentials to automatically run the root.sh configuration scripts (see Figure 9.43).

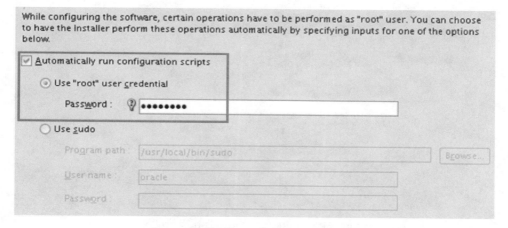

Figure 9.43   Enter the root password.

19. Generate and run any runfixup.sh scripts to remediate any prerequisite issues (see Figure 9.44).

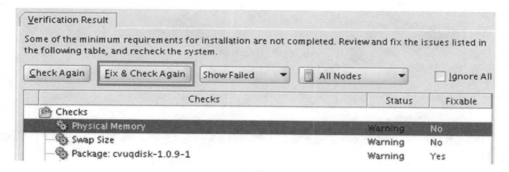

Figure 9.44   Fix any issues.

20. Press Install to initiate the installation process for grid infrastructure (see Figure 9.45).

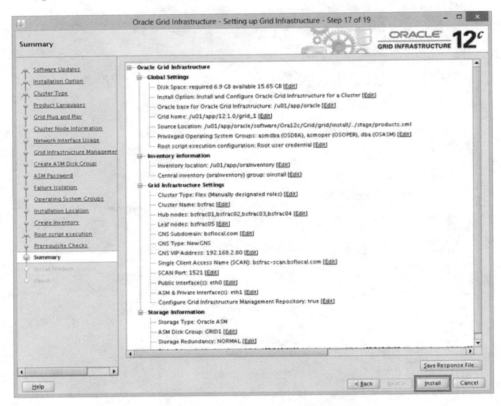

Figure 9.45   Initiate the installation process.

The following output will appear in the SSH window:

```
[oracle@bsfrac01 grid]$ pwd
/u01/app/oracle/software/Ora12c/Grid/grid
[oracle@bsfrac01 grid]$ ./runInstaller
Starting Oracle Universal Installer...

Checking Temp space: must be greater than 120 MB.   Actual 5620 MB     Passed
Checking swap space: must be greater than 150 MB.   Actual 2047 MB     Passed
Checking monitor: must be configured to display at least 256 colors.
Actual 16777216     Passed
Preparing to launch Oracle Universal Installer from
/tmp/OraInstall2013-02-26_01-00-01AM. Please wait ...
```

The following grid infrastructure processes or daemons should appear on the RAC nodes after setup:

PID	USER	PR	NI	VIRT	RES	SHR	S	%CPU	%MEM	TIME+	COMMAND
7619	oracle	20	0	98432	1252	612	S	6.9	0.0	30:33.70	sshd
24066	oracle	20	0	612m	48m	15m	S	4.0	1.7	11:10.74	gipcd.bin
24700	oracle	-2	0	1368m	16m	14m	S	4.0	0.6	10:20.84	asm_vktm_+asm1
28408	oracle	-2	0	1368m	15m	13m	S	4.0	0.5	10:06.05	apx_vktm_+apx1
24336	oracle	RT	0	1157m	182m	80m	S	3.6	6.4	9:49.82	ocssd.bin
24805	root	RT	0	788m	101m	71m	S	3.6	3.6	8:03.76	osysmond.bin
7670	oracle	20	0	1580m	227m	6076	S	2.3	8.0	71:35.10	java
23757	root	20	0	1194m	59m	19m	S	2.3	2.1	5:36.65	ohasd.bin
24963	root	20	0	1146m	43m	16m	S	2.3	1.5	6:24.32	orarootagent.bi
24812	root	20	0	1247m	79m	26m	S	1.6	2.8	4:42.22	crsd.bin
24011	oracle	20	0	1150m	34m	17m	S	1.3	1.2	1:46.04	oraagent.bin
24454	root	20	0	791m	36m	14m	S	1.3	1.3	3:02.20	octssd.bin
25086	oracle	20	0	1754m	151m	19m	S	1.3	5.3	2:53.32	java
3728	oracle	20	0	15180	1256	896	R	1.0	0.0	0:00.08	top
24024	oracle	20	0	667m	38m	15m	S	1.0	1.4	3:04.61	evmd.bin
24311	root	RT	0	918m	106m	71m	S	0.7	3.7	0:16.43	cssdmonitor
24720	oracle	-2	0	1382m	33m	20m	S	0.7	1.2	1:41.75	asm_lms0_+asm1
24864	root	RT	0	849m	160m	71m	S	0.7	5.6	1:48.41	ologgerd
57	root	20	0	0	0	0	S	0.3	0.0	0:12.15	kworker/1:1
24043	oracle	20	0	659m	36m	14m	S	0.3	1.3	0:10.50	gpnpd.bin
24655	oracle	20	0	1368m	19m	17m	S	0.3	0.7	0:07.28	asm_pmon_+asm1
24710	oracle	20	0	1374m	25m	17m	S	0.3	0.9	0:26.34	asm_diag_+asm1
24716	oracle	20	0	1385m	40m	25m	S	0.3	1.4	1:11.91	asm_lmon_+asm1
24718	oracle	20	0	1383m	30m	17m	S	0.3	1.1	0:42.79	asm_lmd0_+asm1
24951	oracle	20	0	1180m	73m	20m	S	0.3	2.6	2:35.66	oraagent.bin
25065	oracle	20	0	1050m	9072	1268	S	0.3	0.3	0:02.38	ons
30490	oracle	20	0	1373m	28m	23m	S	0.3	1.0	0:02.43	oracle_30490_+a

Hub Node(s):

PID	USER	PR	NI	VIRT	RES	SHR	S	%CPU	%MEM	TIME+	COMMAND
2318	gdm	20	0	332m	9924	8924	S	13.9	0.3	0:53.31	gnome-settings-
10097	oracle	-2	0	1368m	15m	13m	S	5.3	0.6	7:47.66	apx_vktm_+apx2
8958	oracle	20	0	602m	47m	15m	S	4.6	1.7	9:34.31	gipcd.bin
9173	root	RT	0	789m	101m	71m	S	4.0	3.6	6:32.76	osysmond.bin
9002	oracle	RT	0	1159m	175m	80m	S	3.6	6.1	10:26.57	ocssd.bin
9506	oracle	-2	0	1368m	16m	14m	S	3.6	0.6	8:41.92	asm_vktm_+asm2
8809	root	20	0	1190m	68m	30m	S	2.0	2.4	4:42.47	ohasd.bin
8909	root	20	0	1150m	39m	20m	S	1.3	1.4	2:53.17	oraagent.bin
8922	oracle	20	0	666m	39m	16m	S	1.3	1.4	2:41.23	evmd.bin
9151	root	20	0	725m	36m	14m	S	1.3	1.3	2:32.39	octssd.bin
9281	root	20	0	748m	29m	16m	S	1.3	1.0	3:35.72	orarootagent.bi
9180	root	20	0	1240m	68m	30m	S	1.0	2.4	3:15.15	crsd.bin
9521	oracle	20	0	1379m	33m	23m	S	0.7	1.2	0:56.36	asm_dia0_+asm2
9528	oracle	-2	0	1382m	33m	20m	S	0.7	1.2	1:29.06	asm_lms0_+asm2
14933	oracle	20	0	15080	1144	812	R	0.7	0.0	0:03.13	top
2207	root	20	0	121m	10m	6116	S	0.3	0.4	0:04.20	Xorg
9347	oracle	20	0	1164m	61m	22m	S	0.3	2.1	2:01.56	oraagent.bin
9516	oracle	20	0	1374m	25m	17m	S	0.3	0.9	0:22.80	asm_diag_+asm2
9523	oracle	20	0	1385m	40m	25m	S	0.3	1.4	1:01.14	asm_lmon_+asm2
9526	oracle	20	0	1383m	30m	17m	S	0.3	1.1	0:38.67	asm_lmd0_+asm2
9532	oracle	20	0	1370m	21m	17m	S	0.3	0.8	0:13.08	asm_lmhb_+asm2

Leaf Node(s):

```
$ ./crs_stat -t -v
```

PID	USER	PR	NI	VIRT	RES	SHR	S	%CPU	%MEM	TIME+	COMMAND
4085	oracle	20	0	602m	44m	14m	S	5.6	1.6	0:17.24	gipcd.bin
4179	root	RT	0	724m	101m	71m	S	4.6	3.5	0:08.74	osysmond.bin
3940	root	20	0	1191m	60m	29m	S	2.6	2.1	0:14.51	ohasd.bin
4161	root	20	0	725m	28m	13m	S	2.0	1.0	0:04.29	octssd.bin

```
4188 root      20   0 1202m  55m  27m S  2.0  1.9   0:07.27 crsd.bin
4051 oracle    20   0  667m  31m  15m S  1.7  1.1   0:05.16 evmd.bin
4128 oracle    RT   0  987m 127m  79m S  1.3  4.5   0:05.97 ocssdrim.bin
4470 oracle    20   0 15080 1100  812 R  0.7  0.0   0:00.08 top
4114 root      RT   0  852m 104m  71m S  0.3  3.7   0:01.12 cssdagent
```

Note

As part of the Flex ASM configuration (new feature), ASM is not running on the leaf node(s).

```
[oracle@bsfrac01 bin]$ ./crs_stat -t -v
```

Name	Type	R/RA	F/FT	Target	State	Host
ora....SM.lsnr	ora....er.type	0/5	0/	ONLINE	ONLINE	bsfrac01
ora.GRID1.dg	ora....up.type	0/5	0/	ONLINE	ONLINE	bsfrac01
ora....ER.lsnr	ora....er.type	0/5	0/	ONLINE	ONLINE	bsfrac01
ora....AF.lsnr	ora....er.type	0/5	0/	OFFLINE	OFFLINE	
ora....N1.lsnr	ora....er.type	0/5	0/0	ONLINE	ONLINE	bsfrac02
ora....N2.lsnr	ora....er.type	0/5	0/0	ONLINE	ONLINE	bsfrac01
ora....N3.lsnr	ora....er.type	0/5	0/0	ONLINE	ONLINE	bsfrac04
ora.MGMTLSNR	ora....nr.type	0/0	0/0	OFFLINE	OFFLINE	
ora.asm	ora.asm.type	0/5	0/0	ONLINE	ONLINE	bsfrac01
ora....01.lsnr	application	0/5	0/0	ONLINE	ONLINE	bsfrac01
ora....c01.ons	application	0/3	0/0	ONLINE	ONLINE	bsfrac01
ora....c01.vip	ora....t1.type	0/0	0/0	ONLINE	ONLINE	bsfrac01
ora....02.lsnr	application	0/5	0/0	ONLINE	ONLINE	bsfrac02
ora....c02.ons	application	0/3	0/0	ONLINE	ONLINE	bsfrac02
ora....c02.vip	ora....t1.type	0/0	0/0	ONLINE	ONLINE	bsfrac02
ora....03.lsnr	application	0/5	0/0	ONLINE	ONLINE	bsfrac03
ora....c03.ons	application	0/3	0/0	ONLINE	ONLINE	bsfrac03
ora....c03.vip	ora....t1.type	0/0	0/0	ONLINE	ONLINE	bsfrac03
ora....04.lsnr	application	0/5	0/0	ONLINE	ONLINE	bsfrac04
ora....c04.ons	application	0/3	0/0	ONLINE	ONLINE	bsfrac04
ora....c04.vip	ora....t1.type	0/0	0/0	ONLINE	ONLINE	bsfrac04
ora.cvu	ora.cvu.type	0/5	0/0	ONLINE	ONLINE	bsfrac01
ora.gns	ora.gns.type	0/5	0/0	ONLINE	ONLINE	bsfrac01
ora.gns.vip	ora....ip.type	0/0	0/0	ONLINE	ONLINE	bsfrac01
ora....network	ora....rk.type	0/5	0/	ONLINE	ONLINE	bsfrac01
ora.oc4j	ora.oc4j.type	0/1	0/2	ONLINE	ONLINE	bsfrac01
ora.ons	ora.ons.type	0/3	0/	ONLINE	ONLINE	bsfrac01
ora.proxy_advm	ora....vm.type	0/5	0/	ONLINE	ONLINE	bsfrac01
ora.scan1.vip	ora....ip.type	0/0	0/0	ONLINE	ONLINE	bsfrac02
ora.scan2.vip	ora....ip.type	0/0	0/0	ONLINE	ONLINE	bsfrac01
ora.scan3.vip	ora....ip.type	0/0	0/0	ONLINE	ONLINE	bsfrac04

Summary

As economies the world over continue to shrink, organizations and entities are looking for new and innovative ways to achieve the next dimension of corporate efficiency. Virtualization is one of the key elements of modern cloud computing, providing the gateway to a cost-effective, agile, and elastic IT environment.

Based on the mainstream open-source Xen hypervisor, OVM along with Oracle RAC and EM12*c* can be used to formulate, build, and set up end-to-end industry-grade, state-of-the-art virtualized database clouds. If you're not already on it, now is the perfect time to hop on the virtualization and cloud computing bandwagon.

The methods outlined in this chapter and the next are a perfect avenue to do so. They provide a step-by-step guide for setting up and installing your own RAC 12*c* environment either at home or in a corporate setting. Please continue reading on to the next chapter to finish the RAC 12*c* database cloud journey that we started in this one.

10

Virtualizing RAC 12*c* (DB Clouds) on Oracle VM VirtualBox—RAC Databases

We started our Oracle Real Application Cluster (RAC) database cloud computing journey in Chapter 9 with Oracle VM (OVM) for x86 and reached the point where we had an Oracle grid infrastructure set up in a virtualized environment, based on Oracle VM for x86. The grid infrastructure serves as a consolidated Clusterware and storage (Automatic Storage Management, or ASM) platform for hosting and serving clustered RAC databases in the database cloud.

We continue our trek in this chapter by repeating some of the same steps with OVM VirtualBox instead of OVM for x86. This alternative approach presents you with the advantage of choice; you can pick a virtual solution based on your requirements. OVM enables you to virtualize RAC and set up database clouds in a corporate environment, whereas OVM VirtualBox enables you to do the same but on your own laptop, thereby eliminating the need for expensive hardware to set up, configure, and deploy Oracle RAC. The OVM VirtualBox approach is a great way of learning RAC in a quick and easy fashion, all implemented with the do-it-yourself methodology shown in this chapter.

Following this line of action, we resume our journey with OVM VirtualBox up to the point of setting up Oracle grid infrastructure. Once that stage is achieved, the subsequent steps in this chapter, detailing setting up RAC databases in the Oracle database cloud, apply equally to both OVM for x86 and OVM VirtualBox.

We also delve into cloud computing in detail from the perspective of Oracle. Some of this material is covered in the earlier chapters, but the information is worth reiterating.

As you've already observed by now, if you have surfed through the last chapter, a step-by-step approach is followed in order to give you a roadmap for setting up virtualized Oracle RAC database clouds. You are free to choose from one of two virtualization solutions—OVM for x86 or OVM VirtualBox.

Following is a list of the sections in this chapter:

- OVM VirtualBox: A Brief Introduction
- What Is Cloud Computing? Synopsis and Overview
- Oracle's Strategy for Cloud Computing
- EM12*c* and OVM: Management and Virtualization Components for Oracle Database Clouds
- RAC Private Cloud on OVM VirtualBox—Software and Hardware Infrastructure Requirements
- Setting Up, Installing, and Configuring an Oracle RAC 12*c* Private Cloud on OVM VirtualBox
- EM12*c*: Implementing DBaaS

It is advisable to follow the steps outlined in this chapter on your own laptop, particularly if you are interested in setting up a brand-new 12*c* cluster on your own machine.

OVM VirtualBox: A Brief Introduction

OVM VirtualBox is a free, open-source virtualization product offering from Oracle that enables guest VM OS virtualization on your own laptop or desktop machine. It can be utilized to install, configure, test, and learn Oracle RAC, alleviating the need for dedicated physical hardware and expensive physical shared storage. OVM VirtualBox can also be used for installation, configuration, and testing of various Oracle products, and it provides other virtualization applications. The latest version available at the time of writing is OVM VirtualBox 4.x.

OVM VirtualBox is a type 2 hypervisor—it installs on an existing preinstalled OS. It can be installed on the Linux, Macintosh, Solaris, and Windows OS families.

OVM VirtualBox can be downloaded from the Oracle Technology Network (OTN) website and can easily be installed by following the intuitive Installation Setup Wizard (see Figure 10.1). The entire process of downloading and installing OVM VirtualBox takes about 5 to 10 minutes.

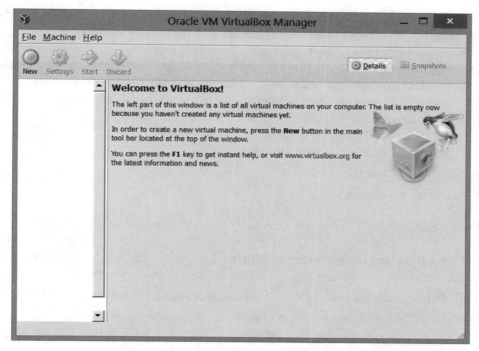

Figure 10.1   A new installation of Oracle VM VirtualBox in a Windows 8 environment

What Is Cloud Computing? Synopsis and Overview

Cloud computing means a lot of different things to a lot of different people. *So what exactly is cloud computing?*

In its most generally accepted form, cloud computing is web- or network-based computing wherein abstracted resources are located and shared on the network, whether on an intranet (private cloud) or the Internet (public cloud), presented in a service-based model. *Cloud* is sometimes used as an alternative term or metaphor for the Internet. By its generally agreed-upon definition, cloud computing is on-demand, metered, and self-serviceable.

Cloud computing is an evolution of existing IT paradigms, strategies, and models: in many respects, it is a rebranding, reorganization, and re-presentation of various components in the overall IT ecosystem. Cloud computing is in flux, not completely mature, and still evolving.

Most cloud computing models do not introduce newer technologies but rather improve on the existing technologies by making them more efficient. Focusing on the subject at hand, RAC plays an integral role in setting up and configuring Oracle database clouds.

Is cloud computing a paradigm shift? The answer is yes and no, depending on your perception, understanding, and implementation of your flavor of cloud computing.

Is cloud computing seeing massive adoption? It is catching on, and the prospects are very promising. Cloud computing is also commonly understood as *elastic computing*, which is fundamentally attained by merit of *virtualization*. Elastic computing is the capability to provide increased computing resources when needed.

Here are a few salient characteristics of an IT cloud:

- Dynamic, elastic, agile, and scalable
- Multitenant, secure, and reliable
- Metered, service based

Four models of deployment are currently prevalent in use:

- **Private cloud (or enterprise cloud)**: Characterized by clouds on private networks (may someday replace the traditional data-center term)
- **Public cloud**: Shared (typically virtualized) resources over the Internet
- **Hybrid cloud**: A combination of private and public cloud models
- **Community cloud**: Organizations forming a shared cloud for common needs, goals, and purposes

Cloud Computing: _____ as a Service

Cloud computing can be summarized with the phrase (and is widely understood as) "fill-in-the-blank as a service," as in

- Database as a service (DBaaS)
- Storage as a service
- Software as a service (SaaS)
- Middleware as a service (MWaaS)
- Platform as a service (PaaS)
- Infrastructure as a service (IaaS)
- IT as a service (the holy grail of cloud computing)

Oracle's Strategy for Cloud Computing

Oracle's cloud computing strategy is a comprehensive yet simple one—Oracle provides infrastructure, products, and support for public and private clouds.

Public Clouds

Services are based primarily on subscription-based application as a service, IaaS, and PaaS paradigms. Some of Oracle's current cloud offerings include products such as Fusion CRM/HCM, RAC/Database Cloud Service, Oracle Social Network, and Oracle Java Cloud Service.

Private Clouds

To briefly summarize the components involved, with OVM for x86 and Enterprise Manager Cloud Control 12*c* (EM12*c*), you can comprehensively formulate, implement, administer, maintain, meter, and support private clouds behind your corporate firewalls.

EM12*c* and OVM: Management and Virtualization Components for Oracle Database Clouds

EM12*c* incorporates the cloud functionality in cloud management packs: Cloud Management Pack for Oracle Database. We talk more about this component at the end of the chapter. We also provide an overview of DBaaS.

The virtualization component OVM for x86 3.x has been integrated into the framework of EM12*c* and works hand-in-hand with EM12*c* to implement cloud IaaS. Working as a proxy agent, with the OVM 3 agent, you do not need an additional EM12*c* agent deployed on your OVM for an x86 machine.

With cloud application programming interfaces (APIs) and command-line interfaces (CLIs), self-service operations, out-of-the-box scaling capabilities, policy-based resource management, governance and chargeback/metering, cloud zones, and more, EM12*c* provides a wide variety of feature-rich functionality for setting up, managing, supporting, and administering Oracle database cloud infrastructures.

After the preceding overview of the various technologies, paradigms, and terms involved, it is now time to start setting up your own virtualized RAC 12*c* database cloud on OVM VirtualBox. The next section begins this journey by outlining the software and hardware requirements.

RAC Private Cloud on OVM VirtualBox—Software and Hardware Requirements

The software requirements are straightforward. The hardware requirements are a little bit more complicated but not overly so.

Software Requirements

As outlined in the following steps, setting up a virtualized RAC 12*c* cluster requires the following prerequisite software components:

- **OVM VirtualBox 4.x**: Download and install from the OTN website.
- **Oracle Enterprise Linux x86_64 Release 6.x**: Oracle Enterprise Linux (OEL) is Oracle's version of the popular Red Hat Enterprise Linux platform.

Hardware Requirements

As outlined in the following steps, setting up a virtualized RAC 12*c* cluster requires a modern desktop or laptop, preinstalled with a Windows, Linux, Macintosh, or Solaris OS. This machine will serve as the host OVM VirtualBox machine. Table 10.1 presents the minimum requirements and the specs of the laptop that was used to follow and implement the steps detailed in this chapter.

Table 10.1　Hardware Requirements

Physical Machine Used	Minimum Requirements
Dell XPS laptop Intel i7 Quad 2.2Ghz 3632QM quad-core processor (hyperthreaded to eight logical cores)	Any equivalent x86 desktop or laptop machine
Memory: 16 GB DDR3 SDRAM	8 GB RAM
Hard drive: 512 GB SSD HD	256 GB SSD or SATA2 HD
Network interfaces: Integrated 10/100 Ethernet and Intel WiMax 6520 cards	Single network interface card, LAN-based or WiFi
NetGear GigaBit WiFi Router WNDR3700	Any equivalent ≥ 100 Mbps home router
OS: Windows 8	OS supported for installing OVM VirtualBox: Linux, Solaris, Windows, Macintosh

Setting Up, Installing, and Configuring Oracle RAC 12*c* Private Cloud on OVM VirtualBox

In this section we run through two alternative approaches to setting up virtualized Oracle RAC on OVM VirtualBox. Then we walk through setting up, installing, and configuring 12*c* virtualized RAC on OVM VirtualBox.

Note

Step 10.1, Approach 1 and Step 10.1, Approach 2 are alternatives to each other: you can choose either one.

Step 10.1, Approach 1—Download and Import an OEL 6.x VM VirtualBox Appliance to Create RAC-Node-01

Approach 1 is simple. It involves one main step composed of a couple of substeps. An OVM VirtualBox appliance is a golden image of software, ready to go. The concept is similar to OVM templates discussed in Chapter 9. Download the prebuilt, preconfigured appliance for OEL 6.x from the OTN website and import it.

1. Choose Oracle VM VirtualBox → File → Import Appliance.
2. Select the .ova file for OEL 6.x and press the Import button (see Figure 10.2).

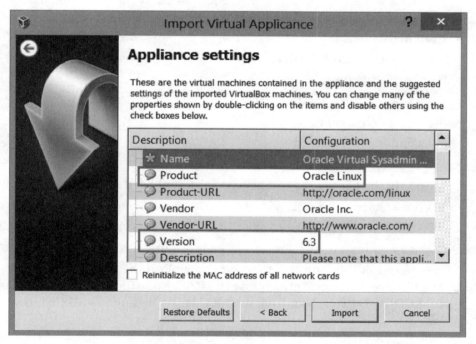

Figure 10.2   A new virtual machine for RAC-Node-01 created in Oracle VM VirtualBox

As you can see, this option is simple and easy.

Note

If you've already used Step 10.1, Approach 1, you can skip Step 10.1, Approach 2.

Step 10.1, Approach 2—Create an OEL 6.x Virtual Machine for Node 01 from a .ISO Image

The second option is a bit more involved. You begin by creating an OEL 6.x virtual machine for node 01 from an .ISO image:

1. Choose Oracle VM VirtualBox → New, and then enter the following information:
   - Name and OS
     - Name: bsfracvx1 (substitute the name of your RAC-Node-01)
     - Type: Linux
     - Version: Oracle (64 bit)
   - Memory size:
     - 4 GB is the ideal/minimum size requirement. If your machine has 8 GB RAM, then 2.5 GB will suffice.
   - Hard drive:
     - Create a virtual hard drive now
   - Hard drive file type:
     - VirtualBox Disk Image (VDI)
   - Storage on physical hard drive:
     - Dynamically allocated
   - File location and size:
     - Specify the folder that will house the virtual hard drive file
     - Virtual hard drive size: 35 GB

   The finished product will look something like what is shown in Figure 10.3.

2. Download and install OEL 6.x, as shown in Figure 10.4.

3. As mentioned in Chapter 9, at this point, download the OEL 6.x ISO from the Oracle eDelivery website, attach it to the RAC-Node-01 virtual machine as a virtual CD/DVD drive, boot from it, and then set up and install OEL 6.x.

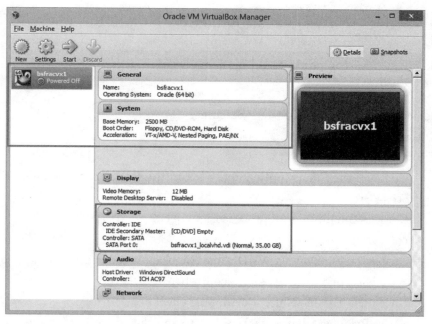

Figure 10.3   A new virtual machine for RAC-Node-01 created in Oracle VM VirtualBox

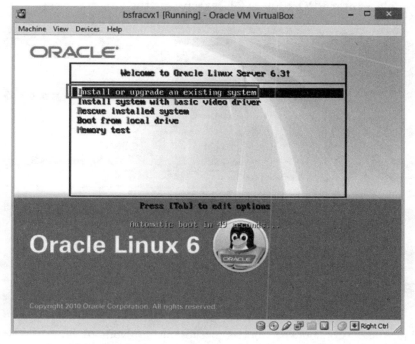

Figure 10.4   Oracle Enterprise Linux 6 installation bootup menu

Step 10.2—OVM VirtualBox: Customize the New Virtual Machine for RAC 12*c*

Now that you have the new virtual machine created, it is time to configure it the way you want it:

1. Select VM for RAC-Node-01 → Settings.
2. Enter the following:
   - System:
     - Uncheck the Floppy option checkbox in the Boot Order option checkbox.
   - Processor:
     - Change the number of processors to qty: 2.
   - Acceleration:
     - Enable the Enable VT-x/AMD-v and Enabled Nested Paging checkbox options.
   - Choose Network → Adapter 1 (see Figure 10.5):
     - Check the Enable Network Adapter checkbox.
     - Select Bridged Adapter as Attached to and the network interface card (NIC) on the system. In this case, it is the WiFi card on the Windows 8 laptop.
     - Select Inter PRO/1000 MT Desktop… as the adapter type.

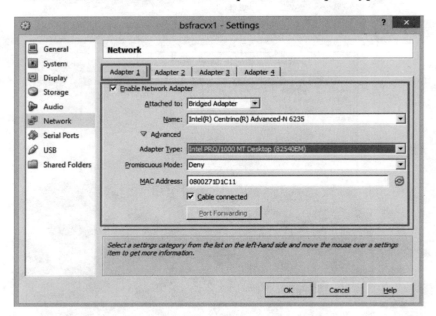

Figure 10.5   Configure network settings for the RAC-Node-01 virtual machine, Adapter 1 (public network interface for RAC)

Note

This virtual network interface card (VNIC) will serve as the public network interface for the RAC 12*c*.

3. Choose Network → Adapter 2 (see Figure 10.6). Make the same selections as shown in the previous step with one exception: this VNIC will be Attached to the Internal Network.

Note

This VNIC will serve as the first NIC for the HAIP-enabled private cluster interconnect.

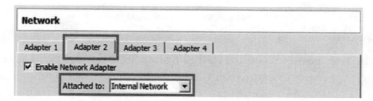

Figure 10.6. Configure network settings for the RAC-Node-01 virtual machine, Adapter 2: Attached to Internal Network—Interface 1 for RAC HAIP-enabled private cluster interconnect

4. Choose Network → Adapter 3. Make the same selections as shown in the previous step.

Note:

This VNIC will serve as the second NIC for the HAIP-*enabled* private cluster interconnect.

Step 10.3—OVM VirtualBox: Create, Configure, and Attach the Shared Virtual Disks for the RAC 12*c* Cluster

In this step, you create, configure, and attach the shared virtual disks for the cluster.

1. Create the shared disks for the RAC 12*c* cluster:
   - GRID1 ASM disk group:
     Qty: 5
     ASM disk size: 15 GB
   - DATA1 ASM disk group:
     Qty: 3
     ASM disk size: 20 GB
   - RECO1 ASM disk group:
     Qty: 1
     ASM disk size: 20 GB

The shared disks are shown here:

```
C:\Program Files\Oracle\VirtualBox\VBoxManage.exe createhd --size 15360
--variant Fixed --format VDI --filename C:\TFMCloud\12c\SharedStorage\asm_grid01.vdi
C:\Program Files\Oracle\VirtualBox\VBoxManage.exe createhd --size 15360
--variant Fixed --format VDI --filename C:\TFMCloud\12c\SharedStorage\asm_grid02.vdi
C:\Program Files\Oracle\VirtualBox\VBoxManage.exe createhd --size 15360
--variant Fixed --format VDI --filename C:\TFMCloud\12c\SharedStorage\asm_grid03.vdi
C:\Program Files\Oracle\VirtualBox\VBoxManage.exe createhd --size 15360
--variant Fixed --format VDI --filename C:\TFMCloud\12c\SharedStorage\asm_grid04.vdi
C:\Program Files\Oracle\VirtualBox\VBoxManage.exe createhd --size 15360
--variant Fixed --format VDI --filename C:\TFMCloud\12c\SharedStorage\asm_grid05.vdi
C:\Program Files\Oracle\VirtualBox\VBoxManage.exe createhd --size 20480
--variant Fixed --format VDI --filename C:\TFMCloud\12c\SharedStorage\asm_data01.vdi
C:\Program Files\Oracle\VirtualBox\VBoxManage.exe createhd --size 20480
--variant Fixed --format VDI --filename C:\TFMCloud\12c\SharedStorage\asm_data02.vdi
C:\Program Files\Oracle\VirtualBox\VBoxManage.exe createhd --size 20480
--variant Fixed --format VDI --filename C:\TFMCloud\12c\SharedStorage\asm_data03.vdi
C:\Program Files\Oracle\VirtualBox\VBoxManage.exe createhd --size 20480
--variant Fixed --format VDI --filename C:\TFMCloud\12c\SharedStorage\asm_reco01.vdi
```

2. **Make the file-based virtual hard disks shareable for the ASM disk groups.**
   Substitute the shared virtual disk filenames in the following commands created
   as a result of the `VBoxManage.exe createhd` commands in the previous section.

```
c:\TFMCloud\12c\SharedStorage\asm_grid01.vdi --type shareable
VBoxManage modifyhd c:\TFMCloud\12c\SharedStorage\asm_grid02.vdi --type shareable
VBoxManage modifyhd c:\TFMCloud\12c\SharedStorage\asm_grid03.vdi --type shareable
VBoxManage modifyhd c:\TFMCloud\12c\SharedStorage\asm_grid04.vdi --type shareable
VBoxManage modifyhd c:\TFMCloud\12c\SharedStorage\asm_grid05.vdi --type shareable
VBoxManage modifyhd c:\TFMCloud\12c\SharedStorage\asm_data01.vdi --type shareable
VBoxManage modifyhd c:\TFMCloud\12c\SharedStorage\asm_data02.vdi --type shareable
VBoxManage modifyhd c:\TFMCloud\12c\SharedStorage\asm_data03.vdi --type shareable
VBoxManage modifyhd c:\TFMCloud\12c\SharedStorage\asm_reco01.vdi --type shareable
```

3. **Attach the file-based virtual hard disks for the ASM disk groups to Node 1:**

Note

Substitute the shared virtual disk filenames in the following commands created as a
result of the VBoxManage createhd commands in the previous sections.

```
VBoxManage storageattach bsfracvx1 --medium c:\TFMCloud\12c\SharedStorage\asm_grid01.vdi --type
hdd --port 1 --device 0
--mtype shareable --storagectl "SATA"
VBoxManage storageattach bsfracvx1 --medium c:\TFMCloud\12c\SharedStorage\asm_grid02.vdi --type
hdd --port 2 --device 0
--mtype shareable --storagectl "SATA"
VBoxManage storageattach bsfracvx1 --medium c:\TFMCloud\12c\SharedStorage\asm_grid03.vdi --type
hdd --port 3 --device 0
--mtype shareable --storagectl "SATA"
VBoxManage storageattach bsfracvx1 --medium c:\TFMCloud\12c\SharedStorage\asm_grid04.vdi --type
hdd --port 4 --device 0
--mtype shareable --storagectl "SATA"
VBoxManage storageattach bsfracvx1 --medium c:\TFMCloud\12c\SharedStorage\asm_grid05.vdi --type
hdd --port 5 --device 0
--mtype shareable --storagectl "SATA"
VBoxManage storageattach bsfracvx1 --medium c:\TFMCloud\12c\SharedStorage\asm_data01.vdi --type
hdd --port 6 --device 0
--mtype shareable --storagectl "SATA"
VBoxManage storageattach bsfracvx1 --medium c:\TFMCloud\12c\SharedStorage\asm_data02.vdi --type
hdd --port 7 --device 0
--mtype shareable --storagectl "SATA"
```

```
VBoxManage storageattach bsfracvx1 --medium c:\TFMCloud\12c\SharedStorage\asm_data03.vdi --type
hdd --port 8 --device 0
--mtype shareable --storagectl "SATA"
VBoxManage storageattach bsfracvx1 --medium c:\TFMCloud\12c\SharedStorage\asm_reco01.vdi --type
hdd --port 9 --device 0
--mtype shareable --storagectl "SATA"
```

4. Verify the attachment and shareable status of the virtual shared ASM disks in OVM VirtualBox by choosing OVM VirtualBox → bsfracvx1 (Node 01) → Settings → Storage (see Figure 10.7).

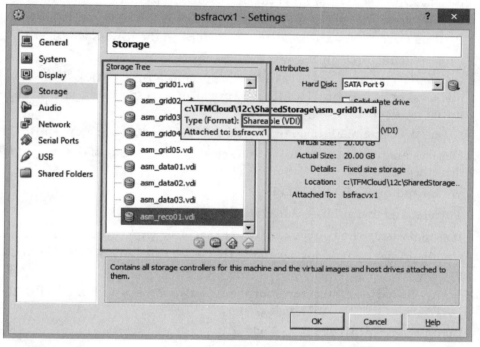

Figure 10.7. Oracle VM VirtualBox: Shared virtual disk configuration for RAC 12*c*

Step 10.4—Configure the New Virtual Machine for RAC 12*c*

Power up the guest VM and configure it by implementing the following steps, which are outlined in Chapter 9:

1. Set the network configuration of the private cluster interconnect VNIC.
2. Modify the /etc/hosts file to include the relevant entries for RAC 12*c*.
3. Check for space requirements.
4. Disable the Linux software firewall.

5. Configure and restart the Network Time Protocol Daemon (NTPD) client.

6. Partition, format, and mount /u01 on the 25 GB local virtual hard disk.

7. Disable the SELINUX option.

8. Install Very Secure File Transfer Protocol Daemon (VSFTPD) server (FTP server).

9. Install X Window System desktop.

10. Reboot RAC-Node-01 for *all* of the preceding setups and configurations to take effect.

11. Perform Oracle software preinstallation steps on the RAC-Node-01 VM.

12. Create the required and relevant OS groups.

13. Create the Oracle and Grid OS users as the Oracle DB HOME software owners and Grid infrastructure HOME software owners, respectively, and set their initial passwords.

14. Create the Optimal Flexible Architecture (OFA) directory structure for RAC 12c.

15. Observe and verify the required and relevant permissions of the created OFA directory structure.

16. Set up and configure the NTPD.

17. Turn off and unconfigure the Avahi daemon.

18. Install packages and options for Linux kernel.

19. Create primary partitions for all the GRID1, DATA1, and RECO1 ASM disk groups.

20. Verify the partition structures for the underlying disks within the GRID1, DATA1, and RECO1 ASM disk groups.

21. Configure ASMLIB ON RAC-Node-01.

22. Download and stage the Oracle software binaries.

At this point, the VM for RAC-Node-01 is ready to be cloned (illustrated in the next section).

Step 10.5—Clone Virtual Hard Drive for RAC-Node-02 from Node 01

Before cloning the virtual hard drive, make a backup copy of the cloned virtual hard drive—for example, bsfracvx1_localvhd.vmdk, on bsfracvx1—to establish a save point. This approach enables you to revert to a point-in-time saved copy of Node 01 so that if there are issues further down the road, you will not have to start over from scratch. However, this approach does translate into a larger space requirement on your desktop or laptop host machine.

Then follow these steps:

1. Run the `clonehd` command to clone the hard drive for RAC-Node-01.
2. Shut down the VM for RAC-Node-01, create another directory for RAC-Node-02, such as C:\Users\tfm1\VirtualBox VMs\bsfracv2, and run the `VBoxManage.exe clonehd` command to clone the hard drive of Node 01.

```
C:\Program Files\Oracle\VirtualBox\ VBoxManage.exe clonehd "C:\Users\tfm1\VirtualBox VMs\
bsfracvx1\bsfracvx1_localvhd.vdi" "C:\Users\tfm1\VirtualBox VMs\bsfracvx2\bsfracvx2_localvhd.vdi"
```

Temporarily copy and relocate the cloned virtual hard drive for Node 02 to another temporary folder to avoid any errors during creation of the VM for RAC-Node-02, as outlined in the following section.

Step 10.6—Create and Configure the VM for RAC-Node-02 Using the Cloned Local Virtual Hard Drive from Node 01

Follow these steps to create and configure the VM for RAC-Node-02.

1. Go to Oracle VM VirtualBox → Machine → New.
2. Follow the same instructions as outlined earlier (Step 10.1, Approach 1) to create and configure the VM for RAC-Node-02 with one exception: instead of creating a new HD, select and attach an existing virtual HD and specify the name of the cloned virtual HD file created in the previous section (see Figure 10.8).

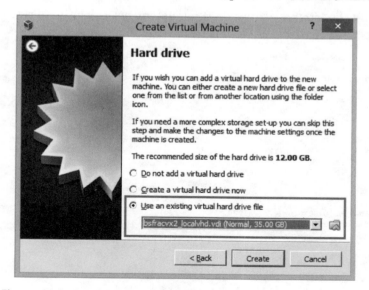

Figure 10.8. Oracle VM VirtualBox: Select the existing cloned virtual hard drive option for RAC-Node-02.

3. Configure and customize RAC-Node-02 by following the same steps as outlined in Step 10.1, Approach 2:

   ▪ System

   ▪ Processor

   ▪ Acceleration

   ▪ Network settings (adapters 1, 2, and 3)

   ▪ Attach the shareable ASM virtual disks to RAC-Node-02 using the `VBoxManage storageattach` command.

   ▪ Verify the attachment and shareable status of the virtual shared ASM disks within OVM VirtualBox.

4. Configure the network settings within the OS for RAC-Node-02.

5. Power up the VM for RAC-Node-02, and in the OS, edit the network settings as shown in the following:

   ▪ Change the hostname in /etc/sysconfig/network.

   ▪ Linux → Top Menu → System → Administration → Network:.

   ▪ Remove the System eth* VNICs: Select Device → Deactivate → Delete

   ▪ Change the connection names to match Node 01, from Auto eth* to System eth*.

   ▪ Modify the IP address information for the public and private network interfaces for RAC-Node-02.

   ▪ Modify the /etc/udev/rules.d/70-persistent-net.rules file to reflect the correct eth* entries:

```
$ vi /etc/udev/rules.d/70-persistent-net.rules
# This file was automatically generated by the /lib/udev/write_net_rules
# program, run by the persistent-net-generator.rules rules file.
#
# You can modify it, as long as you keep each rule on a single
# line, and change only the value of the NAME= key.

# PCI device 0x8086:0x100e (e1000)
SUBSYSTEM=="net", ACTION=="add", DRIVERS=="?*", ATTR{address}==
"08:00:27:c3:58:84", ATTR{type}=="1", KERNEL=="eth*", NAME="eth0"

# PCI device 0x8086:0x100e (e1000)
SUBSYSTEM=="net", ACTION=="add", DRIVERS=="?*", ATTR{address}==
"08:00:27:06:ad:43", ATTR{type}=="1", KERNEL=="eth*", NAME="eth1"

# PCI device 0x8086:0x100e (e1000)
SUBSYSTEM=="net", ACTION=="add", DRIVERS=="?*", ATTR{address}==
"08:00:27:86:01:91", ATTR{type}=="1", KERNEL=="eth*", NAME="eth2"
```

- Modify the .bash_profile file to reflect the hostname and second instance on Node 02 (the following also serves as an example of a .bash_profile file for a RAC 12*c* cluster):

```
[oracle@bsfracvx2 ~]$ cat .bash_profile
# .bash_profile

# Get the aliases and functions
if [ -f ~/.bashrc ]; then
        . ~/.bashrc
fi

# User specific environment and startup programs

PATH=$PATH:$HOME/bin:/usr/kerberos/sbin:/usr/local/sbin:/sbin:/root/bin
export PATH

ORACLE_TERM=xterm
export ORACLE_TERM

ORACLE_SID=racvxdb2
export ORACLE_SID

ORACLE_HOSTNAME=bsfracvx2.bsflocal.com
export ORACLE_HOSTNAME

ORACLE_UNQNAME=RACVXDB
export ORACLE_UNQNAME

ORACLE_BASE=/u01/app/oracle
export ORACLE_BASE

ORACLE_HOME=$ORACLE_BASE/product/12.1.0/dbhome_1
export ORACLE_HOME

TMP=/tmp
export TMP
TMPDIR=$TMP
export TMPDIR

PATH=/usr/sbin:$PATH
export PATH
PATH=$ORACLE_HOME/bin:$PATH
export PATH

LD_LIBRARY_PATH=$ORACLE_HOME/lib:/lib:/usr/lib; export LD_LIBRARY_PATH
CLASSPATH=$ORACLE_HOME/JRE:$ORACLE_HOME/jlib:$ORACLE_HOME/rdbms/jlib; export CLASSPATH

if [ $USER = "grid" -o  $USER = "oracle" ]; then
if [ $SHELL = "/bin/ksh" ]; then
ulimit -p 16384
ulimit -n 65536
else
ulimit -u 16384 -n 65536

fi
umask 022
fi
```

Reboot Node 02. Power Node 01 and verify network connectivity between both nodes by pinging both public and private network interfaces between them.

Step 10.7—Enable X11 Forwarding on the Host Machine

Next, you need to enable X11 forwarding.

1. Install an X Window System display server, such as Xming, on the OS (in this case, Windows 8).
2. Enable X11 forwarding in your terminal emulator program, such as PuTTY (see Figure 10.9).

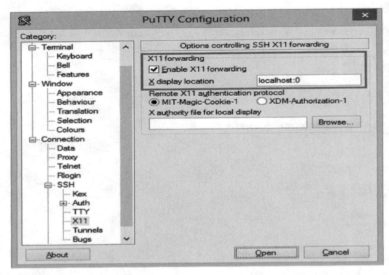

Figure 10.9. Terminal emulator (PuTTY): Enable X11 forwarding for redirection of graphical output from RAC servers to the host machine.

Step 10.8—Install and Set Up 12c Grid Infrastructure

Start the guest VMs constituting the RAC and install and set up Oracle 12c grid infrastructure by following the steps outlined in Chapter 9:

1. Enter the My Oracle Support (MOS) credentials for support on software updates and patches, or choose to skip them.
2. Select the Install and Configure Oracle Grid Infrastructure for a Cluster option.
3. Select the Configure a Flex Cluster option.
4. Select the appropriate product language(s).
5. Enter the required information for Single Client Access Name (SCAN) and Grid Naming Service (GNS).

6. Enter the relevant information for the RAC 12c nodes including HUB and LEAF nodes.

7. Enter the required information for establishing and testing SSH connectivity and user equivalence between all the RAC nodes.

8. Specify the network interfaces for public, private cluster interconnect, and ASM.

9. Select the Configure Grid Infrastructure Management Repository option.

10. Specify the ASM disks for the GRID1 ASM disk group with a HIGH redundancy level.

11. Enter the passwords for the Oracle SYS and ASMSNMP DB users.

12. Select the Do not use Intelligent Platform Management Interface (IPMI) option.

13. Specify the OS groups for ASM.

14. Enter the Oracle BASE and HOME locations.

15. Enter the Oracle inventory location.

16. Enter the root OS password or sudo access credentials to automatically run the root.sh configuration scripts.

17. Generate and run any runfixup.sh scripts to fix any prerequisite issues.

18. Press Install to initiate the installation process for grid infrastructure.

At this point, Oracle 12c grid infrastructure has been set up: we are at the same level of setup in the RAC 12c installation process as we were at the end of Chapter 9. From this point onward, the steps outlined in the following sections apply equally to both virtualization (or physical hardware) approaches: OVM for VirtualBox and OVM for x86.

Step 10.9—Install the OEM 12c Agents on the RAC Nodes

The next two steps outline what is involved in installing and setting up EM12c agent software on the RAC 12c node virtual machines, which are used for monitoring the host machines and all the targets within them by EM12c. This section also assumes that you have an EM12c setup in place. If you are doing it all on your home laptop, then it is advisable to have EM12c installed on the host laptop itself. Step 10.10 details how to configure the Windows 8 firewall (if it is the underlying OS) for EM12c to communicate with the virtual machines for the RAC nodes.

Follow these steps to deploy/install the EM12c agents.

1. Choose OEM 12c → Top-Right Menu → Setup → Add Target → Add Targets Manually.

2. Add targets manually by selecting the Add Host Targets option. Press the Add Hosts button.

3. Set the host and platform by entering the hostnames and platform (Linux x86_x64) for the RAC nodes. Enter a session name to identify the job associated with the addition of the targets in EM12*c*.

4. Then tend to the additional installation details by entering the following information:

   - The installation base directory; for example, /u01/app/oracle/agent12c

   - The instance directory; for example, /u01/app/oracle/agent12c/agent_inst

   - Named credentials for the Oracle OS user

   - The privileged delegation setting

   - The port number

5. Now press the Deploy Agent button. Monitor the progress, as shown in Figure 10.10.

Figure 10.10   Oracle Enterprise Manager 12*c* agent deployment in progress on RAC 12*c* nodes

6. After the deployment process completes, run the root.sh script as the privileged root OS user.

7. Follow the process to promote all the non-host targets.

Step 10.10—Configure the Firewall on the Host Machine (Windows Only)

The default setup and functionality in Windows 8 does not allow a pingback; therefore, a custom inbound rule has to be configured to enable communication between the Windows host machine and the virtual machines for the RAC nodes. The following steps detail this process. For a non-Windows OS on the host machine, implement a similar process (if applicable) to enable communication between the EM12*c* host and the RAC node VMs.

1. Choose Start → Control Panel → Window Firewall → Advanced Settings → Inbound Rules.

2. Enable the File and Printer Sharing (Echo Request—ICMPv4-In) rule (see Figure 10.11).

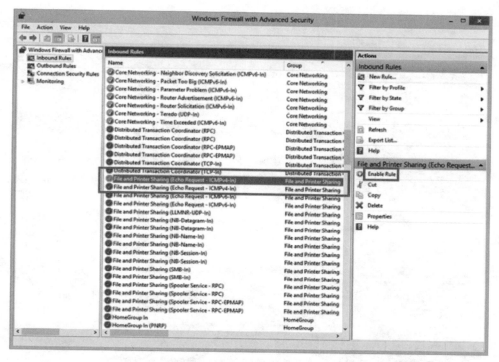

Figure 10.11   Configuring Windows firewall on the host machine to enable communication with the RAC node VMs

Step 10.11—Create and Set Up the Required ASM Disk Groups for RAC Databases

This section details the steps for creating the ASM disk groups needed for the RAC 12c database(s).

1. Create the DATA1 ASM disk group using the ASM Configuration Assistant (ASMA):

    ```
    [grid@bsfracvx1 bin]$ pwd
    /u01/app/12.1.0/grid_1/bin
    [grid@bsfracvx1 bin]$ export ORACLE_HOME=/u01/app/12.1.0/grid_1
    [grid@bsfracvx1 bin]$ ./asmca
    ```

2. Press the Create button.

3. Choose the appropriate level of ASM disk group redundancy—External in this case (see Figure 10.12).

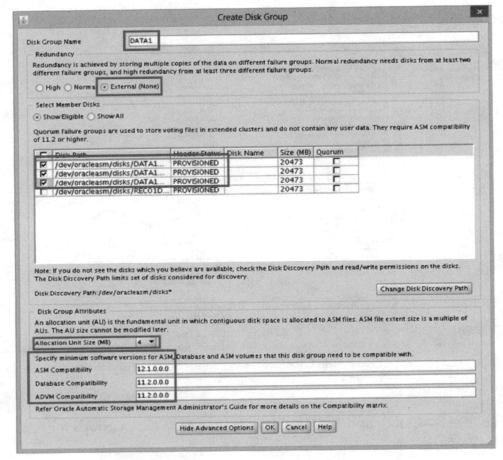

Figure 10.12 Settings for the DATA1 ASM disk group

4. Select the ASM disk group member disks.

5. Enter the values for the ASM disk group compatibility parameters.

6. Set the allocation unit size to 4 MB.

7. Repeat the preceding steps for the RECO1 ASM disk group.

The finished product is shown in Figure 10.13.

Disk Group Name	Size (GB)	Free (GB)	Usable (GB)	Redundancy	State
DATA1	59.98	59.87	59.87	EXTERN	MOUNTED(1 of 2)
RECO1	19.99	19.94	19.94	EXTERN	MOUNTED(1 of 2)
GRID1	24.96	21.27	21.27	EXTERN	MOUNTED(1 of 2)

Figure 10.13. The required ASM disk groups in ASMCA for RAC 12c

Step 10.12—Install the RAC 12c Database Software Using the OUI

This section contains the steps to install the RAC database software into non-shared database homes. Implementing non-shared Oracle Homes is best practice, as it allows rolling patches to be applied to the RAC without the need to bring the entire cluster down for maintenance purposes.

1. Run the Oracle Universal Installer (OUI) from the RAC 12c Database staging area directory:

```
[oracle@bsfracvx1 database]$ pwd
/home/oracle/software/Ora12c/Database/database
[oracle@bsfracvx1 database]$ ./runInstaller
```

2. Enter the following information and make the following selections in the Wizard Entry screens of the OUI, as shown in the following screenshots. In certain cases, you'll need to modify the entries according to the specific needs of your organization:

   a. Enter the MOS credentials for support on software updates and patches, or choose to skip them (see Figure 10.14).

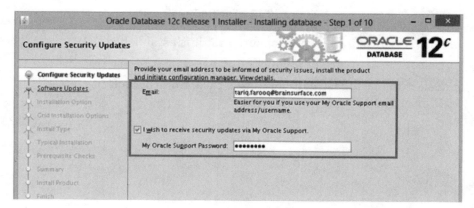

Figure 10.14   Choose to receive or not receive security updates.

b. Select the Install database software only option, as shown in Figure 10.15.

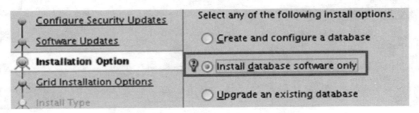

Figure 10.15   Choose Install database software only

c. Select Oracle Real Application Clusters database installation (see Figure 10.16).

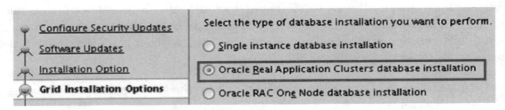

Figure 10.16   Choose Oracle Real Application Clusters database installation

d. Select the RAC nodes on which the installation is to be performed (see Figure 10.17).

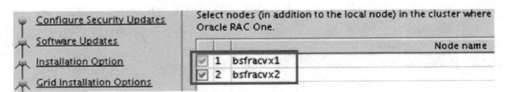

Figure 10.17   The RAC nodes

e. Click SSH Connectivity to ensure that it is established.

f. Select the appropriate product language(s).

g. Select the Database edition, in this case, Enterprise Edition (see Figure 10.18).

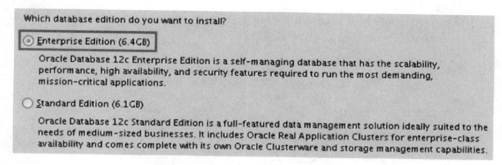

Which database edition do you want to install?

⊙ Enterprise Edition (6.4GB)

Oracle Database 12c Enterprise Edition is a self-managing database that has the scalability, performance, high availability, and security features required to run the most demanding, mission-critical applications.

○ Standard Edition (6.1GB)

Oracle Database 12c Standard Edition is a full-featured data management solution ideally suited to the needs of medium-sized businesses. It includes Oracle Real Application Clusters for enterprise-class availability and comes complete with its own Oracle Clusterware and storage management capabilities.

Figure 10.18   Choose Enterprise Edition.

h. Specify the Oracle base and home locations (see Figure 10.19).

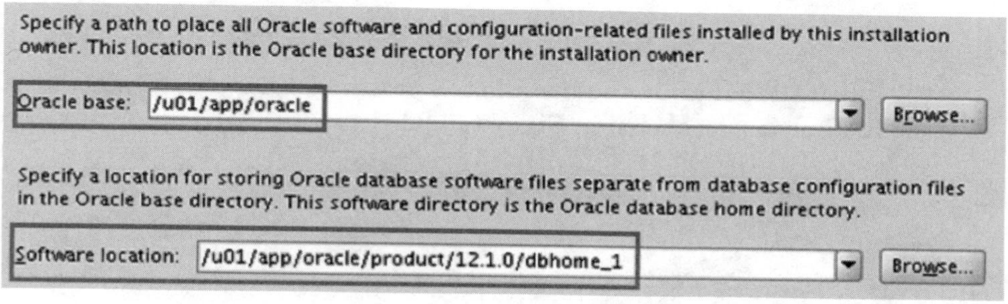

Specify a path to place all Oracle software and configuration-related files installed by this installation owner. This location is the Oracle base directory for the installation owner.

Oracle base: /u01/app/oracle   ▼   Browse...

Specify a location for storing Oracle database software files separate from database configuration files in the Oracle base directory. This software directory is the Oracle database home directory.

Software location: /u01/app/oracle/product/12.1.0/dbhome_1   ▼   Browse...

Figure 10.19   Set Oracle base and home locations.

i. Specify the Oracle OS groups for the various job roles: OSDBA, OSOPER, OSBACKUPDBA, OSDGDBA, OSKMDBA (see Figure 10.20).

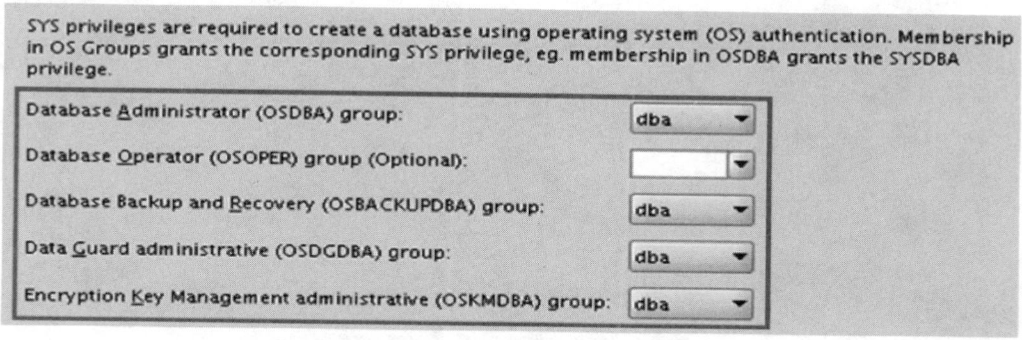

SYS privileges are required to create a database using operating system (OS) authentication. Membership in OS Groups grants the corresponding SYS privilege, eg. membership in OSDBA grants the SYSDBA privilege.

Database Administrator (OSDBA) group: dba ▼

Database Operator (OSOPER) group (Optional):   ▼

Database Backup and Recovery (OSBACKUPDBA) group: dba ▼

Data Guard administrative (OSDGDBA) group: dba ▼

Encryption Key Management administrative (OSKMDBA) group: dba ▼

Figure 10.20   Set Oracle OS groups for the various job roles.

j. The warnings and errors are shown as part of the Verification Results in the next screen (see Figure 10.21).

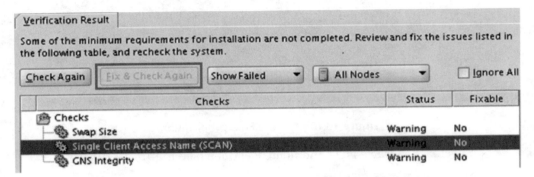

Figure 10.21   Warnings observed as part of the Verification Results

k. Click Install to initiate the installation process for DB HOME software on the RAC nodes, as shown in Figure 10.22.

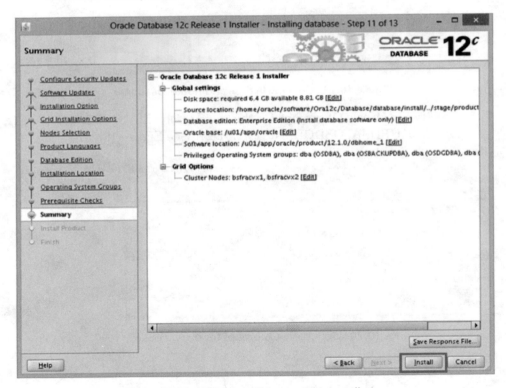

Figure 10.22   Click Install to start the installation.

3. As shown in Figure 10.23, after the installation completes, run the root.sh script on all the RAC nodes, as the privileged OS root user.

```
[root@bsfracvx1 dbhome_1]# ./root.sh
Performing root user operation for Oracle 12c
```

The following environment variables are set as

```
ORACLE_OWNER= oracle
ORACLE_HOME=  /u01/app/oracle/product/12.1.0/dbhome_1
```

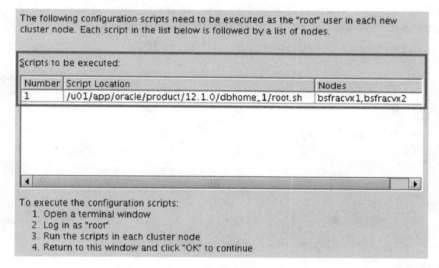

Figure 10.23   Postinstall root scripts

4. Enter the full pathname of the local bin directory:

```
[/usr/local/bin]:

The contents of "dbhome" have not changed. No need to overwrite.
The contents of "oraenv" have not changed. No need to overwrite.
The contents of "coraenv" have not changed. No need to overwrite.
```

Entries will be added to the /etc/oratab file as the generic part of the root script runs.

Next, product-specific root actions will be performed.

Step 10.13—Create/Configure the RAC 12*c* Cluster Database Employing DBCA

At this point, we are ready to create and install a clustered RAC 12*c* database using the DBCA utility. DBCA is considered the best-practice database creation/setup tool because it enables the user to create a RAC (or non-RAC) database, complete with a whole host of industry-standard best practices built into it, along with other database management options as well. This section contains the steps to do so.

1. As the oracle OS user, run the DBCA utility from the RAC 12*c* DB HOME:

```
[oracle@bsfrac01 bin]$ pwd
/u01/app/oracle/product/12.1.0/dbhome_1/bin
[oracle@bsfrac01 bin]$ ./dbca
```

2. Enter the information in the following steps, and make the selections in the Wizard Entry screens of DBCA, as shown in the figures. In certain cases, you'll need to modify the entries according to the specific needs of your organization.

3. Select the Create Database option (see Figure 10.24).

Figure 10.24   Choose Create Database.

4. Select the Advanced Mode option (see Figure 10.25).

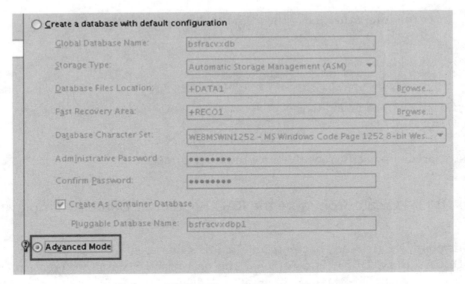

Figure 10.25   Choose Advanced Mode.

5. Select the Oracle Real Application Clusters (RAC) database and Policy-Managed options (see Figure 10.26).

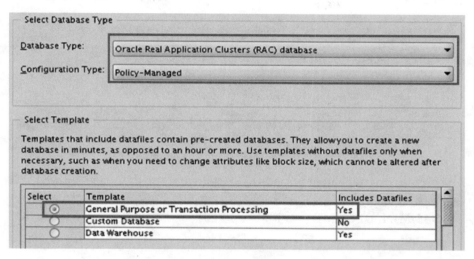

Figure 10.26   Choose the Oracle Real Application Clusters (RAC) database and Policy-Managed settings.

6. Select the General Purpose or Transaction Processing option (see Figure 10.26). Press the Show Details button on this screen.

7. Enter the global database name (see Figure 10.27).

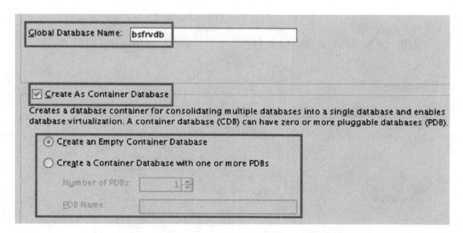

Figure 10.27   Enter the database settings.

8. Enable the Create As Container Database checkbox (see Figure 10.27).

9. Specify the appropriate options for the container database(s): number of pluggable databases, PDB name prefix (see Figure 10.27).

10. Enter the server pool information for the policy-managed RAC DB: server pool name, cardinality, and existing or new server pool (see Figure 10.28).

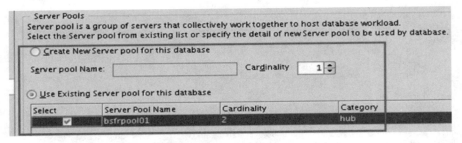

Figure 10.28   Server pool information

11. Specify the management options by registering the database with EM12*c*.

12. Enter and verify the passwords for the database users: SYS, SYSTEM, PDBADMIN, DBSNMP (see Figure 10.29).

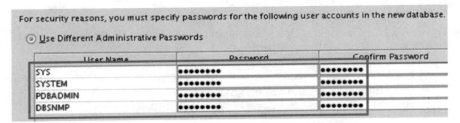

Figure 10.29   Enter and confirm the passwords for the user accounts.

13. Enter the ASM disk groups for the data file locations (see Figure 10.30).

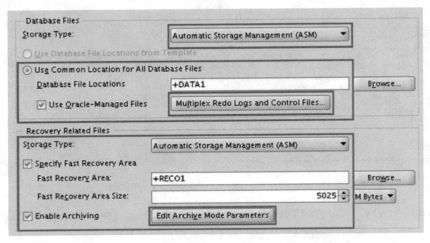

Figure 10.30   Set the ASM disk groups and enable archiving options.

14. Enable the Archiving option for the online Redo log files and enter the parameters for archiving (see Figure 10.30).

15. Press the Multiplex Redo Logs and Control Files button (see Figure 10.30), and enter the locations for the multiplexed files (see Figure 10.31).

Multiplex Redo Logs and Control Files

It is recommended that online redo logs and control files be written to multiple locations spread across different disks to provide greater fault tolerance.

	Location
1	+DATA1
2	+RECO1
3	

Figure 10.31   Enter the locations for multiplexed files.

16. Enter the parameters for the Fast Recovery Area (FRA) (refer to Figure 10.30).

17. Enter the parameters for sample schemas, custom scripts, database vault, and label security.

18. Enter the parameters for database memory management (see Figure 10.32), sizing (see Figure 10.33), connection mode (see Figure 10.34), and character sets (see Figure 10.35).

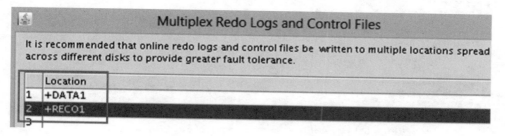

Figure 10.32   Parameters for database memory management

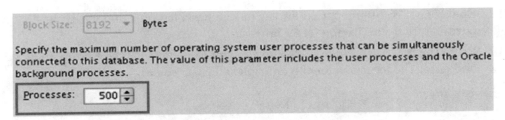

Figure 10.33   Parameters for sizing

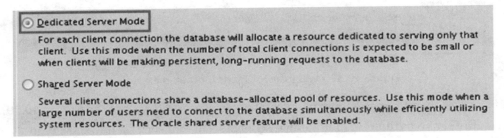

Figure 10.34   Parameters for the connection mode

Figure 10.35   Parameters for character sets

19. Press the All Initialization Parameters button, and then the Show Advanced Parameter button. Modify the RAC DB initialization parameters as needed (see Figure 10.36).

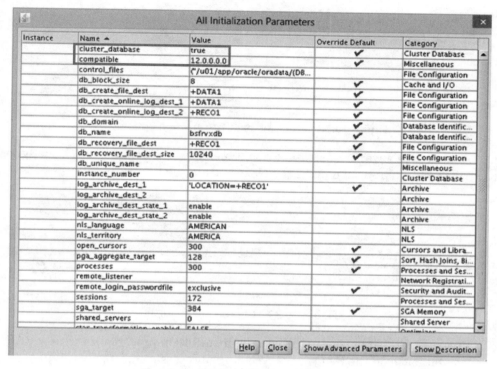

Figure 10.36   Initialization parameters

20. Press the Customize Storage Locations button. Modify the parameters for control files (see Figure 10.37) and data files. Redo log groups and files as needed.

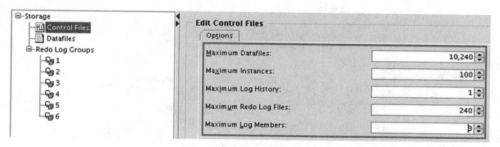

Figure 10.37   Edit the control files.

21. Enable the Create Database and Generate Database Creation Scripts checkbox options, and enter the location of the generated scripts' destination directory (see Figure 10.38).

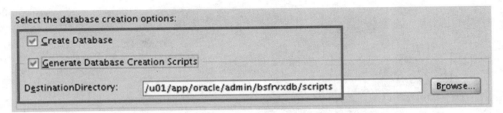

Figure 10.38   Enter the database creation options.

22. You may see a warning message about memory/SWAP sizes: check the Ignore All checkbox, and then press the Next button (see Figure 10.39).

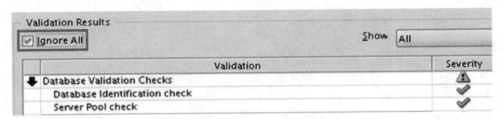

Figure 10.39   Choose Ignore All.

23. Press the Finish button to initiate the installation process for the new RAC 12*c* database on the RAC nodes. When the process completes, you will see a dialog box like the one shown in Figure 10.40.

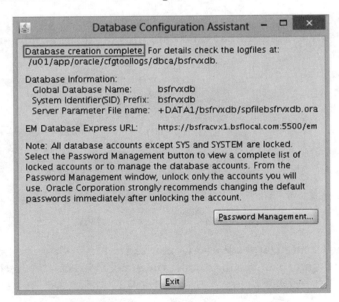

Figure 10.40   The database creation is complete.

Step 10.14—Perform Sanity Checks on the New RAC 12*c* Database

Run the following commands in SQL*Plus to perform basic sanity checks on the new RAC 12*c* database.

```
SQL> select instance_name,status from gv$instance;

INSTANCE_NAME    STATUS
---------------- ------------
bsfrvxdb_1       OPEN
bsfrvxdb_2       OPEN

[grid@bsfracvx1 bin]$ ./lsnrctl status

LSNRCTL for Linux: Version 12.1.0.1.0 - Production on 20-MAR-2013 03:55:50

Copyright © 1991, 2013, Oracle. All rights reserved.

Connecting to (DESCRIPTION=(ADDRESS=(PROTOCOL=IPC)(KEY=LISTENER)))
STATUS of the LISTENER
------------------------
Alias                     LISTENER
Version                   TNSLSNR for Linux: Version 12.1.0.1.0 - Production
Start date                19-APR-2013 18:23:25
Uptime                    0 days 9 hr. 32 min. 27 sec
Trace level               OFF
Security                  ON: Local OS Authentication
SNMP                      OFF
Listener parameter file   /u01/app/12.1.0/grid_1/network/admin/listener.ora
Listener log file         /u01/app/grid/diag/tnslsnr/bsfracvx1/listener/alert/log.xml

Listening endpoints summary...
  (DESCRIPTION=(ADDRESS=(PROTOCOL=ipc)(KEY=LISTENER)))
  (DESCRIPTION=(ADDRESS=(PROTOCOL=tcp)(HOST=192.168.2.116)(PORT=1521)))
  (DESCRIPTION=(ADDRESS=(PROTOCOL=tcp)(HOST=192.168.2.160)(PORT=1521)))
  (DESCRIPTION=(ADDRESS=(PROTOCOL=tcps)(HOST=bsfracvx1)(PORT=5500))(Security
=(my _wallet_directory=/u01/app/oracle/product/12.1.0/dbhome_1/admin/
bsfrvxdb/xdb_wallet))(Presentation=HTTP)(Session=RAW))
Services Summary...
Service "+APX" has 1 instance(s).
  Instance "+APX1", status READY, has 1 handler(s) for this service...
Service "+ASM" has 1 instance(s).
  Instance "+ASM1", status READY, has 1 handler(s) for this service...
Service "-MGMTDBXDB" has 1 instance(s).
  Instance "-MGMTDB", status READY, has 1 handler(s) for this service...
Service "_mgmtdb" has 1 instance(s).
  Instance "-MGMTDB", status READY, has 2 handler(s) for this service...
Service "bsfrvxdb" has 1 instance(s).
  Instance "bsfrvxdb_1", status READY, has 1 handler(s) for this service...
Service "bsfrvxdbXDB" has 1 instance(s).
  Instance "bsfrvxdb_1", status READY, has 1 handler(s) for this service...
Service "bsfrvxpdb" has 1 instance(s).
  Instance "bsfrvxdb_1", status READY, has 1 handler(s) for this service...
The command completed successfully


[root@bsfracvx1 bin]# ./crs_stat -t -v
Name           Type        R/RA   F/FT   Target    State     Host
------------------------------------------------------------------------
ora....SM.lsnr ora....er.type 0/5   0/    ONLINE    ONLINE    bsfracvx1
ora....SM.lsnr ora....er.type 0/5   0/    ONLINE    ONLINE    bsfracvx1
ora.DATA1.dg   ora....up.type 0/5   0/    ONLINE    ONLINE    bsfracvx1
ora.GRID1.dg   ora....up.type 0/5   0/    ONLINE    ONLINE    bsfracvx1
ora....ER.lsnr ora....er.type 0/5   0/    ONLINE    ONLINE    bsfracvx1
```

```
ora....N1.lsnr ora....er.type 0/5     0/0    ONLINE     ONLINE     bsfracvx2
ora....N2.lsnr ora....er.type 0/5     0/0    ONLINE     ONLINE     bsfracvx1
ora....N3.lsnr ora....er.type 0/5     0/0    ONLINE     ONLINE     bsfracvx1
ora.MGMTLSNR   ora....nr.type 0/0     0/0    ONLINE     ONLINE     bsfracvx1
ora.RECO1.dg   ora....up.type 0/5     0/     ONLINE     ONLINE     bsfracvx1
ora.asm        ora.asm.type   0/5     0/0    ONLINE     ONLINE     bsfracvx1
ora....X1.lsnr application    0/5     0/0    ONLINE     ONLINE     bsfracvx1
ora....vx1.ons application    0/3     0/0    ONLINE     ONLINE     bsfracvx1
ora....vx1.vip ora....t1.type 0/0     0/0    ONLINE     ONLINE     bsfracvx1
ora....X2.lsnr application    0/5     0/0    ONLINE     ONLINE     bsfracvx2
ora....vx2.ons application    0/3     0/0    ONLINE     ONLINE     bsfracvx2
ora....vx2.vip ora....t1.type 0/0     0/0    ONLINE     ONLINE     bsfracvx2
ora.bsfrvdb.db ora....se.type 0/2     0/1    ONLINE     ONLINE     bsfracvx2
ora.cvu        ora.cvu.type   0/5     0/0    ONLINE     ONLINE     bsfracvx1
ora.gns        ora.gns.type   0/5     0/0    ONLINE     ONLINE     bsfracvx1
ora.gns.vip    ora....ip.type 0/0     0/0    ONLINE     ONLINE     bsfracvx1
ora.mgmtdb     ora....db.type 0/2     0/1    ONLINE     ONLINE     bsfracvx1
ora....network ora....rk.type 0/5     0/     ONLINE     ONLINE     bsfracvx1
ora.oc4j       ora.oc4j.type  0/1     0/2    ONLINE     ONLINE     bsfracvx1
ora.ons        ora.ons.type   0/3     0/     ONLINE     ONLINE     bsfracvx1
ora.proxy_advm ora....vm.type 0/5     0/     ONLINE     ONLINE     bsfracvx1
ora.scan1.vip  ora....ip.type 0/0     0/0    ONLINE     ONLINE     bsfracvx2
ora.scan2.vip  ora....ip.type 0/0     0/0    ONLINE     ONLINE     bsfracvx1
ora.scan3.vip  ora....ip.type 0/0     0/0    ONLINE     ONLINE     bsfracvx1

[root@bsfracvx1 bin]# ps -ef | grep pmon
grid      4398     1  0 21:11 ?       00:00:02 asm_pmon_+ASM1
grid      4886     1  0 21:13 ?       00:00:01 mdb_pmon_-MGMTDB
oracle    5732     1  0 21:16 ?       00:00:02 ora_pmon_bsfrvdb_2
grid      6138     1  0 21:18 ?       00:00:01 apx_pmon_+APX1
root     11718 11035  0 21:39 pts/0   00:00:00 grep pmon
```

Congratulations! The setup of your own virtualized RAC 12*c* cluster is now complete, and it is fully functional and up and running. The steps for creating clusters on physical resources are very similar, if not identical, to the steps outlined in this and the previous chapter.

EM12*c*: Implementing DBaaS

Now that we have learned how to create RAC 12*c* clusters from scratch, let us focus on the cloud management piece of the picture.

As discussed in Chapter 9, the following components are needed for setting up virtualized Oracle database clouds:

- OVM for x86
- EM12*c*
- Oracle Cloud Management Pack for Oracle Database

EM12*c* is the nerve center of cloud computing for Oracle products in general, including the Oracle database server family. The Cloud Management Pack for Oracle Databases provides the features, options, and framework to set up, configure,

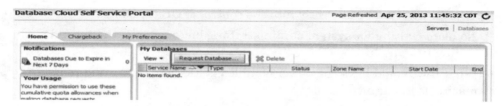

Figure 10.41   Database cloud self-service portal

monitor, meter, account for, and chargeback Oracle database clouds, including self-service capability for Oracle databases (see Figure 10.41).

Following are some salient features and benefits of setting up a database cloud using EM12*c*:

- Elasticity on demand enabled by rapid and agile provisioning of database resources

- End-to-end management of the database cloud lifecycle process

- Self-service access for cloud consumers

- Definition of the service catalog and publishing of templates

- Pooling of cloud resources

- Performance monitoring of cloud databases

- Easy power-up, power-down, and retirement of cloud databases

- Role-based security implementation

- Accounting through chargeback and metering of cloud resources

Note

The process of setting up and configuring DBaaS in EM12*c* is beyond the scope of this book: you are encouraged to read the Oracle documentation on how to set up DBaaS in EM12*c* in order to complete the Oracle database cloud computing picture.

Virtualization and Cloud Computing: From the Perspective of Oracle DBAs

Following are some thought-provoking points and questions (as well as some answers) that we (the DBAs) should ask ourselves:

- Who are the end consumers and owners of the IT hardware?

  Yes, the business implicitly owns everything, but from the administration, maintenance, support, and ownership standpoints, the answer is that we, the Oracle DBAs, are the end consumers of the machines.

- What if we put OVM directly into the control of Oracle DBAs?

  No more waiting for system administrators, but of course, that would mean adding to your skills set.

- What if we could have the power of agile elasticity to set up and remove machines in our own hands?

  We could rapidly prototype new environments without having to wait for and depend on the OS and sysadmin folks.

- Is super-rapid provisioning of new infrastructures really possible with virtualization? That sounds like someone is blowing a lot of hot air—right?

  Wrong.

- Virtualization in production? No way is that going to happen on my watch: it would be an overhead and a performance nightmare—right?

  Wrong.

- Multi-tenant virtualization: That would present security risks; guest VMs would not be isolated and secure enough—right?

  Wrong.

- In order to implement my own private cloud using OVM, I would have to learn so much—right?

  Wrong. (OVM along with EM12c is ultra-easy to learn and implement. You can set up your entire virtualized infrastructure within a few hours; the real fun and productivity start after that.)

- Carrying the burden of legacy infrastructures, my professional back hurts on a daily basis. When will I get my hands on new machines that I have been promised by the OS and sysadmin folks for a while now?

  Virtualization and cloud computing together are the consolidated answer to all of the above—unprecedented productivity, throughput, and resource efficiency, which quite simply are just not possible in the physical, non-cloud universe. Oracle RAC 12c is *the* database cloud and enables you to complete the overall corporate cloud picture.

Summary

As emphasized in this chapter and in Chapter 9, the significance of cloud computing can no longer be overlooked or ignored in the modern-day IT workplace. Whether it is your own private cloud behind the corporate firewall, a subscription-based model in a public cloud, or a hybrid of both paradigms, cloud computing is an inevitability that is happening now in the IT universe. This and the previous chapter presented a detailed, step-by-step way to build your own virtualized RAC 12*c* clouds, managed and integrated under the umbrella of EM12*c*. An overview of the various paradigms, technologies, and products involved in setting up virtualized RAC database clouds was also presented. You can choose one of two virtualization options: OVM for x86 or OVM VirtualBox. The latter option allows you to set up, configure, and learn RAC 12*c* comfortably and conveniently on your own home laptop or desktop machine.

Index

REGISTER YOUR PRODUCT at informit.com/register
Access Additional Benefits and SAVE 35% on Your Next Purchase

- Download available product updates.

- Access bonus material when applicable.

- Receive exclusive offers on new editions and related products.
  (Just check the box to hear from us when setting up your account.)

- Get a coupon for 35% for your next purchase, valid for 30 days. Your code will be available in your InformIT cart. (You will also find it in the Manage Codes section of your account page.)

Registration benefits vary by product. Benefits will be listed on your account page under Registered Products.

InformIT.com—The Trusted Technology Learning Source
InformIT is the online home of information technology brands at Pearson, the world's foremost education company. At InformIT.com you can

- Shop our books, eBooks, software, and video training.
- Take advantage of our special offers and promotions (informit.com/promotions).
- Sign up for special offers and content newsletters (informit.com/newsletters).
- Read free articles and blogs by information technology experts.
- Access thousands of free chapters and video lessons.

Connect with InformIT—Visit informit.com/community
Learn about InformIT community events and programs.

the trusted technology learning source

Addison-Wesley · Cisco Press · IBM Press · Microsoft Press · Pearson IT Certification · Prentice Hall · Que · Sams · VMware Press

ALWAYS LEARNING   PEARSON